A CASEBOOK ON FILM

CHARLES THOMAS SAMUELS
WILLIAMS COLLEGE

VAN NOSTRAND REINHOLD COMPANY

New York   Cincinnati   Toronto   London   Melbourne

FOR MY PARENTS AND GRANDMOTHER

Published by Van Nostrand Reinhold Company
450 West 33rd Street, New York, N.Y. 10001

Published simultaneously in Canada by
D. Van Nostrand Company (Canada), Ltd.

10   9   8   7   6   5   4   3   2

HOW TO USE THIS CASEBOOK

Recognizing the need to train students in the writing of research papers, but realizing the impossibility of sending large numbers to one library at the same time, instructors have recently turned to the casebook. Such a collection contains assorted essays on a single topic, together with suggestions for further work, within the covers of a single volume. The casebook provides several distinct advantages. For the student, it eliminates vexing—and frequently uneducational—problems of procurement. Moreover, since he is reading, at least initially, the same materials as his classmates, he can enter into valuable out-of-class discussion with them. In class, students and teacher benefit from a common approach to their topic. And because the teacher knows how each student began his project (and is familiar with much of his source material), he is instantly informed about the student's comprehension and scholarly method and can, therefore, turn to the more immediate problem of evaluating the student's writing.

A Casebook on Film presents two opportunities for student papers: on film form and on specific movies. The first part of the volume contains essays that define the art of film, discuss its principal techniques, and consider methods by which we can judge its results. Questions accompanying each essay are designed to suggest ways in which the topic might be pursued, and the Papers and Projects section provides opportunities for analytical writing and research. The second part of the volume presents essays on three widely discussed films of recent years: The Graduate, Bonnie and Clyde and Blow-Up. Instructors may use these movies not only as examples of film art but also as a basis for analyzing the real-life situations and problems which their plots and characters embody. Accordingly, both the study questions and the paper topics for this section go beyond the boundaries of aesthetics and film criticism.

Though primarily designed as a casebook, this volume may also serve as a text for a course on film. To this end, the introduction surveys briefly the issues and problems that such a course might treat. A glossary of basic terms and a bibliography for further reading are included at the end of this text, both for those who want to use this book as a writing source and for those eager to pursue their study of film.

As you read the articles you will notice italicized numbers inserted in brackets. For convenience in making footnotes, the numbers indicate the turning of the page; thus [67–68] marks the end of page 67 and the beginning of page 68 in the article as it was printed in the original source.

Preparation of this volume has been made easier by Nancy MacFadyen of the Williams College interlibrary loan department and by Louisa Blair and Karen George, who helped type the manuscript. To these ladies, friends in this and other projects, the editor wishes to express deep appreciation.

Charles Thomas Samuels

CONTENTS

How To Use This Casebook   iii

Introduction   3

Theory of Film

DEFINING THE FORM

Erwin Panofsky   "Style and Medium in the Motion Pictures"   9
     Critique (January–February, 1947)

Arnold Hauser   "The Film Age"   23
     from *The Social History of Art*

Michael Roemer   "The Surfaces of Reality"   37
     Film Quarterly (Fall, 1964)

Maya Deren   "Cinema as an Art Form"   47
     New Directions (1946)

Nicola Chiaromonte   "A Note on the Movies"   56
     Encounter (March, 1960)

MAKING FILMS

Andrew Sarris   "The Fall and Rise of the Film Director"   63
     from *Interviews with Film Directors*

Dudley Nichols   "The Writer and the Film"   71
     from *Great Film Plays*

V. I. Pudovkin   "On Cinema Acting"   78
     from *Film Technique and Film Acting*

Basil Wright   "Handling the Camera"   85
     from *Footnotes to the Film*

George Bluestone   "Editing"   94
     from *Novels into Film*

Irving Pichel   "Seeing with the Camera"   99
     Hollywood Quarterly (1946)

PERSPECTIVES FOR CRITICISM

John Simon   "A Critical Credo"   107
     from *Private Screenings*

Penelope Houston   "The Critical Question"   116
     Sight and Sound (Autumn, 1960)

Robert Brustein   "The New Hollywood: Myth and Anti-Myth"   **126**
       Film Quarterly (Spring, 1959)

Robert Warshow   "The Gangster as Tragic Hero"   **133**
       from *The Immediate Experience*

Theory Applied

THE GRADUATE

Stanley Kauffmann   "Cum Laude"   **141**
       The New Republic (December 23, 1967)

Edgar Z. Friedenberg   "Calling Dr. Spock!"   **148**
       The New York Review of Books (March 28, 1968)

Stephen Farber and **Estelle Changas**   "The Graduate"   **154**
       Film Quarterly (Spring, 1968)

Jacob Brackman   "The Graduate"   **160**
       The New Yorker (July 27, 1968)

BONNIE AND CLYDE

Joseph Morgenstern   "Two Views"   **175**
       Newsweek (August 21 *and* 28, 1967)

Pauline Kael   "Bonnie and Clyde"   **179**
       from *Kiss Kiss Bang Bang*

Charles Thomas Samuels   "Bonnie and Clyde"   **194**
       The Hudson Review (Spring, 1968)

Jerry Richard   "Foggy Bottom"   **201**
       The Antioch Review (Fall, 1968)

BLOW-UP

John Simon   "A Bit Overblown"   **207**
       from *Private Screenings*

Robert Garis   "Watching Antonioni"   **212**
       Commentary (April, 1967)

James F. Scott   "Blow-Up: Antonioni and the Mod World"   **216**
       Cross Currents (Spring, 1967)

Charles Thomas Samuels   "The Blow-Up: Sorting Things Out"   **224**
       The American Scholar (Winter, 1967–68)

SELECTIVE GLOSSARY   **238**
PAPERS AND PROJECTS   **242**
SELECTIVE BIBLIOGRAPHY   **249**

A CASEBOOK
ON FILM

INTRODUCTION

Throughout the world—not only in Hollywood—most movies are produced for diversion. With most movies, therefore, the liberal arts curriculum has no more concern than with best sellers, advertising art, or Tin Pan Alley. For someone anxious to learn craft, a poster, a slick romance, or an Otto Preminger movie might prove instructive. But the present volume is designed for film students, not craftsmen, and is thus devoted only to films that a student might profitably view.

In order to give even provisional definition to that category, certain historical considerations must be recalled. This volume is concerned neither with film technology nor film history (though, in the latter case, the only motive is limitation of space); but a glance at the history of thinking about film is necessary to put our essays in perspective.

As Erwin Panofsky points out, the cinema began in a unique manner, for it existed as a mechanical capability before anyone knew how it might be turned into an art. Consequently, cinema aestheticians begin by asking if it *is* an art and whether it can be distinguished from its fellows. Since, at bottom, film is a branch of photography, and since photography is reproductive rather than creative, how can film claim parity with literature, drama, music, painting, and sculpture? Moreover, if, to be an art, film must create stories (and not merely photograph things), how can it distinguish itself, in particular, from books and plays?

Film theorists seeking answers to the first question have tended to travel along two separate roads. Down one, camera in hand, go those who believe that film must make its opportunity where it can; that is to say, in its very unlimited power of reproduction. Capable of achieving the truest imitation of reality (absolutely faithful pictures that can also move), film should become a great mirror, finding its clearest expression in the mode of documentary. Although this position has had a number of distinguished practitioners, among them John Grierson and Robert Flaherty, it succumbed—partly because of commercial considerations, partly because of belief—to the practice of filming stories. What was most exciting in the documentary theory became, ironically, an ingredient in fiction films, mainly through the "neo-realists": Italian directors who believed that movies should tell real stories, set in authentic locales, using nonprofessional actors. We shall see this line of argument reflected in the essay by Michael Roemer.

3

The second road has been better able to maintain its distinctness from the main highway of commercial filmmaking. The proponents of this argument hold that directors must avoid or transform reality, precisely because the camera is so good at reproduction that it can turn the artist into a mere workman who cranks the machine. Ably represented by Maya Deren, this position is more viably aesthetic than the documentary point of view, but it has had no more acceptance from audiences charmed with the power of narrative. As a result, it has gone underground; underground films are, indeed, movies in which narrative is either absent or tenuous and the photographic image becomes virtually the sole expressive means.

For better or worse, neither the documentary nor the underground (or avant-garde) approach to filmmaking has prevailed. As a consequence, the attempt to distinguish cinema from literature and drama took precedence over the attempt to define cinema in terms of intrinsic potentiality. Rather, the potentialities of the camera became important only insofar as they served to distinguish films from books and plays. This we see reflected, positively, in essays by Erwin Panofsky and Arnold Hauser and, negatively, in Nicola Chiaromonte's "note." It is fair, I think, to call a synthesis of these essays the "classic" aesthetics of the film.

The argument goes something like this: Film resembles drama because it tells stories through the speech and gestures of actors impersonating people. It resembles literature because some of its exposition is not achieved through dialogue and thus recalls the novelist's narrative voice (as when it describes setting or recounts events). But film is different from plays and books because it is produced with a camera. A true aesthetics of the cinema must investigate the means by which the camera operates and the consequences of telling a story on film.

To a degree unparalleled in the arts, film aesthetics is inseparable from film mechanics, which is why this volume moves from essays on formal definition to discussions of technique. Here too, there has been a division among commentators. In this area, the debate between the nonfictional advocates (whether documentarian or avant-garde) and the fiction film theorists is paralleled by a debate between those who think that montage is essential to the art and those who think it only an important ingredient.

Borrowing from American directors (whose misfortune it has been to pioneer but never perfect the form), a few Russians, working on silent films, developed the theory and practice of creative montage. On the simplest level, every director relies on montage, for montage is merely the assembling of all those individual shots and scenes which make up the film. But men like Eisenstein and Pudovkin believed that montage should not only create continuity but should actually express the director's ideas. Thus, by matching shots, the Russians could accelerate or retard time, create the cinematic equivalent of metaphor or analogy, and even produce new realities composed of ingredients from the pre-existing natural world. Such techniques are briefly but lucidly touched upon in the article by George Bluestone.

In part, the early emphasis on assembling and editing shots and scenes was due to the absence of sound. Lacking speech—the swiftest, most flexible means of imparting information—the silent director was forced to explore all the expressive capabilities of the image. Moreover, those less adept at montage tended to produce living cartoons, with intercut written titles doing far more work than was suitable for an imagistic art form. With the advent of sound, however, editing became less crucial for expression than it had been. And as sound technology improved, enabling directors to use microphones for outdoor "location" shots, a movement away from creative montage could be discerned.

Renewed was the sense of how much could be communicated by the unaided shot or scene. Moreover, sight could be played off against hearing, much as one shot had been played off against another in creative montage (e. g. a man protesting his love could be shown by the camera to have a knife behind his back). Improved lenses which allow the cameramen to hold far and near objects in simultaneous sharp focus also increased the expressive possibilities of the individual scene. With their natural power of speech restored, actors became capable of more subtle performances, while technical improvements in lighting made both human and inanimate objects more eloquent. Movies would still be made from a string of shots, but now each shot could be fully expressive either because of its total content or through the editorializing camera, highlighting this or that detail. As a result, editing and camera work became more nearly equal than they had been for directors like Eisenstein.[1] The mechanics and aesthetics of camera work are discussed in the articles by Basil Wright and Irving Pichel.[2]

By about the 30's, then, the cinema attained artistic maturity, with a coherent sense of its uniqueness and a full range of technical capabilities to explore.[3] There had been great masters of the silent film, but the period immediately following the coming of sound was confused and uncertain. Montage was no longer considered the foundation of cinematic art, though it still exerted influence, while sound made it all too easy to turn film back into a reproductive medium—the more superfluous because most filmmakers were forced to reproduce novels and plays. By the 40's, however, following the example of men like Orson Welles and Jean Renoir, new masters appeared who could blend sound and image, montage and camera work—and even later developments, like color—into a fluent technology at the service of a personal artistic vision.

At about the same time, a criticism began to develop that tried to equal cinema's new stature. Though film reviewing still lags behind criticism in the other arts, before the days of men like James Agee it had not even mattered. In the late 40's and early 50's, however, important American critics began to emerge, and serious intellectual journals that formerly ignored films began to accord them regular coverage.

What are the problems of film criticism? John Simon gives an accurate survey in his essay and, in so doing, implies an over-arching problem that has beck-

[1] A more sophisticated, polemical sketch of the history of film technique is given by André Bazin in "The Evolution of the Language of Cinema" (see bibliography). Students who have attained a high degree of cinematic literacy are advised to read Bazin. He is, unfortunately, too allusive and suggestive for the beginner.

[2] Other available essays on important component arts of the film are included in the section "Making Films."

[3] Subsequent innovations, like 3D or Cinerama, have either been short-lived or dubious as contributions to a developing art. At the moment, the stock of film techniques seems full; the critical question is what a director does with it.

oned critics down seemingly divergent but actually complementary paths. Film can either be considered an aesthetic object in which content is important only as it is formed, or it can be considered an object for the sociologist: a maker and reflector of social attitudes. In contributions by Simon and Penelope Houston, we see this set of alternatives mentioned, worried, and, in a measure, resolved. In essays by Robert Brustein and Robert Warshow, we see ways in which sociological or psychosociological approaches can make film criticism more alert to the complexity of its subject.

The first part of this collection attempts to suggest a major definition of film form, to survey the major techniques that the student must understand, and to situate subsequent discussion along the most relevant lines of inquiry. But criticism cannot be practiced without concrete examples. In Part Two, the freshman writer seeking theme topics and the aspiring critic seeking test cases will each find material. The three films selected to exemplify the methods and problems of film criticism are important, controversial, and widely seen. Each treats matters of urgent contemporary concern, and thus opens wide the avenue of sociological consideration; at the same time, each is so technically skillful that it warrants aesthetic evaluation. In every case, critiques were chosen to provide a spectrum of opinion, although the inherent quality of an article always took precedence over the imperative of representation. For example, it may come as a surprise that essays on *The Graduate* are predominantly unfavorable; but an ironic fact about this hugely successful American film is that it was disliked by most critics who write well and fully about movies. No bibliography has been provided for other criticism of these films, on the grounds that compiling such a bibliography would be a helpful exercise for most students likely to use this book. But anyone eager to peruse other opinions will find it easy to do so, for *The Graduate, Bonnie and Clyde,* and *Blow-Up* are almost certainly the most widely discussed English-language films of the last decade. By discussing them himself, the student of this volume will have begun his active comprehension of the problems involved in film criticism.

THEORY OF FILM

DEFINING THE FORM

STYLE AND MEDIUM IN THE MOTION PICTURES

Erwin Panofsky

Film art is the only art the development of which men now living have witnessed from the very beginnings; and this development is all the more interesting as it took place under conditions contrary to precedent. It was not an artistic urge that gave rise to the discovery and gradual perfection of a new technique; it was a technical invention that gave rise to the discovery and gradual perfection of a new art.

From this we understand two fundamental facts. First, that the primordial basis of the enjoyment of moving pictures was not an objective interest in a specific subject matter, much less an aesthetic interest in the formal presentation of subject matter, but the sheer delight in the fact that things seemed to move, no matter what things they were. Second, that films—first exhibited in "kinetoscopes," viz., cinematographic peep-shows, but projectable to a screen since as early as 1894—are, originally, a product of genuine folk art (whereas, as a rule, folk art derives from what is known as "higher art"). At the very beginning of things we find the simple recording

ERWIN PANOFSKY was a distinguished critic and art historian. Among his many books are *Studies in Iconology* (1939), *Albrecht Dürer* (1943), and *Meaning in the Visual Arts* (1955).

This essay was originally published in *Critique,* Vol. I, No. 3 (January–February, 1947). © by Erwin Panofsky; reprinted by permission of Dr. Gerda Panofsky. Two footnotes included in the original have been omitted in the present version.

of movements: galloping horses, railroad trains, fire engines, sporting events, street scenes. And when it had come to the making of narrative films these were produced by photographers who were anything but "producers" or "directors," performed by people who were anything but actors, and enjoyed by people who would have been much offended had anyone called them "art lovers."

The casts of these archaic films were usually collected in a "café" where unemployed supers or ordinary citizens possessed of a suitable exterior were wont to assemble at a given hour. An enterprising photographer would walk in, hire four or five convenient characters and make the picture while carefully instructing them what to do: "Now, you pretend to hit this lady over the head"; and (to the lady): "And you pretend to fall down in a heap." Productions [5–6] like these were shown, together with those purely factual recordings of "movement for movement's sake," in a few small and dingy cinemas mostly frequented by the "lower classes" and a sprinkling of youngsters in quest of adventure (about 1905, I happen to remember, there was only one obscure and faintly disreputable *kino* in the whole city of Berlin, bearing, for some unfathomable reason, the English name of "The Meeting Room"). Small wonder that the "better classes," when they slowly began to venture into these early picture theatres, did so, not by way of seeking normal and possibly serious entertainment, but with that characteristic sensation of self-conscious condescension with which we may plunge, in gay company, into the folkloristic depths of Coney Island or a European Kermis; even a few years ago it was the regulation attitude of the socially or intellectually prominent that one could confess to enjoying such austerely educational films as "The Sex Life of the Starfish" or films with "beautiful scenery," but never to a serious liking for narratives.

Today there is no denying that narrative films are not only "art"—not often good art, to be sure, but this applies to other media as well—but also, besides architecture, cartooning, and "commercial design," the only visual art entirely alive. The "movies" have re-established that dynamic contact between art production and art consumption which, for reasons too complex to be considered here, is sorely attenuated, if not entirely interrupted, in many other fields of artistic endeavor. Whether we like it or not, it is the movies that mold, more than any other single force, the opinions, the taste, the language, the dress, the behavior, and even the physical appearance of a public comprising more than 60% of the population of the earth. If all the serious lyrical poets, composers, painters and sculptors were forced by law to stop their activities, a rather small fraction of the general public would become aware of the fact and a still smaller fraction would seriously regret it. If the same thing were to happen with the movies the social consequences would be catastrophic.

In the beginning, then, there were the straight recordings of movement no matter what moved, viz., the prehistoric ancestors of our "documentaries"; and, soon after, the early narratives, viz., the prehistoric ancestors of our "feature films." The craving for a narrative element could be satisfied only by borrowing from older arts, and one should expect that the natural thing would have been to borrow from the theatre, a theatre play being apparently the *genus proximum* to a narrative film in that it consists of a narrative enacted by persons that move. But in reality the imitation of stage performances was a comparatively late and thoroughly frustrated development. What happened at the start was a very different thing: instead of imitating a theatrical performance already endowed with a certain amount of motion, the earliest films [6–7] added movement to works of art originally stationary, so that the dazzling technical invention might achieve a triumph of its own without intruding upon the sphere of higher culture. The living language, which is always right, has endorsed this sensible choice when it still speaks of a "moving picture" or, simply, a "picture," instead of accepting the pretentious and fundamentally erroneous "screen play."

The stationary works enlivened in the earliest movies were indeed pictures: bad nineteenth-century paintings and postcards (or wax works à la Madame Tussaud's), supplemented by the comic strips—a most important root of cinematic art—and the subject matter of popular songs, pulp magazines and dime novels; and the films descending from this ancestry appealed directly and very intensely to a folk art mentality. They gratified—often simultaneously—first: a primitive sense of justice and decorum when virtue and industry were rewarded while vice and laziness were punished; second, plain sentimentality when "the thin trickle of a fictive love interest" took its course "through somewhat serpentine channels," or when, father, dear father, returned from the saloon to find his child dying of diptheria; third, a primordial instinct for bloodshed and cruelty when Andreas Hofer faced the firing squad, or when (in a film of 1893/94) the head of Mary Queen of Scots actually came off; fourth, a taste for mild pornography (I remember with great pleasure a French film of *ca.* 1900 wherein a seemingly but not really well-rounded lady as well as a seemingly but not really slender one were shown changing to bathing suits—an honest, straightforward *porcheria* much less objectionable than the now extinct Betty Boop films and, I am sorry to say, some of the more recent Walt Disney productions); and, finally, that crude sense of humor, graphically described as "slapstick," which feeds upon the sadistic and the pornographic instinct, either singly or in combination.

Not until as late as *ca.* 1905 was a film adaptation of "Faust" ventured upon (cast still "unknown," characteristically enough), and not until 1911 did Sarah Bernhardt lend her prestige to an unbelievably funny film tragedy *Queen Elizabeth of England.* These films represent the first conscious attempt at transplanting the movies from the folk art level to that of "real art"; but they also bear witness to the fact that this commendable goal could not be reached in so simple a manner. It was soon realized that the imitation of a theatre performance with a set stage, fixed entries and exits, and distinctly literary ambitions is the one thing the film must avoid.

The legitimate paths of evolution were opened, not by running away from the folk art character of the primitive film but by developing it within the limits of its own possibilities. Those primordial archetypes of film productions on the folk art level—success or retribution, sentiment, sensation, pornography, and crude humor—could blossom forth into genuine history, tragedy and romance, crime and adventure, and comedy, as soon as it was realized that [7–8] they could be transfigured: not by an artificial injection of literary values but by the exploitation of the unique and specific possibilities of the new medium. Significantly, the beginnings of this legitimate development antedate the attempts at endowing the film with higher values of a foreign order (the crucial period being the years from 1902 to ca. 1905), and the decisive steps were taken by people who were laymen or outsiders from the view-point of the serious stage.

These unique and specific possibilities can be defined as *dynamization of space* and, accordingly, *spatialization of time.* This statement is self-evident to the point of triviality but it belongs to that kind of truths which, just because of their triviality, are easily forgotten or neglected.

In a theatre, space is static, that is, the space represented on the stage, as well as the spatial relation of the beholder to the spectacle, are unalterably fixed. The spectator cannot leave his seat, and the setting of the stage cannot change, during one act (except for such incidentals as rising moons or gathering clouds and such illegitimate re-borrowings from the film as turning wings or gliding backdrops). But, in return for this restriction, the theatre has the advantage that time, the medium of emotion and thought conveyable by speech, is free and independent of anything that may happen in visible space. Hamlet may deliver his famous monologue lying on a couch in the middle distance, doing nothing and only dimly discernible to the spectator and listener, and yet by his mere words enthrall him with a feeling of intensest emotional action.

With the movies the situation is reversed. Here, too, the spectator occupies a fixed seat, but only physically, not as the subject of an aesthetic experience. Aesthetically, he is in permanent motion as his eye identifies itself with the lens of the camera which permanently shifts in distance and direction. And as movable as the spectator is, as movable is, for the same reason, the space presented to him. Not only bodies move in space, but space itself does, approaching, receding, turning, dissolving and recrystallizing as it appears through the controlled locomotion and focussing of the camera and through the cutting and editing of the various shots—not to mention such special effects as visions, transformations, disappearances, slow-motion and fast-motion shots, reversals and trick films. This opens up a world of possibilities of which the stage can never dream. Quite apart from such photographic tricks as the participation of disembodied spirits in the action of the *Topper* series, or the more effective wonders wrought by Roland Young in *The Man Who Could Work Miracles,* there is, on the purely factual level, an untold wealth of themes as inaccessible to the "legitimate" stage as a fog or a snowstorm is to the sculptor; all sorts of violent elemental phenomena and, conversely, events too microscopic to be visible under normal conditions (such as the life-saving injection with the serum flown in at the very last moment, or the fatal bite of [8–9] the yellow fever mosquito); full-scale battle scenes; all kinds of operations, not only in the surgical sense but also in the sense of any actual construction, destruction or experimentation, as in *Louis Pasteur* or *Madame Curie;* a really grand party, moving through many rooms of a mansion or palace. Features like these, even the mere shifting of the scene from one place to another by means of a car perilously negotiating heavy traffic or a motor-boat steered through a nocturnal harbour, will not only always retain their primitive cinematic appeal but also remain enormously effective as a means of stirring the emotions and creating suspense. In addition, the movies have the power, entirely denied to the theatre, to convey psychological experiences by directly projecting their content to the screen, substituting, as it were, the eye of the beholder for the consciousness of the character (as when the imaginings and hallucinations of the drunkard in the otherwise overrated *Lost Weekend* appear as stark realities instead of being described by mere words). But any attempt to convey thought and feelings exclusively, or even primarily, by speech leaves us with a feeling of embarrassment, boredom, or both.

What I mean by thoughts and feelings "conveyed exclusively, or even primarily, by speech" is simply this: contrary to naive expectation, the invention of the sound track in 1928 has been unable to change the basic fact that a moving picture, even when it has learned to talk, remains a picture that moves, and does not convert itself into a piece of writing that is enacted. Its substance remains a series of visual sequences held together by an uninterrupted flow of movement in space (except, of course, for such checks and pauses as have the same compositional value as a rest in music), and not a sustained study in human character and destiny transmitted by effective, let alone "beautiful," diction. I cannot remember a more misleading statement about the movies than Mr. Eric Russell Bentley's in the Spring Number of the *Kenyon Review*, 1945: "The potentialities of the talking screen differ from those of the silent screen in adding the dimension of dialogue—which could be poetry." I would suggest: "The potentialities of the talking screen differ from those of the silent screen in integrating visible movement with dialogue which, therefore, had better not be poetry."

All of us, if we are old enough to remember the period prior to 1928, recall the old-time pianist who, with his eyes glued on the screen, would accompany the events with music adapted to their mood and rhythm; and we also recall the weird and spectral feeling overtaking us when this pianist left his post for a few minutes and the film was allowed to run by itself, the darkness haunted by the monotonous rattle of the machinery. Even the silent film, then, was never mute. The visible spectacle always required, and received, an audible accompaniment which, from the very beginning, distinguished the film from simple pantomime and rather classed it—*mutatis mutandis*—with the ballet. The advent of the talkie meant, not so much an "addition" as a [9–10] transformation: the transformation of musical sound into articulate speech and, therefore, of quasi-pantomime into an entirely new species of spectacle which differs from the ballet, and agrees with the stage play, in that its acoustic component consists of intelligible words, but differs from the stage play and agrees with the ballet in that this acoustic component is not detachable from the visual. In a film, that which we hear remains, for good or worse, inextricably fused with that which we see; the sound, articulate or not, cannot express any more than is expressed, at the same time, by visible movement; and in a good film it does not even attempt to do so. To put it briefly: the play—or, as it is very properly called, the "script"—of a moving picture is subject to what might be termed the *principle of coexpressibility*.

Empirical proof of this principle is furnished by the fact that, wherever the dialogical or monological element gains temporary prominence there appears, with the inevitability of a natural law, the "close-up." What does the close-up achieve? In showing us, in magnification, either the face of the speaker or the face

of the listeners or both in alternation, the camera transforms the human physiognomy into a huge field of action where—given the qualification of the performers—
every subtle movement of the features, almost imperceptible from a natural distance,
becomes an expressive event in visible space and thereby completely integrates
itself with the expressive content of the spoken word; whereas, on the stage, the
spoken word makes a stronger rather than a weaker impression if we are not permitted to count the hairs in Romeo's moustache.

   This does not mean that the scenario is a negligible factor in the making
of a moving picture. It only means that its artistic intention differs in kind from that
of a stage play, and much more from that of a novel or a piece of poetry. As the success of a Gothic jamb figure depends, not only upon its quality as a piece of sculpture
but also, or even more so, upon its integrability with the architecture of the portal,
so does the success of a move script—not unlike that of an opera libretto—depend,
not only upon its quality as a piece of literature but also, or even more so, upon its
integrability with the events on the screen.

   As a result—another empirical proof of the coexpressibility principle—
good movie scripts are unlikely to make good reading and have seldom been published in book form; whereas, conversely, good stage plays have to be severely
altered, cut, and, on the other hand, enriched by interpolations to make good movie
scripts. In Shaw's *Pygmalion,* for instance, the actual process of Eliza's phonetic
education and, still more important, her final triumph at the grand party, are wisely
omitted; we see—or, rather, hear—some samples of her gradual linguistic improvement and finally encounter her, upon her return from the reception, victorious and
splendidly arrayed but deeply hurt for want of recognition and sympathy. In the film
adaptation, precisely these [10–11] two scenes are not only supplied but also strongly
emphasized; we witness the fascinating activities in the laboratory with its array of
spinning disks and mirrors, organ pipes and dancing flames, and we participate in
the ambassadorial party, with many moments of impending catastrophe and a little
counter-intrigue thrown in for suspense. Unquestionably these two scenes, entirely
absent from the play, and indeed unachievable upon the stage, were the highlights
of the film; whereas the Shavian dialogue, however severely cut, turned out to fall a
little flat in certain moments. And wherever, as in so many other films, a poetic
emotion, a musical outburst, or a literary conceit (even, I am grieved to say, some of
the wisecracks of Groucho Marx) entirely lose contact with visible movement, they
strike the sensitive spectator as, literally, out of place. It is certainly terrible when a
soft-boiled He-Man, after the suicide of his mistress, casts a twelve-foot glance upon
her photograph and says something less-than-coexpressible to the effect that he
would never forget her. But when he recites, instead, a piece of poetry as sublimely
more-than-coexpressible as Romeo's monologue at the bier of Juliet, it is still worse.
Reinhardt's *Midsummer Night's Dream* is probably the most unfortunate major
film ever produced; and Olivier's *Henry V* owes its comparative success, apart from
the all but providential adaptability of this particular play, to so many *tours de force*
that it will remain, God willing, an exception rather than set a pattern. It combines
"judicious pruning" with the interpolation of pageantry, non-verbal comedy and
melodrama; it uses a device perhaps best designated as "oblique close-up" (Mr.
Olivier's beautiful face inwardly listening to but not pronouncing the great soliloquy);

and, most notably, it shifts between three levels of archaeological reality: a recon-struction of Elizabethan London, a reconstruction of the events of 1415 as laid down in Shakespeare's play, and the reconstruction of a performance of this play on Shakespeare's own stage. All this is perfectly legitimate; but, even so, the highest praise of the film will always come from those who, like the critic of the *New Yorker,* are not quite in sympathy with either the movies *au naturel* or Shakespeare *au naturel.*

As the writings of Conan Doyle potentially contain all modern mystery stories (except for the tough specimens of the Dashiell Hammett school), so do the films produced between 1900 and 1910 preestablish the subject matter and methods of the moving picture as we know it. This period produced the incunabula of the Western and the crime film (Edwin S. Porter's amazing *Great Train Robbery* of 1903) from which developed the modern Gangster, Adventure, and Mystery pictures (the latter, if well done, is still one of the most honest and genuine forms of film enter-tainment, space being doubly charged with time as the beholder asks himself, not only "what is going to happen?" but also "what has happened before?"). The same period saw the emergence of the fantastically imaginative film (Méliès) which was to lead [11–12] to the expressionist and surrealist experiments (*The Cabinet of Dr. Caligari, Sang d'un Poète,* etc.), on the one hand, and to the more superficial and spectacular fairy tales à la Arabian Nights, on the other. Comedy, later to triumph in Charlie Chaplin, the still insufficiently appreciated Buster Keaton, the Marx Brothers, and the pre-Hollywood creations of René Clair, reached a respectable level in Max Linder and others. In historical and melodramatic films the foundations were laid for movie iconography and movie symbolism, and in the early work of D. W. Griffith we find, not only remarkable attempts at psychological analysis (*Edgar Allen Poe*) and social criticism (*A Corner in Wheat*) but also such basic tech-nical innovations as the long-shot, the flashback and the close-up. And modest trick-films and cartoons paved the way to Felix the Cat, Pop-Eye the Sailor, and Felix's prodigious offspring, Mickey Mouse.

Within their self-imposed limitations the earlier Disney films, and certain sequences in the later ones, represent, as it were, a chemically pure distillation of cinematic possibilities. They retain the most important folkloristic elements—sadism, pornography, the humor engendered by both, and moral justice—almost without dilution and often fuse these elements into a variation on the primitive and inex-haustible David-and-Goliath motif, the triumph of the seemingly weak over the seemingly strong; and their fantastic independence of the natural laws gives them the power to integrate space with time to such perfection that the spatial and temporal experiences of sight and hearing come to be almost interconvertible. A series of soap bubbles, successively punctured, emits a series of sounds exactly corresponding in pitch and volume to the size of the bubbles; the three uvulae of Willie the Whale —small, large and medium—vibrate in consonance with tenor, bass and baritone notes; and the very concept of stationary existence is completely abolished. No object in creation, whether it be a house, a piano, a tree, or an alarm clock, lacks the [12–13] faculties of organic, in fact anthropomorphic, movement, facial expres-sion and phonetic articulation. Incidentally, even in normal, "realistic" films the inanimate object, provided that it is dynamizable, can play the role of a leading character as do the ancient railroad engines in Buster Keaton's *General* and *Niagara Falls*. How the earlier Russian films exploited the possibility of heroizing all sorts of machinery lives in everybody's memory; and it is perhaps more than an accident that the two films which will go down in history as the great comical and the great serious masterpiece of the silent period bear the names and immortalize the personalities of two big ships: Keaton's *Navigator* (1924) and Eisenstein's *Potemkin* (1925).

The evolution from the jerky beginnings to this grand climax offers the fascinating spectacle of a new artistic medium gradually becoming conscious of its legitimate, that is, exclusive, possibilities and limitations—a spectacle not unlike the development of the mosaic, which started out with transposing illusionistic genre pictures into a more durable material and culminated in the hieratic supernaturalism of Ravenna; or the development of line engraving, which started out as a cheap and handy substitute for book illumination and culminated in the purely "graphic" style of Dürer.

Just so the silent movies developed a definite style of their own, adapted to the specific conditions of the medium. A hitherto unknown language was forced upon a public not yet capable of reading it, and the more proficient the public became the more refinement could develop in the language. For a Saxon peasant of around 800 it was not easy to understand the meaning of a picture showing a man as he pours water over the head of another man, and even later many people found it difficult to grasp the significance of two ladies standing behind the throne of an emperor. For the public of around 1910 it was no less difficult to understand the meaning of the speechless action in a moving picture, and the producers employed means of clarification similar to those we find in mediaeval art. One of these were printed titles or letters, striking equivalents of the mediaeval *tituli* and scrolls (at a still earlier date there even used to be explainers who would say, *viva voce:* "Now he [13–14] thinks his wife is dead but she isn't" or: "I don't wish to offend the ladies in the audience but I doubt that any of them would have done that much for her child"). Another, less obtrusive method of explanation was the introduction of a fixed iconography which from the outset informed the spectator about the basic facts and characters, much as the two ladies behind the emperor, when carrying a sword and a cross, respectively, were uniquely determined as Fortitude and Faith. There arose, identifiable by standardized appearance, behavior, and attributes, the well-remembered types of the Vamp and the Straight Girl (perhaps the most convincing modern equivalents of the mediaeval personifications of the Vices and Virtues), the Family Man, and the Villain, the latter marked by a black moustache and walking stick. Nocturnal scenes were printed on blue or green film. A checkered table cloth meant, once for all, a "poor but honest" milieu; a happy marriage, soon to be endangered by the shadows from the past, was symbolized by the young wife's pouring the breakfast coffee for her husband; the first kiss was invariably announced by the lady's gently playing with her partner's necktie and was invariably accompanied by her kicking out with her left foot. The conduct of the characters was predetermined accordingly. The poor but honest laborer who, after leaving his little house with the checkered table cloth, came upon an abandoned baby could not but take it to his home and bring it up as best he could; the Family Man could not but yield, however temporarily, to the temptations of the Vamp. As a result these early melodramas had a highly gratifying and soothing quality in that events took shape, without the complications of individual psychology, according to a pure Aristotelian logic so badly missed in real life.

Devices like these became gradually less necessary as the public grew accustomed to interpret the action by itself and were virtually abolished by the invention of the talking film. But even now there survive—quite legitimately, I think —the remnants of a "fixed attitude and attribute" principle and, more basic, a primitive or folkloristic concept of plot construction. Even today we take it for granted that the diphtheria of a baby tends to occur when the parents are out, and, having occurred, solves all their matrimonial problems. Even today we demand of a decent mystery film that the butler, though he may be anything from an agent of the British Secret Service to the real father of the daughter of the house, must not turn out to be the murderer. Even today we love to see Pasteur, Zola, or Ehrlich win out against stupidity and wickedness, with their respective wives trusting and trusting all the time. Even today we much prefer a happy finale to a gloomy one, and insist, at the very least, on the observance of the Aristotelian rule that the story have a beginning, a middle, and an ending—a rule the abrogation of which has done so much to estrange the general public from the more elevated spheres of modern writing. Primitive symbolism, too, survives in such amusing details [14–15] as the last sequence of Casablanca where the delightfully crooked and right-minded Préfet de Police casts an empty bottle of Vichy water into the wastepaper basket; and in such telling symbols of the supernatural as Sir Cedric Hardwicke's Death in the guise of a "gentleman in a dustcoat trying" (On Borrowed Time) or Claude Rains' Hermes Psychopompos in the striped trousers of an airline manager (Here Comes Mister Jordan).

The most conspicuous advances were made in directing, lighting, camera work, cutting, and acting proper. But while in most of these fields the evolution proceeded continuously—though, of course, not without detours, breakdowns and archaic relapses—the development of acting suffered a sudden interruption by the invention of the talking film; so that the style of acting in the silents can already be evaluated in retrospect, as a lost art not unlike the painting technique of Jan van Eyck or, to take up our previous simile, the burin technique of Dürer. It was soon realized that acting in a silent film neither meant a pantomimic exaggeration of stage acting (as was generally and erroneously assumed by professional stage actors who more and more frequently condescended to perform in the movies), nor could dispense with stylization altogether; a man photographed while walking down a gangway in ordinary, every-day-life fashion looked like anything but a man walking down a gangway when the result appeared on the screen. If the picture was to look both natural and meaningful the acting had to be done in a manner equally different from the style of the stage and the reality of ordinary life; speech had to be made dispensable by establishing an organic relation between the acting and the technical procedure of cine-photography—much as in Dürer's prints color had been made dispensable by establishing an organic relation between the design and the technical procedure of line engraving.

This was precisely what the great actors of the silent period accomplished, and it is a significant fact that the best of them did not come from the stage, whose crystallized tradition prevented Duse's only film, *Cenere,* from being more than a priceless record of Duse. They came instead from the circus or the variety, as was the case of Chaplin, Keaton and Will Rogers; from nothing in particular, as was the case of Theda Bara, of her greater European parallel, the Danish actress Asta Nielsen, and of Garbo; or from everything under the sun, as was the case of Douglas Fairbanks. The style of these "old masters" was indeed comparable to the style of line engraving in that it was, and had to be, exaggerated in comparison with stage acting (just as the sharply incised and vigorously curved *tailles* of the burin are exaggerated in comparison with pencil strokes or brushwork), but richer, subtler and infinitely more precise. The advent of the talkies, reducing if not abolishing this difference between acting and stage acting, thus confronted the actors and actresses of the silent screen with a serious problem. Buster Keaton yielded [15–16] to temptation and fell. Chaplin first tried to stand his ground and to remain an exquisite archaist but finally gave in, with only moderate success *(The Dictator).* Only the glorious Harpo has thus far successfully refused to utter a single articulate sound; and only Greta Garbo succeeded, in a measure, in transforming her style in principle. But even in her case one cannot help feeling that her first talking picture, *Anna Christie,* where she could ensconce herself, most of the time, in mute or monosyllabic sullenness, was better than her later performances; and in the second, talking version of *Anna Karenina,* the weakest moment is certainly when she delivers a big Ibsenian speech to her husband, and the strongest when she silently moves along the platform of the railroad station while her despair takes shape in the consonance of her movement (and expression) with the movement of the nocturnal space around her, filled with the real noises of the trains and the imaginary sound of the "little men with the iron hammers" that drives her, relentlessly and almost without her realizing it, under the wheels.

Small wonder that there is sometimes felt a kind of nostalgia for the silent period and that devices have been worked out to combine the virtues of sound and speech with those of silent acting, such as the "oblique close-up" already mentioned in connection with *Henry V;* the dance behind glass doors in *Sous les Toits de Paris;* or, in the *Histoire d'un Tricheur,* Sacha Guitry's recital of the events of his youth while the events themselves are "silently" enacted on the screen. However, this nostalgic feeling is no argument against the talkies as such. Their evolution has shown that, in art, every gain entails a certain loss on the other side of the ledger; but that the gain remains a gain, provided that the basic nature of the medium is realized and respected. One can imagine that, when the cave-men of Altamira began to paint their buffaloes in natural colors instead of merely incising the contours, the more conservative cave-men foretold the end of palaeolithic art. But palaeolithic art went on, and so will the movies. New technical inventions always tend to dwarf the values already attained, especially in a medium that owes its very existence to technical experimentation. The earliest talkies were infinitely inferior to the then mature silents, and most of the present technicolor films are still inferior to the now mature talkies in black and white. But even if Aldous Huxley's nightmare should come true and the experiences of taste, smell and touch should be added to those of sight and hearing, even then we may say with the Apostle, as we have said when first confronted with the sound track and the technicolor film: "We are troubled on every side, yet not distressed; we are perplexed, but not in despair."

From the law of time-charged space and space-bound time, there follows the fact that the *"screen play,"* in contrast to the theater play, *has no aesthetic existence independent of its performance, and that its characters have no* [16–17] *aesthetic existence outside the actors.*

The playwright writes in the fond hope that his work will be an imperishable jewel in the treasure house of civilization and will be presented in hundreds of performances that are but transient variations on a "work" that is constant. The script writer, on the other hand, writes for one producer, one director and one cast. Their work achieves the same degree of permanence as does his; and should the same or a similar scenario ever be filmed by a different director and a different cast there will result an altogether different "play."

Othello or Nora are definite, substantial figures created by the playwright. They can be played well or badly, and they can be "interpreted" in one way or another; but they most definitely exist, no matter who plays them or even whether they are played at all. The character in a film, however, lives and dies with the actor. It is not the entity "Othello" interpreted by Robeson or the entity "Nora" interpreted by Duse; it is the entity "Greta Garbo" incarnate in a figure called Anna Christie or the entity "Robert Montgomery" incarnate in a murderer who, for all we know or care to know, may forever remain anonymous but will never cease to haunt our memories. Even when the names of the characters happen to be Henry VIII or Anna Karenina, the King who ruled England from 1509 to 1547 and the woman created by Tolstoi do not exist outside the being of Garbo and Laughton. They are but empty and incorporeal outlines like the shadows in Homer's Hades, assuming the character of reality only when filled with the life blood of an actor. Conversely, if a movie role is badly played there remains literally nothing of it, no matter how interesting the character's psychology or how elaborate the words.

What applies to the actor applies, *mutatis mutandis,* to most of the other artists, or artisans, who contribute to the making of a film: the director, the sound man, the enormously important camera man, even the make-up man. A stage production is rehearsed until everything is ready, and then it is repeatedly performed in three consecutive hours. At each performance everybody has to be on hand and does his work; and afterwards he goes home and to bed. The work of the stage actor may thus be likened to that of a musician, and that of the stage director to that of a conductor. Like these, they have a certain répertoire which they have studied and present in a number of complete but transitory performances, be it "Hamlet" today and "Ghosts" tomorrow, or "Life With Father" *per saecula saeculorum.* The activities of the film actor and the film director, however, are comparable, respectively, to those of the plastic artist and the architect, rather than to those of the musician and conductor. Stage work is continuous but transitory; film work is discontinuous but permanent. Individual sequences are done piecemeal and out of order according to the most efficient use of sets and personnel. Each bit is done over and over again until it stands; and when the whole has been cut and composed [17–18] everyone

is through with it forever. Needless to say that this very procedure cannot but emphasize the curious consubstantiality that exists between the person of the movie actor
and his role. Coming into existence piece by piece, regardless of the natural sequence of events, the "character" can grow into a unified whole only if the actor
manages to be, not merely to play, Henry VIII or Anna Karenina throughout the entire
wearisome period of shooting. I have it on the best of authorities that Laughton was
really difficult to live with in the particular six or eight weeks during which he was
doing—or rather being—Captain Bligh.

It might be said that a film, called into being by a cooperative effort in
which all contributions have the same degree of permanence, is the nearest modern
equivalent of a mediaeval cathedral; the role of the producer corresponding, more
or less, to that of the bishop or archbishop; that of the director to that of the architect-
in-chief; that of the scenario writers to that of the scholastic advisers establishing the
iconographical program; and that of the actors, camera men, cutters, sound men,
make-up men and the divers technicians to that of those whose work provided the
physical entity of the finished product, from the sculptors, glass painters, bronze
casters, carpenters and skilled masons down to the quarry men and woodsmen. And
if you speak to any one of these collaborators he will tell you, with perfect *bona
fides,* that his is really the most important job—which is quite true to the extent that
it is indispensable.

This comparison may seem sacrilegious, not only because there are, pro-
portionally, fewer good films than there are good cathedrals, but also because the
movies are commercial. However, if commercial art be defined as all art not primarily produced in order to gratify the creative urge of its maker but primarily
intended to meet the requirements of a patron or a buying public, it must be said
that non-commercial art is the exception rather than the rule, and a fairly recent and
not always felicitous exception at that. While it is true that commercial art is always
in danger of ending up as a prostitute, it is equally true that non-commercial art is
always in danger of ending up as an old maid. Non-commercial art has given us
Seurat's *Grande Jatte* and Shakespeare's Sonnets, but also much that is esoteric to
the point of incommunicability. Conversely, commercial art has given us much that
is vulgar or snobbish (two aspects of the same thing) to the point of loathsomeness,
but also Dürer's prints and Shakespeare's plays. For, we must not forget that Dürer's
prints were partly made on commission and partly intended to be sold in the open
market; and that Shakespeare's plays—in contrast to the earlier masques and *inter-
mezzi* which were produced at court by aristocratic amateurs and could afford to
be so incomprehensible that even those who described them in printed monographs
occasionally failed to grasp their intended significance—were meant to appeal,
and did appeal, not only to the select few but also to [*18*] everyone who was
prepared to pay a shilling for admission.

It is this requirement of communicability that makes commercial art more
vital than non-commercial, and therefore potentially much more effective for better
or for worse. The commercial producer can both educate and pervert the general
public, and can allow the general public—or rather his idea of the general public
—both to educate and to pervert himself. As is demonstrated by a number of excellent films that proved to be great box office successes, the public does not refuse to

accept good products if it gets them. That it does not get them very often is caused, not so much by commercialism as such as by too little discernment and, paradoxical though it may seem, too much timidity in its application. Hollywood believes that it must produce "what the public wants" while the public would take whatever Hollywood produces. If Hollywood were to decide for itself what it wants it would get away with it—even if it should decide to "depart from evil and do good." For, to revert to whence we started: in modern life the movies are what most other forms of art have ceased to be, not an adornment but a necessity.

That this should be so is understandable, not only from a sociological but also from an art-historical point of view. The processes of all the earlier representational arts conform, in a higher or lesser degree, to an idealistic conception of the world. These arts operate from top to bottom, so to speak, and not from bottom to top; they start with an idea to be projected into shapeless matter and not with the objects that constitute the physical world. The painter works on a blank wall or canvas which he organizes into a likeness of things and persons according to his idea (however much this idea may have been nourished by reality); he does not work with the things and persons themselves even if he works "from the model." The same is true of the sculptor with his shapeless mass of clay or his untooled block of stone or wood; of the writer with his sheet of paper or his dictaphone; and even of the stage designer with his empty and sorely limited section of space. It is the movies, and only the movies, that do justice to that materialistic interpretation of the universe which, whether we like it or not, pervades contemporary civilization. Excepting the very special case of the animated cartoon, the movies organize material things and persons, not a neutral medium, into a composition that receives its style, and may even become fantastic or pretervoluntarily symbolic, not so much by an interpretation in the artist's mind [27–28] as by the actual manipulation of physical objects and recording machinery. The medium of the movies is physical reality as such: the physical reality of eighteenth-century Versailles—no matter whether it be the original or a Hollywood facsimile indistinguishable therefrom for all aesthetic intents and purposes—or of a suburban home in Westchester; the physical reality of the Rue de Lappe in Paris or of the Gobi Desert, of Paul Ehrlich's apartment in Frankfurt or of the streets of New York in the rain; the physical reality of engines and animals, of Edward G. Robinson and Jimmy Cagney. All these objects and persons must be organized into a work of art. They can be arranged in all sorts of ways ("arrangement" comprising, of course, such things as make-up, lighting and camera work); but there is no running away from them. From this point of view it becomes evident that an attempt at subjecting the world to artistic pre-stylization, as in the expressionist settings of *The Cabinet of Doctor Caligari* (1919), could be no more than an exciting experiment that could exert but little influence upon the general course of events. To pre-stylize reality prior to tackling it amounts to dodging the problem. The problem is to manipulate and shoot unstylized reality in such a way that the result has style. This is a proposition no less legitimate and no less difficult than any proposition in the older arts.   [28]

1. How relevant to modern films is Prof. Panofsky's summary of the original methods of film narrative?

2. Is Prof. Panofsky correct when he contends that film dialogue must not
    be eloquent? How many films are you familiar with that have eloquent
    dialogue?

3. How does Prof. Panofsky make his case for film as an art form? Are his
    arguments and analogies persuasive?

4. Is Prof. Panofsky correct in foreseeing a possible improvement in the
    quality of Hollywood movies? Does he omit or misrepresent any
    factors that might bring such an improvement about?

THE FILM AGE

Arnold Hauser

. . . The accent is now on the simultaneity of the contents of consciousness, the immanence of the past in the present, the constant flowing together of the different periods of time, the amorphous fluidity of inner experience, the boundlessness of the stream of time by which the soul is borne along, the relativity of space and time, that is to say, the impossibility of differentiating and defining the media in which the mind moves. In this new conception of time almost all the strands of the texture which form the stuff of modern art converge: the abandonment of the plot, the elimination of the hero, the relinquishing of psychology, the "automatic method of writing" and, above all, the montage technique and the intermingling of temporal and spatial forms of the film. The new concept of time, whose basic element is simultaneity and whose nature consists in the spatialization of the temporal element, is expressed in no other genre so impressively as in this youngest art, which dates from the same period as Bergson's philosophy of time. The agreement between the technical methods of the film and the characteristics of the new concept of time is so complete that one has the feeling that the time categories of modern art altogether must have arisen from the spirit of cinematic form, and one is inclined to consider the film itself as the stylistically [939–940] most representative, though qualitatively perhaps not the most fertile genre of contemporary art.

The theatre is in many respects the artistic medium most similar to the film; particularly in view of its combination of spatial and temporal forms, it represents the only real analogy to the film. But what happens on the stage is partly spatial,

ARNOLD HAUSER, a noted historian, has taught in Europe and the United States. His experience and interest in films are reflected in the last chapter of his monumental *The Social History of Art*, from which the present selection is taken.

From *The Social History of Art*, Volume II, by Arnold Hauser. Published 1951, 1957 by Alfred A. Knopf, Inc. Reprinted by permission of the publisher. English edition © by Routledge & Kegan Paul Ltd., which also granted permission for this reprinting.

partly temporal; as a rule spatial and temporal, but never a mixture of the spatial and the temporal, as are the happenings in a film. The most fundamental difference between the film and the other arts is that, in its world-picture, the boundaries of space and time are fluid—space has a quasi-temporal, time, to some extent, a spatial character. In the plastic arts, as also on the stage, space remains static, motionless, unchanging, without a goal and without a direction; we move about quite freely in it, because it is homogeneous in all its parts and because none of the parts presupposes the other temporally. The phases of the movement are not stages, not steps in a gradual development; their sequence is subject to no constraint. Time in literature —above all in the drama—on the other hand, has a definite direction, a trend of development, an objective goal, independent of the spectator's experience of time; it is no mere reservoir, but an ordered succession. Now, these dramaturgical categories of space and time have their character and functions completely altered in the film. Space loses its static quality, its serene passivity and now becomes dynamic; it comes into being as it were before our eyes. It is fluid, unlimited, unfinished, an element with its own history, its own scheme and process of development. Homogeneous physical space here assumes the characteristics of heterogeneously composed historical time. In this medium the individual stages are no longer of the same kind, the individual parts of space no longer of equal value; it contains specially qualified positions, some with a certain priority in the development and others signifying the culmination of the spatial experience. The use of the close-up, for example, not only has spatial criteria, it also represents a phase to be reached or to be surpassed in the temporal development of the film. In a good film the close-ups are not distributed arbitrarily and capriciously. They are not cut in independently of the inner development of the scene, not at any time and anywhere, [940–941] but only where their potential energy can and should make itself felt. For a close-up is not a cut-out picture with a frame; it is always merely part of a picture, like, for instance, the repoussoir figures in baroque painting which introduce a dynamic quality into the picture similar to that created by the close-ups in the spatial structure of a film.

But as if space and time in the film were interrelated by being interchangeable, the temporal relationships acquire an almost spatial character, just as space acquires a topical interest and takes on temporal characteristics, in other words, a certain element of freedom is introduced into the succession of their moments. In the temporal medium of a film we move in a way that is otherwise peculiar to space, completely free to choose our direction, proceeding from one phase of time into another, just as one goes from one room to another, disconnecting the individual stages in the development of events and grouping them, generally speaking, according to the principles of spatial order. In brief, time here loses, on the one hand, its uninterrupted continuity, on the other, its irreversible direction. It can be brought to a standstill: in close-ups; reversed: in flash-backs; repeated: in recollections; and skipped across: in visions of the future. Concurrent, simultaneous events can be shown successively, and temporally distinct events simultaneously—by double-exposure and alternation; the earlier can appear later, the later before its time. This cinematic conception of time has a thoroughly subjective and apparently irregular character compared with the empirical and the dramatic conception of the same medium. The time of empirical reality is a uniformly progressive, uninterruptedly continuous, absolutely irreversible order, in which events follow one another as if "on a conveyor belt." It is true that dramatic time is by no means identical with empirical time—the embarrassment caused by a clock showing the correct time on the stage comes from this discrepancy—and the unity of time prescribed by classicistic dramaturgy can even be interpreted as the fundamental elimination of ordinary time, and yet the temporal relationships in the drama have more points of contact with the chronological order of ordinary experience than the order of time in a film. Thus in the drama, or at least in one and the same act [941–942] of a drama, the temporal continuity of empirical reality is preserved intact. Here too, as in real life, events follow each other according to the law of a progression which permits neither interruptions and jumps, nor repetitions and inversions, and conforms to a standard of time which is absolutely constant, that is, undergoes no acceleration, retardation or stoppages of any kind within the several sections (acts or scenes). In the film, on the other hand, not only the speed of successive events, but also the chronometric standard itself is often different from shot to shot, according as to whether slow or fast motion, short or long cutting, many or few close-ups, are used.

The dramatist is prohibited by the logic of scenic arrangement from repeating moments and phases of time, an expedient that is often the source of the most intensive aesthetic effects in the film. It is true that a part of the story is often treated retrospectively in the drama, and the antecedents followed backwards in time, but they are usually represented indirectly—either in the form of a coherent narrative or of one limited to scattered hints. The technique of the drama does not permit the playwright to go back to past stages in the course of a progressively developing plot and to insert them *directly* into the sequence of events, into the dramatic present—that is, it is only recently that it has begun to permit it, perhaps under the immediate influence of the film, or under the influence of the new conception of time, familiar also from the modern novel. The technical possibility of interrupting any shot without further ado suggests the possibilities of a discontinuous treatment of time from the very outset and provides the film with the means of heightening the tension of a scene either by interpolating heterogeneous incidents or assigning the individual phases of the scene to different sections of the work. In this way the film often produces the effect of someone playing on a keyboard and striking the keys ad libitum, up and down, to right and left. In a film we often see the hero first at the beginning of his career as a young man, later, going back to the past, as a child; we then see him, in the further course of the plot, as a mature man and, having followed his career for a time, we, finally, may see him still living after his death, in the memory of one of his relations or friends. As a result of the [942–943] discontinuity of time, the retrospective development of the plot is combined with the progressive in complete freedom, with no kind of chronological tie, and through the repeated twists and turns in the time-continuum, mobility, which is the very essence of the cinematic experience, is pushed to the uttermost limits. The real spatialization of time in the film does not take place, however, until the simultaneity of parallel plots is portrayed. It is the experience of the simultaneity of different, spatially separated happenings that puts the audience into that condition of suspense, which moves between space and time and claims the categories of both orders for itself. It is the simultaneous nearness and remoteness of things—their nearness to one another in time and their distance from one another in space—that constitutes that spatio-temporal element, that two-dimensionality of time, which is the real medium of the film and the basic category of its world-picture.

It was discovered in a comparatively early stage in the history of the film that the representation of two simultaneous sequences of events is part of the original stock of cinematic forms. First this simultaneity was simply recorded and brought to the notice of the audience by clocks showing the same time or by similar direct indications; the artistic technique of the intermittent treatment of a double plot and the alternating montage of the single phases of such a plot only developed step by step. But later on we come across examples of this technique at every turn. And whether we stand between two rival parties, two competitors or two doubles, the structure of the film is dominated in any case by the crossing and intersecting of the two different lines, by the bilateral character of the development and the simultaneity of the opposing actions. The famous finish of the early, already classical Griffith films, in which the upshot of an exciting plot is made to depend on whether a train or a car, the intriguer or the "king's messenger on horseback," the murderer or the rescuer, reaches the goal first, using the then revolutionary technique of continuously changing pictures, flashing and vanishing like lightning, became the pattern of the dénouement since followed by most films in similar situations.

The time experience of the present age consists above all in [943–944] an awareness of the moment in which we find ourselves: in an awareness of the present. Everything topical, contemporary, bound together in the present moment is of special significance and value to the man of today, and, filled with this idea, the mere fact of simultaneity acquires new meaning in his eyes. His intellectual world is imbued with the atmosphere of the immediate present, just as that of the Middle Ages was characterized by an other-worldly atmosphere and that of the enlightenment by a mood of forward-looking expectancy. He experiences the greatness of his cities, the miracles of his technics, the wealth of his ideas, the hidden depths of his psychology in the contiguity, the interconnections and dovetailing of things and processes. The fascination of "simultaneity," the discovery that, on the one hand, the same man experiences so many different, unconnected and irreconcilable things in one and the same moment, and that, on the other, different men in different places often experience the same things, that the same things are happening at the same time in places completely isolated from each other, this universalism, of which modern technics have made contemporary man conscious, is perhaps the real source of the new conception of time and of the whole abruptness with which modern art describes life. This rhapsodic quality, which distinguishes the modern novel most sharply from the older novel, is at the same time the characteristic accountable for its most cinematic effects. The discontinuity of the plot and the scenic development, the sudden emersion of the thoughts and moods, the relativity and the inconsistency of the time-standards, are what remind us in the works of Proust and Joyce, Dos Passos and Virginia Woolf of the cuttings, dissolves and interpolations of the film, and it is simply film magic when Proust brings two incidents, which may lie thirty years apart, as closely together as if there were only two hours between them. The way in which, in Proust, past and present, dreams and speculation join hands across the intervals of space and time, the sensibility, always on the scent of new tracks, roams about in space and time, and the boundaries of space and time vanish in this endless and boundless stream of interrelations: all this corresponds exactly to that mixture of space and time in which the film moves. Proust never mentions dates and [944–945] ages; we never know exactly how old the hero of his novel is, and even the chronological relationships of the events often remain rather vague. The experiences and happenings do not cohere by reason of their proximity in time and the attempt to demarcate and arrange them chronologically would be all the more nonsensical from his point of view as, in his opinion, every man has his typical experiences which recur periodically. The boy, the youth and the man always experience fundamentally the same things; the meaning of an incident often does not dawn on him until years after he has experienced and endured it; but he can hardly ever distinguish the deposit of the years that are past from the experience of the present hour in which he is living. Is one not in every moment of one's life the same child or the same invalid or the same lonely stranger with the same wakeful, sensitive, unappeased nerves? Is one not in every situation of life the person capable of experiencing this and that, who possesses, in the recurring features of his experience, the one protection against the passage of time? Do not all our experiences take place as it were at the same time? And is this simultaneity not really the negation of time? And this negation, is it not a struggle for the recovery of that inwardness of which physical space and time deprive us?

Joyce fights for the same inwardness, the same directness of experience, when he, like Proust, breaks up and merges well-articulated, chronologically organized time. In his work, too, it is the interchangeability of the contents of consciousness which triumphs over the chronological arrangement of the experiences, for him, too, time is a road without direction, on which man moves to and fro. But he pushes the spatialization of time even further than Proust, and shows the inner happenings not only in longitudinal but also in cross-sections. The images, ideas, brainwaves and memories stand side by side with sudden and absolute abruptness; hardly any consideration is paid to their origins, all the emphasis is on their contiguity, their simultaneity. The spatialization of time goes so far in Joyce, that one can begin the reading of *Ulysses* where one likes, with only a rough knowledge of the context—not necessarily only after a first reading, as has been said, and almost in any sequence one cares to choose. The [945–946] medium in which the reader finds himself, is in fact wholly spatial, for the novel describes not only the picture of a great city, but also adopts its structure to some extent, the network of its streets and squares, in which people stroll about, walking in and out and stopping when and where they like. It is supremely characteristic of the cinematic quality of this technique that Joyce wrote his novel not in the final succession of the chapters, but—as is the custom in the production of films—made himself independent of the sequence of the plot and worked at several chapters at the same time.

We meet the Bergsonian conception of time, as used in the film and the modern novel—though not always so unmistakably as here—in all the genres and trends of contemporary art. The "simultanéité des états d'âmes" is, above all, the basic experience connecting the various tendencies of modern painting, the futurism of the Italians with the expressionism of Chagall, and the cubism of Picasso with the surrealism of Giorgio de Chirico or Salvador Dali. Bergson discovered the counterpoint of spiritual processes and the musical structure of their interrelationships. Just as, when we listen properly to a piece of music, we have in our ears the mutual connection of each new note with all those that have already sounded, so we always possess in our deepest and most vital experiences everything that we have ever experienced and made our own in life. If we understand ourselves, we read our own souls as a musical score, we resolve the chaos of the entangled sounds and transform them into a polyphony of different parts.—All art is a game with and a fight against chaos; it is always advancing more and more dangerously towards chaos and rescuing more and more extensive provinces of the spirit from its clutch. If there is any progress in the history of art, then it consists in the constant growth of these provinces wrested from chaos. With its analysis of time, the film stands in the direct line of this development: it has made it possible to represent visually experiences that have previously been expressed only in musical forms. The artist capable of filling this new possibility, this still empty form, with real life has not yet arrived, however.

The crisis of the film, which seems to be developing into a chronic illness, is due above all to the fact that the film is not finding [946–947] its writers or, to put it more accurately, the writers are not finding their way to the film. Accustomed to doing as they like within their own four walls, they are now required to take into account producers, directors, script-writers, cameramen, art-directors and technicians of all kinds, although they do not acknowledge the authority of this spirit of co-operation, or indeed the idea of artistic co-operation at all. Their feelings revolt against the idea of the production of works of art being surrendered to a collective, to a "concern," and they feel that it is a disparagement of art that an extraneous dictate, or at best a majority, should have the last word in decisions of the motives of which they are often unable to account for themselves. From the point of view of the nineteenth century, the situation with which the writer is asked to come to terms is quite unusual and unnatural. The atomized and uncontrolled artistic endeavours of the present now meet for the first time with a principle opposed to their anarchy. For the mere fact of an artistic enterprise based on co-operation is evidence of an integrating tendency of which—if one disregards the theatre, where it is in any case more a matter of the reproduction than the production of works of art—there had really been no perfect example since the Middle Ages, and, in particular, since the masons' lodge. How far removed film production still is, however, from the generally accepted principle of an artistic co-operative group, is shown not only by the inability of most writers to establish a connection with the film, but also by such a phenomenon as Chaplin, who believes that he must do as much as possible in his films on his own: the acting of the main part, the direction, the script, the music. But even if it is only the beginning of a new method of organized art production, the, for the present, still empty framework of a new integration, nevertheless, here too, as in the whole economic, social and political life of the present age, what is being striven for is the comprehensive planning without which both our cultural and material world threaten to go to pieces. We are confronted here with the same tension as we find throughout our social life: democracy and dictatorship, specialization and integration, rationalism and irrationalism, colliding with each other. But if even in the field of economics and politics planning cannot always be solved by [947–

948] imposing rules of conduct, it is all the less possible in art, where all violation of spontaneity, all forcible levelling down of taste, all institutional regulation of personal initiative, are involved in great though certainly not such mortal dangers as is often imagined.

But how, in an age of the most extreme specialization and the most sophisticated individualism, are harmony and an integration of individual endeavours to be brought about? How, to speak on a practical level, is the situation to be brought to an end in which the most poverty-stricken literary inventions sometimes underlie the technically most successful films? It is not a question of competent directors against incompetent writers, but of two phenomena belonging to different periods of time—the lonely, isolated writer dependent on his own resources and the problems of the film which can only be solved collectively. The co-operative film-unit anticipates a social technique to which we are not yet equal, just as the newly invented camera anticipated an artistic technique of which no one at the time really knew the range and power. The reunion of the divided functions, first of all the personal union of the director and the author, which has been suggested as a way to surmount the crisis, would be more an evasion of the problem than its solution, for it would prevent but not abolish the specialization that has to be overcome, would not bring about but merely avoid the necessity of the planning which is needed. Incidentally, the monistic-individual principle in the discharge of the various functions, in place of a collectively organized division of labour, corresponds not merely externally and technically to an amateurish method of working, but it also involves a lack of inner tension which is reminiscent of the simplicity of the amateur film. Or may the whole effort to achieve a production of art based on planning only have been a temporary disturbance, a mere episode, which is now being swept away again by the torrent of individualism? May the film be perhaps not the beginning of a new artistic era, but merely the somewhat hesitant continuation of the old individualistic culture, still full of vitality, to which we owe the whole of post-medieval art?—Only if this were so, would it be possible to solve the film crisis by the personal union of certain functions, that is, by partly surrendering the principle of collective labour.   *[948–949]*

The film crisis is, however, also connected with a crisis in the public itself. The millions and millions who fill the many thousands of cinemas all over the world from Hollywood to Shanghai and from Stockholm to Cape Town daily and hourly, this unique world-embracing league of mankind, have a very confused social structure. The only link between these people is that they all stream into the cinemas, and stream out of them again as amorphously as they are pumped in; they remain a heterogeneous, inarticulate, shapeless mass with the only common feature of belonging to no uniform class or culture. This mass of cinema-goers can hardly be called a "public" proper, for only a more or less constant group of patrons can be described as such, one which is able to some extent to guarantee the continuity of production in a certain field of art. Public-like agglomerations are based on mutual understanding; even if opinions are divided, they diverge on one and the same plane. But with the masses who sit together in the cinemas and who have undergone no previous common intellectual formation of any kind, it would be futile to look for such a platform of mutual understanding. If they dislike a film there is such a small chance of agreement amongst them as to the reasons for their rejection of the film that one must assume that even general approval is based on a misunderstanding.

The homogeneous and constant public units which, as mediators between the art producers and the social strata with no real interest in art, had always discharged a fundamentally conserving function were, as we know, dissolved with the advancing democratization of the enjoyment of art. The bourgeois subscription audiences of the state and municipal theatres of the last century still formed a more or less uniform, organically developed body, but with the end of the repertory theatre even the last remains of this public were scattered and since then an integrated audience has come into being only in particular circumstances, though in some cases the size of such audiences has been bigger than ever before. It was on the whole identical with the casual cinema-going public which has to be caught by new and original attractions every time and over and over again. The repertory theatre, the serial performance theatre and the cinema mark the successive stages in the democratization of art and the gradual [949–950] loss of the festive character that was formerly more or less the property of every form of theatre. The cinema takes the final step on this road of profanation, for even to attend the modern metropolitan theatre showing some popular play or other still demands a certain internal and external preparation—in most cases seats have to be booked in advance, one has to keep to a fixed time and to prepare for an occupation that will fill the whole evening —whereas one attends the cinema *en passant,* in one's everyday clothes and at any time during the continuous performance. The everyday point of view of the film is in perfect accordance with the improvisation and unpretentiousness of cinema-going.

The film signifies the first attempt since the beginning of our modern individualistic civilization to produce art for a mass public. As is known, the changes in the structure of the theatre and reading public, connected at the beginning of the last century with the rise of the boulevard play and the feuilleton novel, formed the real beginning of the democratization of art which reaches it culmination in mass attendance of cinemas. The transition from the private theatre of the princes' courts to the bourgeois state and municipal theatre and then to the theatre trusts, or from the opera to the operetta and then to the revue, marked the separate phases of a development characterized by the effort to capture ever wider circles of consumers, in order to cover the costs of the growing investments. The outfit for an operetta could still be sustained by a medium-sized theatre, that of a revue or a large ballet had already to travel from one big city to the next; in order to amortise the invested capital, the cinema-goers of the whole world have to contribute to the financing of a big film. But it is this fact that determines the influence of the masses on the production of art. By their mere presence at theatrical performances in Athens or the Middle Ages they were never able to influence the ways of art directly, only since they have come on the scene as consumers and paid the full price for their enjoyment, have the terms on which they hand over their shillings become a decisive factor in the history of art.

There has always been an element of tension between the quality and the popularity of art, which is not by any means to say that the broad masses of the people have at any time taken a [950–951] stand against qualitatively good art in favour of inferior art on principle. Naturally, the appreciation of a more complicated art presents them with greater difficulties than the more simple and less developed, but the lack of adequate understanding does not necessarily prevent them from accepting this art—albeit not exactly on account of its aesthetic quality. Success with them is completely divorced from qualitative criteria. They do not react to what is artistically good or bad, but to impressions by which they feel themselves reassured or alarmed in their own sphere of existence. They take an interest in the artistically valuable, provided it is presented so as to suit their mentality, that is, provided the subject-matter is attractive. The chances of success of a good film are from this point of view better from the very outset than those of a good painting or poem. For, apart from the film, progressive art is almost a closed book today for the uninitiated; it is intrinsically unpopular, because its means of communication have become transformed in the course of a long and self-contained development into a kind of secret code, whereas to learn the newly developing idiom of the film was child's play for even the most primitive cinema public. From this happy constellation one would be inclined to draw far-reaching optimistic conclusions for the future of the film, if one did not know that that kind of intellectual concord is nothing more than the state of a paradisian childhood, and is probably repeated as often as new arts arise. Perhaps all the cinematic means of expression will no longer be intelligible even to the next generation, and certainly the cleft will sooner or later arise that even in this field separates the layman from the connoisseur. Only a young art can be popular, for as soon as it grows older it is necessary, in order to understand it, to be acquainted with the earlier stages in its development. To understand an art means to realize the necessary connection between its formal and material elements; as long as an art is young, there is a natural, unproblematical relation between its content and its means of expression, that is to say, there is a direct path leading from its subject-matter to its forms. In the course of time these forms become independent of the thematic material, they become autonomous, poorer in meaning, and harder to interpret, until they become accessible only to a [951–952] quite small stratum of the public. In the film this process has hardly begun, and a great many cinema-goers still belong to the generation which saw the birth of the film and witnessed the full significance of its forms. But the process of estrangement already makes itself felt in the present-day director's forgoing of most of the so-called "cinematic" means of expression. The once so popular effects produced by different camera-angles and manoeuvrings, changing distances and speeds, by the tricks of montage and printing, the close-ups and the panoramas, the cut-ins and the flash-backs, the fade-ins, fade-outs and dissolves, seem affected and unnatural today, because the directors and cameramen are concentrating their attention, under the pressure of a second, already less film-minded generation, on the clear, smooth and exciting narration of a story and believe they can learn more from the masters of the "pièce bien faite" than from the masters of the silent film.

It is inconceivable that, in the present stage of cultural development, an art could begin all over again, even though, like the film, it has completely new means at its disposal. Even the simplest plot has a history and bears within it certain epic and dramatic formulae of the older periods of literature. The film, whose public is on the average level of the petty bourgeois, borrows these formulae from the light fiction of the upper middle class and entertains the cinema-goers of today with the dramatic effects of yesterday. Film production owes its greatest successes to the realization that the mind of the petty bourgeois is the psychological meeting place of the masses. The psychological category of this human type has, however, a wider range than the sociological category of the actual middle class; it embraces fragments of both the upper and the lower classes, that is to say, the very considerable elements who, where they are not engaged in a direct struggle for their existence, join forces unreservedly with the middle classes, above all in the matter of entertainment. The mass public of the film is the product of this equalizing process, and if the film is to be profitable, it has to base itself on that class from which the intellectual levelling proceeds. The middle class, especially since the "new middle class," with its army of "employees," minor civil servants and private officials, [952–953] commercial travellers and shop-assistants, has come into being, has hovered "between the classes" and has always been used to bridge the gaps between them. It has always felt menaced from above and below, but has preferred to give up its real interests rather than its hopes and alleged prospects. It has wanted to be reckoned as part of the bourgeois upper class, although in reality it shared the lot of the lower class. But without a clear-cut and clarified social position no coherent consciousness and consistent outlook on life is possible, and the film producer has been able to rely quite safely on the disorientation of these rootless elements of society. The petty bourgeois attitude to life is typified by a thoughtless, uncritical optimism. It believes in the ultimate unimportance of social differences and, accordingly, wants to see films in which people simply walk out of one social stratum into another. For this middle class the cinema gives the fulfilment to the social romanticism which life never realizes and the lending libraries never realize so deceptively as the film with its illusionism. "Everyone is the architect of his own furtune," that is its supreme belief and climbing the basic motif of the wish-fantasies which entice it into the cinema. Will Hays, the one-time "film czar," was well aware of that when he included in his directions for the American film industry the instruction, "to show the life of the upper classes."

The development of moving photography to the film as an art was dependent on two achievements: the invention of the close-up—attributed to the American director D. W. Griffith—and a new method of interpolation, discovered by the Russians, the so-called short cutting. The Russians did not, however, invent the frequent interruption of the continuity of a scene, the Americans had long had this means of producing excited atmospheres or dramatic accelerations at their disposal; but the new factor in the Russian method was the restriction of the flashes to close-ups—forgoing the insertion of informative long-shots—and the shortening, pushed to the limits of perceptibility, of the individual shots. The Russians thereby succeeded in finding an expressionistic film style for the description of certain agitated moods, nervous rhythms and tearing speeds, which made possible quite new effects, unattainable in any other art. The [953–954] revolutionary quality of this montage technique consisted, however, less in the shortness of the cutting, in the speed and rhythm of the change of shots and in the extension of the boundaries of the cinematically feasible, than in the fact that it was no longer the phenomena of a homogeneous world of objects, but of quite heterogeneous elements of reality, that were brought face to face. Thus Eisenstein showed the following sequence in The

Battleship Potemkin: men working desperately, engine-room of the cruiser; busy hands, revolving wheels; faces distorted with exertion, maximum pressure of the manometer; a chest soaked with perspiration, a glowing boiler; an arm, a wheel; a wheel, an arm; machine, man; machine, man; machine, man. Two utterly different realities, a spiritual and a material, were joined together here, and not only joined but identified, in fact, the one proceeding from the other. But such a conscious and deliberate trespassing presupposed a philosophy which denies the autonomy of the individual spheres of life, as surrealism does, and as historical materialism has done from the very beginning.

That it is not simply a question of analogies but of equations, and that the confrontation of the different spheres is not merely metaphorical, becomes even more obvious when the montage no longer shows two interconnected phenomena but only one and, instead of the one to be expected from the context, a substituted one. Thus, in the *End of St. Petersburg,* Pudovkin shows a trembling crystal chandelier for the shattered power of the bourgeoisie; a steep, endless staircase on which a small human figure is laboriously climbing up for the official hierarchy, its thousands of intermediary stages and its unattainable summit. In Eisenstein's *October,* the twilight of the Czars is represented by dark equestrian statues on leaning pedestals, quivering statues of the Buddha used as knick-knacks and shattered negro idols. In the *Strike,* executions are replaced by slaughter-house scenes. Throughout things take the place of ideas; things which expose the ideological character of ideas. A social-historical situation has hardly ever found a more direct expression in art than the crisis of capitalism and the Marxist philosophy of history in this montage technique. A tunic covered with decorations but without a head signifies the automatism of the war machine in these [954–955] Russian films; new, strong soldiers' boots, the blind brutality of military power. Thus, in *Potemkin,* we see again and again only these heavy, indestructible and merciless boots, instead of the steadily advancing Cossacks. Good boots are the precondition of military power, that is the meaning of this "pars pro toto"–montage, just as the meaning of the earlier example from *Potemkin* was that the victorious masses are nothing but the personification of the triumphant machine. Man, with his ideas, faith, and hope is merely a function of the material world in which he lives; the doctrine of historical materialism becomes the formal principle of the art of the Russian film. One must not forget, however, how far the film's whole method of presentation, especially its technique of the close-up, which favours the description of the material requisites from the outset and is calculated to give them an important motivating rôle, comes to meet this materialism half-way. On the other hand, the question whether the whole of this technique, in which the properties are put in the foreground, is not itself already a product of materialism cannot simply be dismissed. For the fact that the film is the creation of the historical epoch which has witnessed the exposure of the ideological basis of human thought is no more pure coincidence than the fact that the Russians have been the first classical exponents of this art.

Film directors throughout the world, irrespective of national and ideological divergences, have adopted the stock forms of the Russian film and thereby confirmed that as soon as the content has been translated into form, form can be taken over and used as a purely technical expedient, without the ideological background from which it has emerged. The paradox of historicity and timelessness in art, to which Marx refers in his *Introduction to the Critique of Political Economy,* is rooted in this capacity of form to become autonomous: "Is Achilles conceivable in an era of powder and lead?" he asks. "Or for that matter the *Iliad* at all in these days of printing-press and press-jacks? Do not song and legend and muse necessarily lose their meaning in the age of the Press? But the difficulty is not that Greek art and epic are connected with certain forms of social development, but rather that they still give us aesthetic satisfaction today, that in a sense they [955–956] act as a norm, as an unattainable paragon."—The works ot Eisenstein and Pudovkin are in some respects the heroic epics of the cinema; the fact that they are regarded as models, independent of the social conditions which made their realization possible, is no more surprising than the fact that Homer still gives us supreme artistic satisfaction.

The film is the only art in which Soviet Russia has important achievements to its credit. The affinity between the young communist state and the new form of expression is obvious. Both are revolutionary phenomena moving along new paths, without a historical past, without binding and crippling traditions, without pre-suppositions of a cultural or routine nature of any kind. The film is an elastic, extremely malleable, unexhausted form which offers no inner resistance to the expression of the new ideas. It is an unsophisticated, popular means of communication, making a direct appeal to the broad masses, an ideal instrument of propaganda the value of which was immediately recognized by Lenin. Its attraction as an irreproachable, that is to say, historically uncompromised, entertainment was so great from the point of view of communist cultural policy from the very outset, its picture-book-like style so easy to grasp, the possibility of using it to propagate ideas to the uneducated so simple, that it seemed to have been specially created for the purposes of a revolutionary art. The film is, moreover, an art evolved from the spiritual foundations of technics and, therefore, all the more in accordance with the problems in store for it. The machine is its origin, its medium and its most suitable subject. Films are "fabricated" and they remain tied to an apparatus, to a machine in a narrower sense than the products of the other arts. The machine here stands both between the creative subject and his work and between the receptive subject and his enjoyment of art. The motory, the mechanical, the automatically moving, is the basic phenomenon of the film. Running and racing, travelling and flying, escape and pursuit, the overcoming of spatial obstacles is the cinematic theme par excellence. The film never feels so much in its element as when it has to describe movement, speed and pace. The wonders and mischievous tricks of instruments, automata and vehicles are among its oldest and most effective subjects. The old [956–957] film comedies expressed sometimes naïve admiration, at others arrogant contempt for technics, but they were in most cases the self-teasing of man caught in the wheels of a mechanized world. The film is above all a "photograph" and is already as such a technical art, with mechanical origins and aiming at mechanical repetition, in other words, thanks to the cheapness of its reproduction, a popular and fundamentally "democratic" art. It is perfectly comprehensible that it suited bolshevism with its romanticism of the machine, its fetishism of technics and its admiration for efficiency. Just as it is also comprehensible that the Russians and the Americans, as the two most technically-minded peoples, were partners and rivals in the development of this art. The film was, however, not only in accord with their technicism, but also with their interest in the documentary, the factual and the authentic. All the more important works of Russian film art are to some extent documentary films, historical documents of the building up of the new Russia, and the best we owe to the American film consists in the documentary reproduction of American life, of the everyday routine of the American economic and administrative machine, of the skyscraper cities and the Middle West farms, the American police and the gangster world. For a film is the more cinematic, the greater the share extra-human, material facts have in its description of reality, in other words, the closer the connection in this description between man and the world, the personality and the milieu, the end and the means.

This tendency to the factual and the authentic—to the "document"—is evidence not only of the intensified hunger for reality characteristic of the present age, of its desire to be well informed about the world, with an activistic ulterior motive, but also of that refusal to accept the artistic aims of the last century which is expressed in the flight from the story and from the individual, psychologically differentiated hero. This tendency, which is tied up, in the documentary film, with an escape from the professional actor, again signifies not only the desire that is always recurring in the history of art, to show the plain reality, the unvarnished truth, unadulterated facts, that is, life "as it really is," but very often a renunciation of art altogether. In our age the prestige of [957–958] the aesthetic is being undermined in many ways. The documentary film, photography, newspaper reports, the reportage novel, are no longer art in the old sense at all. Moreover, the most intelligent and most gifted representatives of these genres do not in any way insist that their products should be described as "works of art"; they rather take the view that art has always been a by-product and arose in the service of an ideologically conditioned purpose.

In Soviet Russia, it is regarded wholly as a means to an end. This utilitarianism is, of course, conditioned above all by the need to place all available means in the service of communist reconstruction and to exterminate the aestheticism of bourgeois culture which, with its "l'art pour l'art," its contemplative and quietistic attitude to life, implies the greatest possible danger for the social revolution. It is the awareness of this danger that makes it impossible for the architects of communist cultural policy to do justice to the artistic developments of the last hundred years and it is the denial of this development which makes their views on art seem so old-fashioned. They would prefer to put back the historical standing of art to the level of the July monarchy, and it is not only in the novel that they have in mind the realism of the middle of the last century, in the other arts, particularly in painting, they encourage the same tendency. In a system of universal planning and in the midst of a struggle for mere existence, art cannot be left to work out its own salvation. But regimentation of art is not without risks even from the point of view of the immediate aim; in the process it must also lose much of its value as an instrument of propaganda.

It is certainly correct that art has produced many of its greatest creations under compulsion and dictation, and that it had to conform to the wishes of a ruthless despotism in the Ancient Orient and to the demands of a rigid authoritarian culture in the Middle Ages. But even compulsion and censorship have a different meaning and effect in the different periods of history. The main difference between the situation today and that of former ages is that we find ourselves at a point in time after the French Revolution and nineteenth-century liberalism and that every idea that we think, every impulse that we feel, is [958–959] permeated by this liberalism. One might well argue that Christianity also had to destroy a very advanced and comparatively liberal civilization and that medieval art sprang from very modest beginnings; one must not forget, however, that early Christian art did in fact make an almost completely fresh start, whereas Soviet Russian art starts out from a style which was historically already highly developed, although it is much behind the times today. But even if one were willing to assume that the sacrifices demanded are the price of a new "Gothic," there is no kind of guarantee that this "Gothic" would not again become, as in the Middle Ages, the exclusive possession of a comparatively small cultured élite.

The problem is not to confine art to the present-day horizon of the broad masses, but to extend the horizon of the masses as much as possible. The way to a genuine appreciation of art is through education. Not the violent simplification of art, but the training of the capacity for aesthetic judgement is the means by which the constant monopolizing of art by a small minority can be prevented. Here too, as in the whole field of cultural policy, the great difficulty is that every arbitrary interruption of the development evades the real problem, that is, creates a situation in which the problem does not arise, and therefore merely postpones the task of finding a solution. There is today hardly any practicable way leading to a primitive and yet valuable art. Genuine, progressive, creative art can only mean a complicated art today. It will never be possible for everyone to enjoy and appreciate it in equal measure, but the share of the broader masses in it can be increased and deepened. The preconditions of a slackening of the cultural monopoly are above all economic and social. We can do no other than fight for the creation of these preconditions. [959]

1. Writing nearly twenty years ago, Arnold Hauser believed that no artist had come forward to exploit the temporal capabilities of film. Has the situation improved since this writing? Are you aware of any directors or screenwriters who now treat time as Hauser said film can treat it?

2. In doubting whether individualistic societies can train people to work in so collective an art, Prof. Hauser raises an important question about the influence of society on film. How effectively does he deal with this question?

3. Another question posed by Prof. Hauser concerns the influence of the audience. How might you go about investigating the power of American audiences to shape our films?

4. Do you agree with Prof. Hauser's contention that the mechanical is the true sphere of film?

THE SURFACES
OF REALITY

Michael Roemer

As Siegfried Kracauer effectively demonstrates, the camera photographs the skin; it cannot function like an X-ray machine and show us what is underneath. This does not mean, however, that the film-maker has no control over the surfaces rendered by his camera. On the contrary, he *chooses* his surfaces for their content, and through their careful selection and juxtaposition builds a structure of feeling and meaning that are the core of his work.

There are times in the history of the medium when story, treatment and performance drift so far into a studio never-never land that we cannot help but make a virtue of "pure" reality, as free from interference on the part of the film-maker as possible—even at the risk of creating something shapeless. This should not, however, obscure the fact that a film, like a poem or painting, is basically an artifact.

The assertion that film is nothing more than a documentary recording of reality undoubtedly stems from the fact that the medium must render all meaning in physical terms. This affinity for real surfaces, combined with great freedom of movement both in time and space, brings film closer than any other medium to our own random experience of life. Even the realistic playwright, who—until the advent of the camera—came closest to rendering the appearance of reality, is often

MICHAEL ROEMER, the director of *Nothing But a Man* and *Harry,* teaches film writing at Yale. He was formerly film critic for *The Reporter.*

forced in his structure to violate the very sense of life he is trying to create. But the film-maker can use the flexible resources at his command to approximate the actual fabric of reality. Moreover, he need not heighten his effects in order to communicate, for he can call on the same sensibilities in his audience that we use in life itself.

All of us bring to every situation, whether it be a business meeting or a love affair, a social and psychological awareness which helps us understand complex motivations and relationships. This kind of perception, much of it nonverbal and based on apparently insignificant clues, is not limited to the educated or gifted. We all depend on it for our understanding of other people and have become extremely proficient in the interpretation of subtle signs—a shading in the voice, an averted glance. This nuanced awareness, however, is not easily called upon by the arts, for it is predicated upon a far more immediate and total experience than can be provided by literature and the theater, with their dependence on the word, or by the visual arts—with their dependence [15–16] on the image. Only film renders experience with enough immediacy and totality to call into play the perceptual processes we employ in life itself.

The fact that film exercises this sort of perceptual capacity is, I believe, one of its chief appeals to us. It gives us practice in the delicate and always somewhat uncertain skill of finding out what is going on. As an extreme example, take these lines from *Marty*. They are spoken in a dance hall during the first encounter between a lonely man and a lonely girl. She says: "I'm twenty-nine years old. How old are you?" And he answers: "Thirty-six."

On the stage or the printed page these lines would fall ludicrously flat. But on the screen, when spoken by performers who can make every detail yield a wealth of meaning, they instantly convey—as they would in life itself—a complex web of feeling: the girl's fear that she might be too old for the man, her need to come right to the point, her relief when he turns out to be older, and finally a mutual delight that their relationship has crossed its first hurdle.

Film thrives on this kind of intimate detail, for the camera reports it so closely that nothing essential is lost to the eye or ear. The camera makes it possible to use the stuff of life itself, without amplification or overstatement and without any loss in dramatic value. What is achieved in a large action or an explicit moment on the stage can be rendered just as dramatically on the screen in small and *implicit* terms, for it is not the magnitude of a gesture that makes it dramatic but its meaning and intention.

This is *not* to say that the medium is most aptly used on the kind of everyday story told in *Marty,* or that low-key dialogue without conflict or strong feeling is always effective on the screen. I quote the scene merely as an example of the medium's capacity for finding meaning in the detail of everyday life and would like to suggest that out of such detail, out of the ordinary surfaces of life, the film-maker can structure *any* kind of situation and story—lyrical or dramatic, historical or contemporary.

Like so many films that deal with the past, Dreyer's *Passion de Jeanne D'Arc* might well have been filled with violent action and theatrical confrontations. Instead the story is told in terms of mundane detail. Thus Jeanne is betrayed at a critical moment by a priest who averts his eyes when she turns to him for help.

There is no call for anything more explicit. The betrayal is what matters, and the camera renders it far more credibly and forcefully in a mundane detail than it would be in a highly dramatized gesture.

In *Rashomon* and *The Seven Samurai* Kurosawa deals with events of the thirteenth and sixteenth centuries in the most everyday terms. He knows that our basic daily experience of reality has not changed much over the centuries: a war between bandits and samurai in a feudal Japanese village was as full of mud and rain, as gritty and as grotesque as a twentieth-century skirmish. Film at its best uses the language of ordinary experience—but uses it subtly and artfully.

In a contemporary setting, Bresson's *A Man Escaped* chronicles the efforts of a French resistance fighter to break out of a German prison. Much of the film takes place within the confines of a cell and the camera records how he painstakingly prepares his escape by fashioning tools out of spoons and rope out of blankets. It is all very ordinary and physical, but out of the grimy detail emerges a devout and heroic assertion of life and human freedom and of the need to preserve them in the face of all odds. In the hands of a sensitive film-maker the ordinary moment becomes a channel for deep feeling and a sequence of apparently insignificant scenes is structured into a world of great complexity.

This use of ordinary surfaces requires great skill and discipline since the audience can sense every false move and movement, every false note in the dialogue, every unsubstantiated relationship. The very thing that works *for* the [*16–17*] film-maker if he can master it—reality—can quickly turn against him, so that the most ordinary moment becomes utterly unreal. Not surprisingly most directors avoid the challenge and set their stories in unfamiliar parts, among unusual people and in unusual circumstances.

Because most good films use the language of the commonplace, they tend to have an unassuming appearance, whereas films that make a large claim—that speak nobly and poetically about life, love and death—almost invariably prove to be hollow. A good film is concrete: it creates a sequence of objective situations, actual relationships between people, between people and their circumstances. Thus each moment becomes an objective correlative; that is, feeling (or meaning) rendered in actual, physical terms: objectified.

By contrast, most movies are a series of conventional communicative gestures, dialogues, and actions. Most movie-makers *play* on the feelings of their audience by setting up a sequence of incidents that have a proven effect. The events are not rendered; they are merely *cited*. The films do not use the vocabulary of actuality but rather a second-hand language that has proven effective in other films —a langauge that is changed only when the audience no longer responds.

This language of conventions gives most pictures the appearance of ludicrous unreality fifteen or twenty years after they have been acclaimed as masterpieces. The dramatic conventions of the 1940's are recognized as a system of hollow clichés by the sixties. When *The Best Years of Our Lives* was first shown, references to the war were enough to make an audience feel strongly about a situation or character without any substantiation whatever; there were feelings abroad which, when touched, produced the desired effect. By 1964 this is no longer true and the tissue of the film disintegrates.

Audiences can be "played" by a skillful movie-maker with a fair amount of predictability, so that even discriminating audiences are easily taken in. At the beginning of Bergman's *Wild Strawberries* Professor Borg dreams that he is on a deserted street with all its doors and windows shuttered tight. He looks up at a clock that has no hands and pulls out his own watch only to find that its hands are missing also. A man appears on the corner with his head averted; when he turns, he has no face and his body dissolves into a pool on the sidewalk. A glass hearse comes down the street and spills a coffin that opens. Borg approaches and discovers his own body in the coffin. The corpse comes to life and tries to pull him in.

The nightmare quality in this sequence is derivative. The deserted, shuttered street, the clock and watch without hands, the glass hearse, the faceless man are all conventions familiar to surrealist painting and literature. Bergman uses them skillfully and with conviction to produce an effect in the audience, but they are not true film images, derived from life and rendered in concrete, physical terms.

There is a similar nightmare in Dreyer's *Vampire*. A young man dreams that he has entered a room with an open coffin in it. He approaches and discovers that he himself is the corpse. The camera now assumes the point-of-view of the dead man: we look up at the ceiling. Voices approach and two carpenters appear in our field of vision. They close the coffin with a lid but we continue to look out through a small glass window. Talking indistinctly, they nail down the lid and plane the edges of the wood. The shavings fall onto the window. One of them has put a candle down on the glass and wax drips onto it. Then the coffin is lifted up and we pass close under the ceiling, through the doorway, beneath the sunlit roofs and the church steeple of a small town—out into the open sky.

Here the detail is concrete: an experience is rendered, not cited; the situation is objective and out of it emerges, very powerfully, the feeling that Dreyer is after: a farewell to life, a last confined look at the earth before the coffin is lowered into the grave. Once again we note that the unassuming detail can render a complex feeling (or meaning) which eludes [17–18] the more obviously ambitious but abstract statement.

Good film dialogue, too, has this concrete quality. Like the speech of everyday life, it does not tell you *directly* what is felt or meant. One might call it symptomatic dialogue: symptomatic because it is a surface manifestation of what is going on inside the person. The dialogue in most films is, of course, the opposite: a direct statement of feeling or meaning: "I love you"; "I am so happy"; "You are this"; "I am that." But just as the action should be a physical or surface correlative that permits the audience to discover for itself the implicit meaning, so the dialogue should be a *surface* that renders its content by implication—not directly. The two lines quoted from *Marty* are good film dialogue. In contrast, here is an incident from Bergman's *The Seventh Seal*.

Shortly before his death the knight Antonius Block shares a meal with a young couple in front of their covered wagon. "I shall always remember this moment," he says. "The silence, the twilight, the bowls of strawberries and milk, your faces in the evening light. Mikhael sleeping, Jof with his lyre. I'll try to remember what we have talked about. I'll carry this moment between my hands as carefully as if it were a bowl filled to the brim with fresh milk. And it will be an adequate sign—it will be enough for me."

Without this lengthy and explicit verbalization, one would have little insight into the feelings of Antonius Block. The situation itself does not communicate them and Bergman uses dialogue as a way of getting us to understand and feel something the film itself does not render. In Kurosawa's *Ikiru,* a petty official who is dying of cancer and trying desperately to give meaning to his life by pushing a playground project through the sterile bureaucracy, stops on his way home from work to look at the evening sky. "It's beautiful," he says to his companion, "but I have no time." Here the dialogue is part of the objective situation. No direct statement is needed since the man and his feelings are clear.

What is true for dialogue is equally true for performance. A good film performance is a carefully integrated sequence of concrete actions and reactions that render the feelings and thoughts of a character. It is not a system of hollow gestures that, like bad dialogue, *tell* the audience what is going on. Most film performances are drawn from the vast repertory of acting conventions. Conversely, the good film actor—whether trained in the Method or not—tries to render feelings through the use of surface correlatives. He is not concerned with the demonstration of feeling but with the symptom of feeling.

Chaplin's best work is continuously physical and concrete. If his performance in *The Gold Rush* had been generalized (or conventionalized) the scene in which he boils and eats his shoe would have become preposterous. He executes it, however, in the most careful physical detail. While the shoe is cooking, he pours water over it as if he were basting a bird. He carves and serves it with meticulous care, separating the uppers from the sole as though boning a fish. Then he winds the limp laces around his fork like spaghetti and sucks each nail as if it were a delicate chicken bone. Thus a totally incongruous moment is given an absolute, detailed physicality; the extraordinary is made ordinary, credible—and therefore funny.

It must be noted again that while the screen exceeds all other media in verisimilitude, its reality is nevertheless a *mode.* We appear to be looking at reality but are actually looking at a representation of it that may be as carefully structured as a still-life by Cézanne. The film-maker uses the surfaces of life itself—literal photographic images and accurately reproduced sounds. But the arrangement of these images and sounds is totally controlled. Each moment, each detail is carefully coordinated into the structure of the whole—just like the details in a painting or poem. By artfully controlling his images, the film-maker presents an unbroken realistic surface; he preserves the appearance of reality.   [*18–19*]

This means that he should at no time interpose himself between audience and action. He must be absent from the scene. An example of this is the use of the camera. In the standard film the camera is often editorial; the director uses it to *point out* to the audience what he wants them to see. Imagine a scene between husband and wife: we see them in a medium-shot, talking; then we cut to a close-up of the woman's hand and discover that she is slipping her wedding ring off and on. The director has made his point: we now know that she is unhappily married. But by artificially lifting the detail out of context and bringing it to our attention, the autonomous reality of the scene is violated and the audience becomes aware of the film-maker. Of course a good director may also be said to use the camera editorially —to point out what he wants us to see. But he never seems to be doing so; he preserves the appearance of an autonomous reality on the screen. The moment with the ring would have been incidental to the scene—for the camera must follow the action, not lead it.

Since the process of editing is an obvious and continued intrusion by the film-maker on the material, an editor tries to make most of his cuts in such a way that the cut itself will be obscured. In order to cut from a medium-shot to a close-up of a man, he will probably use a moment when the man rises from a chair or turns rapidly. At such a time the audience is watching the action and is unaware of the jump; once again, the effort is to preserve an apparently autonomous reality.

At the end of *Notti di Cabiria* the girl and the man she has just married are sitting in a restaurant. We see her from the back, talking. Then Fellini cuts to a shot from the front and we see that she has taken out a large wad of bank notes—her savings. We immediately realize, with something of a shock, that the man is after her money. If Fellini had actually *shown* us Cabiria taking the money out of her pocketbook, the moment would have become self-conscious and overloaded with meaning; we would have had too much time to get the point. By jumping the moment and confronting us suddenly with the money, Fellini renders the meaning *and* preserves the apparent autonomy of the situation.

Spontaneity, the sense that what is happening on the screen is happening for the first time and without plan or direction, is an essential factor in establishing a reality. It is also extremely difficult to achieve since a huge industry has sprung up around the medium, putting enormous financial and technical pressure on the moment before the camera. Years of routine and a high degree of established skill in every department of film-making all conspire against it. From writing and casting to the angles of the camera a monstrous if unintended predictability crushes all life. Even a strong director is often helpless against the machinery; and even location shooting, which should be a liberating force, turns into a dead-end when a huge crew descends on the place, seals it off hermetically and effectively turns it into a studio. The channels have been set up too long and too well; all vision is trapped into standardized imagery and the living moment cannot survive.

For this reason an almost improvised film—like *Shadows* or *Breathless,* made without great skill or art by relatively inexperienced people—can carry far greater conviction than the standard theatrical product. In spite of obvious flaws there is a spontaneity to the action that endows it with life. Of course the experienced director, working in freedom and under good conditions, can achieve spontaneity without relying on improvisation. Kurosawa shot parts of *The Seven Samurai* with several cameras; this made it unnecessary for the actors to repeat, and so deaden, the action with every shift in camera position. Chaplin, on the other hand, used to rehearse and shoot endlessly to achieve a perfect but seemingly effortless result. Both men were after the same thing: spontaneity—and with it, reality.

Our sense of reality is so delicately attuned that certain moments are better left off the [19–20] screen or the situation is destroyed. This is especially true for violence and death. When someone's head is cut off in a fiction film we know perfectly well that a trick is employed and unless a scene of this kind is handled with great care, it ends up being incredible or even funny. Similarly, when someone dies on the screen and remains in full view, many of us cannot resist watching for the slightest sign of life in the supposed corpse. We are pitting our own sense of reality against the movie-maker's; needless to say, *we* come out on top and the scene is destroyed.

In Dreyer's unproduced script on the life of Christ he describes the crucifixion by showing us the back of the cross, with the points of the nails splintering through the wood. On the screen these would be undeniably real nails going through real wood, and the authenticity of the moment would not be challenged. If, however, Dreyer had chosen to show us the cross from the front we would know absolutely that the nails going through the *flesh* are a deception—and the suffering figure would turn into a performer.

The nail splintering through the wood forces us to use our imagination—forces us to visualize what is happening on the other side of the cross. This involves us in a far deeper participation than could be achieved by the spurious horror of a nail going through the flesh of an actor.

There is something to be learned here about the entire process of perception in film. If we are explicitly told something, as we are in most pictures, we remain passive and essentially outsiders. If, however, we have to draw our *own* conclusions on the basis of evidence presented, as we do in life itself, we cannot help but participate. We become actively involved. When we are told something explicitly, we are in a sense deprived of the experience. It has been digested for us and we are merely informed of the results, or the meaning. But it is *experience* we are after, even if it remains vicarious experience. ·

This brings us to another characteristic of the medium—one that is profoundly related to our previous discussion. Although the experience of the motion picture audience remains essentially vicarious, film comes closer than any other medium to giving us the illusion of a *primary* experience. This has been studied by psychologists who have found that the dark theater, the bright hypnotic screen, the continuous flow of images and sounds, and the large anonymous audience in which we are submerged all contribute to a suspension of self-awareness and a total immersion in the events on the screen.

Beyond this, however, the medium itself encourages the illusion of a primary participation. The camera can induce an almost physical response—so that when Chaplin sits on a hypodermic needle in the lair of a dope fiend, or when Dreyer's Jeanne d'Arc has her head shaved and some of the hair falls onto her lip, the sensation produced in us is almost physical. Moreover, this physical participation is not limited to sharp sensory detail; it extends to the realm of movement.

Most directors think of the screen as of a *picture frame* within which each shot is carefully composed. They emphasize the *pictorial* quality of film. But while the medium is visual, it is not pictorial in the conventional sense. A sequence of beautifully composed shots tends to leave the audience outside the frame—spectators who are continually aware of the director's fine eye for composition. A good director tries to eliminate this distance between audience and action, to destroy the screen as a picture frame, and to drag the audience *through* it into the reality of the scene. That is the function of the running shots in *Rashomon* and of the extraordinarily emphatic camerawork of Fellini, who leans subtly into every movement and propels us into the action kinesthetically. By contrast, we have the autonomous camera motion and stiff pictorial composition of most films.

Images of movement rather than beautifully composed shots are at the heart of the medium, [20–21] and significantly some of the most haunting moments in film derive their effect from motion. In Vigo's *L'Atalante,* a bride on her wedding night, still dressed in her white gown, walks along the deck of a moving barge. The barge moves forward, she is walking toward the stern, and the camera is set on the edge of the canal, so that there is a dark stationary line in the foreground. The combination of the silent forward gliding of the barge with the backward motion of the girl, whose gown and veil are streaming in the wind, has a profound emotional impact; it renders perfectly both her feelings and our own.

At the end of *Ikiru* the dying bureaucrat has succeeded in building the playground. It is a winter night; the camera moves slowly past a jungle-gym; beyond it we see the old man, swaying to and fro on a child's swing and singing to himself under the falling snow. The various components of this scene are hard to separate: the hoarse, cracked voice of the dying man; his happiness; the song itself. But the motion of the camera, the falling snow, and the slow movement of the swing certainly contribute to the extraordinary sense of peace and reconciliation that is communicated by the image.

A last example: in Dreyer's *Day of Wrath,* a witch is burned in a seventeenth-century town. We see her bound to the top rungs of a tall ladder. Then Dreyer cuts to a long-shot and side view: on the left a huge pile of faggots is burning; to the right soldiers are raising the ladder toward the fire by means of long poles. When it stands perpendicular, they topple it forward so that the woman falls screaming across the entire frame toward the flames. The falling arc described by the victim is rendered in coldly objective terms, from far away—but it transmits her terror completely and draws us relentlessly into the action.

Kurosawa has developed a way of staging that makes it hard for an audience to remain detached. On the theory that no one should be seen entirely from the back, many directors stage their scenes in a three-quarter view. As a result, no one is seen full-face: we look at the actors, but they look away. In *Rashomon* and *The Seven Samurai,* however, the actors either have their backs to camera or face us frontally. When they face us, they are all but looking at us—with only their eyes turned slightly left or right of lens to indicate that they are addressing each other and not us. Of course a face seen frontally is much more exposed than a three-quarter view, and far less likely to leave us detached.

Film can further strengthen the illusion of a primary experience by using a subjective point-of-view. In the ancient and Elizabethan theaters, while we remain in objective possession of the entire stage, the poetry and particularly the soliloquy can focus our attention on one person and shift it to his point-of-view. At any given moment the world can be seen through his eyes, subjectively. In the realistic theater, with its fidelity to the surfaces of everyday life, this has become difficult if not impossible. We *know* how Ibsen's Nora sees the world but except for rare moments do not *experience* it from her point-of-view. She cannot, as it were, reach out and envelop us in her vision—as Hamlet and Lear can.

On the screen it again becomes possible to shift from an objective vision of a person to a vision of what *he* sees. This is done continually, often with little understanding or control. We see a girl enter a room in an objective shot. Then the camera renders what *she* sees: there is a party and her husband is talking to another woman. The next moment might be objective again, or it might be seen from the husband's point-of-view. Montage makes it possible to shift from objective to subjective, or from one subjective point-of-view to another. Film can render a place, a person, or a situation not just as they are but in the context of the protagonist's experience—*as* his experience. A point-of-view can be so carefully articulated that we comprehend every object, every passing figure, every gesture and mood in terms of the protagonist. The medium thus extends the meaning of realistic surfaces beyond [21–22] their objective value; it renders them in their subjective context as well.

This brings us to an apparent paradox, for we have insisted throughout that film is at its best when rendering an objective situation. It is true, of course, that a moment can be rendered subjectively on the screen and still retain its objective reality. When the girl sees her husband talking to another woman, we see them through her eyes and so become privy to a subjective state. But the husband and the other woman are *in themselves* rendered objectively: they look no different; they are not affected by the point-of-view. The basic language of the medium, the realistic surface, has not been violated. The same may be said of most flash-backs: a subjective recollection is rendered—but in objective, undistorted terms.

There are, however, moments on the screen in which the realistic surface is in fact destroyed and a purely subjective state is created. The processional at the end of Vigo's *Zero de Conduite* is shot in slow-motion, with the boys in their white gowns gliding through a snow of pillow feathers to the accompaniment of a totally distorted but oddly ecstatic song. In such scenes, and it must be noted that while they are often attempted they do not often succeed, the reality of the feeling is so compelling that an audience accepts and assimilates a totally subjective image. The participation is so intensive that instead of rejecting an image we know to be "unreal," we enter into it eagerly.

When successful, scenes of this kind are deeply moving for they are predicated on a rare and free flow of feeling between audience and material. But they are moments of grace and cannot be counted on—like those rare moments in a performance when pure feeling breaks out of the actor and is communicated directly, without the mediation of a physical correlative.

By and large the language of the medium remains the surface of reality, and there seem to be few experiences that cannot be rendered in this language. Moreover, there is a great challenge in making the commonplaces of life, that have so long eluded art, yield up their meaning and take their rightful place in the larger patterns of existence. Film is indeed, as Kracauer put it, the redemption of physical reality. For we are finally able to use the much-despised and ephemeral detail of everyday life, the common physical dross, and work it into the gold of art. [22]

    1. Is Mr. Roemer convincing in his criticism of *Wild Strawberries*? Does the scene he cites from *Vampire* provide a telling contrast?

2. Do you agree that the scene Mr. Roemer describes on page 41 would make the spectator aware of the filmmaker? Do you agree that such awareness is undesirable?

3. Do you find any contradiction between Mr. Roemer's derision of obtrusive editing and his advocacy of subjective shots? What enables him to reject one and accept the other?

CINEMA AS AN ART FORM

Maya Deren

Even the most cursory observation of film production reveals that the entire field is dominated by two main approaches: the fiction-entertainment film, promoted internationally by commercial interests; and the documentary-educational film, promoted by individuals and organizations interested in social reform, visual education and cultural dissemination. What is conspicuously lacking is the development of cinema as an art form—concerned with the type of perception which characterizes all other art forms such as poetry, painting, etc., and devoted to the development of a formal idiom as independent of other art forms as they are of each other.

The seriousness of this gap in our cultural development is in no way lessened by the utilitarian validity of the camera as an instrument for recording and infinitely reproducing imaginative or factual material which would otherwise be accessible to a very limited audience. Nor should this lack of cinematic form be obscured by the growing body of sometimes sensational film techniques which are developed and exploited in the interest of a more effective rendition of the subject matter.

However, the most serious aspect of the entire situation is the passive acceptance and casual neglect of this state of the cinema by those whose active, compulsive interest and devotion is responsible for the varying but constant vitality of other art forms. This passivity on the part of those who should, presumably, be the most actively interested, is the more serious since it derives not from an innocent ignorance of cinematic possibilities, but constitutes a reaction to the apparent failure

MAYA DEREN, an avant-garde filmmaker, wrote frequently about her work.

of the film avant-garde of France and other countries. It is true that, out of the flurry of cinematic experiments which marked the twenties and early thirties, only a few emerge as art expressions of lasting, intrinsic value. The great majority of them are of interest as period-pieces, symptomatic of a given stage of film history. But it is false to deduce from this, and from the dwindling away of the movement as a whole, that there is something in the very nature of film-making which precludes the possibility of its development as an art form.

It is true that an analysis of the failure of the first film avant-garde would seem to indicate certain formidable and paralyzing conclusions. First among these is that since the production of films is necessarily expensive (much more so than the production of a poem or a painting) they must [111–112] appeal to large audiences in order to meet their expenses—those very audiences who daily indicate their approval of the present Hollywood product. Second, but no less important, it seems that the machinery, the enormous personnel of assistant directors, cameramen, lighting men, actors and producers, represents a kind of collective monster who, standing between the artist and the realization of his vision, is bound to mangle any delicate or sensitive impulse. This is an obstacle which the poet, in his direct control over words, and the painter in his direct relationship to the canvas, does not confront. Finally, the use of the camera as a utilitarian instrument for recording remains such a fertile field of activity that a completely creative use of it will remain, both to potential producers and to potential audience, a rather superfluous excursion.

The basic fallacy in this entire line of argument consists in the fact that those who advance it have (unconsciously, to be sure) been the victims of elaborate propaganda. The cosmic production figures which Hollywood takes great care in making public, represent a typically grandiose conceit. In Hollywood let no one be guilty of achieving something with less expense, less fanfare and less trouble than can possibly be employed, for in that glittering system of values, economy of any kind constitutes a debasement. In Hollywood logic, this is sound enough, for if a film is dependent upon the recording of reality, or rather its papier-mâché stand-in, then all possible lavish care must be taken in the construction of that reality—from the star (with her background of publicity, make-up men, etc.) to the *real* mink-lined dress in which she will dance. If, however, a film were itself, through camera and cutting, to create a reality, the star salaries, the set-builders, the costumers, the full orchestrations, the million-dollar gag writers, the fantastic hierarchy of executives and overhead would disappear. A film can be treated on 16mm for varying sums of from $500 to $10,000. Once this is achieved, the problem of the mass audience vanishes, for the audience which supports (in modest style, to be sure) the other art forms, is also sufficient to return such relatively modest production costs.

Moreover, the monstrous division of labor which characterizes the industry and makes of a film an assembly line product—passing from idea-man to writer to screen-play writer to shooting-script writer to director to actor (while the electricians and the camera-men are engaged in another section of it), and so on until the dismal end—this is not only unnecessary, but completely destructive to the idiom. Intrinsic integrity is possible only when the individual who conceives the work remains its prime mover until the end, with purely technical assistance where necessary.

It is true that even with these simplifications, the magnitude of the purely practical problems of film-making is rather unique; but it is also true that, whatever they are, these remain problems of *execution* only, and should [*112–113*] not be confused with the creative and esthetic problems of conception. Nor do they excuse films from incorporating those values which we expect to be present in other works of art.

When we agree that a work of art is, first of all, creative, we actually mean that it *creates* a reality and *itself constitutes* an experience. The antithesis of such a creative work is the merely communicative expression whose purpose it is to register, through *description* an existent reality or an experience. When the created reality differs from the existent reality only by subtle variations, or when great skill and accuracy are brought to the description of an extra-ordinary reality, the distinction between the products seems almost obliterated. It resolves itself into a question of form, which I shall discuss later.

What is important, however, is that the descriptive expression approaches the creative expression when (as in all creative expression) it is devoted to the *experience* of reality rather than *reality* itself. It is revealing that the best use of cinematic form (camera, editing, etc.) appears in those commercial films which seek to describe an abnormal state of mind and its abnormal perception of reality.

The consistent popularity of horror films, on one level, and of "psychological" films, on another, testifies to the seductive quality of experiential reality as subject matter for cinema, since cinema is uniquely capable of presenting the unbelievable with a show-it-to-me convincingness. It is significant that Hollywood conceives intense experience to be the particular attribute of abnormality either in the environment (horror films) or in the individual "psyche" (psychological films). The implication is, that non-objectively-real, imaginative force (and here the subconscious appears as a manifestation of the supernatural) may be interesting, but that they are essentially malevolent. In the end, the imagination as a way of life does not pay. The imaginative individual is represented either as a psychic criminal who will receive his just deserts at the hands of a society determined to reestablish the same way of life; or as a physically diseased organism which should be restored to a normal condition.

Thus, the imaginative experience which is for the artist a *desired normality,* is for the motion picture industry a dangerous, *psychic illegality.* As producer of a "mass art," the industry assumes a social responsibility. Accepting a pre-disposition towards evil in even the most innocent, it provides them with catharsis through the vicarious experience of its seductive aspects. At the same time it threatens them with dire consequences should they replace the vicarious experience with the direct.

In devoting at least some attention to the powerful potentialities of the [*113–114*] imaginative experience, the industry has been more acute than that considerable body of theoreticians who hold that a "mass art" should concern itself with the *common* problems of a *common,* objective reality in terms of a *common* denominator of perception. Actually the distilled, experiential emotion of an incident is more universal and timeless than the incident itself. Fear, for example, as a subjective experience is as universal as the incidents of reality in which it arises are singular. Yet these critics claim that a work of the imagination is an esoteric object, accessible to the comprehension only of a select few.

It is therefore relevant to underline here the fact that the appreciation of a work based on experiential, or inner, realities consists not in a laborious analysis based on the logic of a reality which a "prepared" spectator brings to the work. It consists, rather in an abandonment of all previously conceived realities. It depends upon an attitude of *innocent receptivity which permits the perception and the experience of the new reality.* Once this reality has been perceived and experienced, its logic may be deduced if one wishes. Such a deduction is not necessary to the perception and can only follow it as a secondary activity, much as an analysis of love, for example, can only follow upon the experience but can never induce it.

The audience for art is limited not by ignorance nor by an inability to analyze, but by a lack of innocent receptivity. The defensism which is responsible for this reluctance to surrender one's own reality, at least temporarily, in order to experience another, is symptomatic of a social condition for which the artist is not responsible. It is based on the fact that if one concedes validity to contemporary realities other than one's own, the self-righteous convictions—those "absolute" truths—upon which social organization is based, are undermined. To this the average social being is instinctively and traditionally opposed.

At the opposite pole to the objective realists stand the psycho-socio-analysts, a movement which has gained impetus from the self-conscious alignment of the surrealists with Freudian and political theory. Here, any expression is regarded as a compulsive confessional, and a comprehension of it is considered dependent upon an analysis of the relationship of the images to the psyche of their source.

The most interesting results of this method occur in the work of a few highly intelligent, sophisticated film-critics who regard commercial films as the somnambulistic confessionals of modern society. They proceed on the assumption that the significant meanings are not so much incorporated in the *intended statement* (which is the case with a work of art) but are *concealed in its decorative periphery and in the relationships between the statement and its source.*

The psycho-analytical approach is also rewarding in a comprehension [*114–115*] of fantasy. In Hollywood films the significant meanings are derived from an analysis of the morally-determined (both conscious and un-conscious) censorships which give form, through limitation, to the work. In fantasy such censorships are presumably absent and the organizational integrity (hence the significant meaning) of these completely compulsive projections of psychic imagery, resides forever in its particular psychic source.

But if the psycho-analytical approach is brought to a truly creative, imaginative work of art, it yields a distorted interpretation. For such a work, although it is also based (like fantasy) on the personal psyche, is a process in which the raw materials of fantasy are assorted, selected and integrated in terms of a dominant idea or emotion. The energies of the artist are devoted to so mating his psychic images with the art instrument that the resultant product is imbued with a vitality independent of its source. Thus it is conceived, shaped, fed and formed towards the day of its emergence from the parent body as an independent, organized form. As such, its *reality and meaning are contained within itself and in the dynamics of the inter-relationships of its component parts;* even though the nature of that reality and dynamic is determined by the conceptual sources from which it derives.

   Art is distinguished from other human activities and expression by this organic function of *form* in the projection of imaginative experience into reality. This function of *form* is characterized by two essential qualities: first, that it incorporates in itself the philosophy and emotions which relate to the experience which is being projected; and second, that it derives from the instrument by which that projection is accomplished.
   While the relationship of form to content has been given much consideration and recognition, the role of the instrument, in the case of cinema particularly, deserves special attention. The relationship of the instrument to the form—the *oneness* between them—is clear enough in painting, where the form of painting is one with paint and brush; or in poetry, where the form is one with words. Here the conception of technique is expressed in the somewhat idealized notion that the brush of a painter should act, almost, as an organic extension of the hand. But to think of the mechanism of the cinema as an extension of human faculties, is to deny the advantage of the machine. The entire excitement of working with a machine as a creative instrument rests, on the contrary, in the recognition of its capacity for a *qualitatively different* dimension of projection. That is why, in cinema, the instrument (and by this I mean both the camera and the cutting of the film) becomes not a passive, adjustable conveyor of formal decisions, but an active, contributing formative factor.   [*115–116*]
   The mechanical similarity between the lens and the eye is largely responsible for the use of the camera as a recording, rather than as a creative, instrument, for the function of the eye is to register. However, it is in the *mind behind the eye* that the registered material achieves meaning and impact. In cinema this extension has been ignored. The meaning of the incident or experience is here made an *attribute of the reality in front of the lens* rather than a creative act on the part of the mechanism (including the human being) behind the lens.
   In keeping with this theory of the camera as a registering eye, there is a substantial school of thought which holds that the documentary film, by exploiting the capacity of the camera to record reality, constitutes *the* cinematic art form. Certain sequences from "Fighting Lady" (a war documentary), in which enemy planes are engaged in combat and are strafed at close quarters, are advanced as an example of great cinematic achievement. Actually, these sequences were achieved as follows: the camera shutter was connected to the gun in such a way that it was automatically released when the gun was fired. These sequences are, then, the result of the automatic functioning of a brainless mechanism which operated in synchronization with another mechanism, a gun, which was operated because of the desire to kill. This, as a motivation, has obviously little in common with the motivation of art.
   When the camera is used to register (for infinite reproduction) either theater, or a picturization of fiction, or a so-called "objective" reality, there is no more *oneness* between form and instrument than there is between the poem and the typewriter. But whereas the typewriter can hardly be considered capable of creative action, the camera is, potentially, a highly creative instrument.

We are, however, in a period in which the reporter, the international cor-respondent, stands as a Man of Letters in the public mind. All who have read fine poetry could not confuse even the finest reportorial account with a poem. Documen-taries are the visual counterparts of reportorial dispatches, and bear the same rela-tionship to cinema art as the dispatches do to poetry. If, particularly in film, the flowering of the documentary has almost obscured all else save the "entertainment" film, it is because the events and accidents of reality are, today, more monstrous, more shocking, than the human imagination is capable of inventing. The war gives rise to incidents which are not only beyond the inventive power of the human imagination, but also beyond its capacity, almost, to believe. In this period, where we are concerned with the unbelievableness of incidents, we require a reportage and a proof of their reality. But the great art expressions will come later, as they always have; and they will be dedicated, again, to the *agony* and the *experience* rather than the *incident.*   [*116–117*]

What has been most responsible for the lack of development of the cine-matic idiom is the emphatic literacy of our age. So accustomed are we to thinking in terms of the continuity-logic of the literary narrative that the narrative pattern has come to completely dominate cinematic expression in spite of the fact that it is, basically, a visual form. We overlook the fact that painting, for instance, is organized in visual logics, or that music is organized in tonal-rhythmic logics, that there are visual and auditory experiences which have nothing to do with the descriptive narrative.

Once we arrive at an independent cinematic idiom, the present sub-servience of cinema to the literary story will appear unbelievably primitive. It will seem comparable to those early days when the airplanes flew above and along the highway and railroad routes. The fact that they moved by air—a dustless, faster, pleasanter method than railroad or automobile—does not negate the fact that they travelled *by earth,* not *by air.* It is also true that, before one could travel really by air, many instruments, techniques, etc., had to be developed. But the fact is that if these efforts to discover the element air—as contrasted to the elements earth and water—had not been made, airplane travel would have remained a merely minor, quantitative improvement over earthly locomotion and would never have so qualita-tively affected our concepts of time and space and our relationship to them.

There are also those who, riding in an airplane, turn their attention to recognizing earth landmarks and who complain for the lack of bird songs and flower perfumes. In their fixation upon the familiar and the recognizable, they fail to enlarge their experience. As long as we seek for literature in cinema, whose peculiar beauty and creative potentialities have hardly been touched, it will be denied development.

The fact that an individual may find walking in the country more satisfying than swimming in the ocean or flying through the air is a question of his own per-sonal preference; but it is only in terms of personal disposition that preferential comparisons can be made between experiences which differ qualitatively. More-over, ideally, such personal preferences and predispositions should not be per-mitted to minimize the value of an experience which differs, qualitatively, from that towards which the individual may be pre-disposed.

I hope therefore that it is clear that, in my repeated references to literature and other art forms, in my insistence upon the independence of cinema from them, and in my suggestion that, as an art form, cinema seems especially appropriate to some of the central problems of our time, I am not implying a comparative value judgment. On the contrary, by insisting upon its independence from other art forms, I strike at the very heart of the growing tendency to think of motion pictures as a somehow superior method of communicating literary or theatrical experience. (Dance, for [117–118] example, which, of all art forms would seem to profit most by cinematic treatment, actually suffers miserably. The more successful it is as a theatrical expression, conceived in terms of a stable, stage-front audience, the more its carefully wrought choreographic patterns suffer from the restiveness of a camera which bobs about in the wings, on-stage for a close-up, etc. . . . . There *is* a potential filmic dance form, in which the choreography and movements would be designed, precisely, for the mobility and other attributes of the camera, but this, too, requires an independence from theatrical dance conceptions.)

The development of cinematic form has suffered not only because the camera has been used almost exclusively to pictorialize literature and to document reality, but also because it came into a world in which other art forms had already been firmly established for centuries. Painters, for instance, inspired by the possibilities of this new medium, brought to it the traditions of the idiom with which they were first pre-occupied. Consequently, in many abstract films, the film frame has been used as an animated canvas. But these are developments in painting rather than in film. In most cases the creative energy of the artists who came from other fields was dedicated first of all, to the arrangement of objects in front of the lens rather than the manner of manipulating the mechanism behind the lens.

Nor does the direction of cinematic form consist in a wide-eyed game with the camera as if it were a new toy in the hands of a curious, clever child. It does not consist in making things appear or disappear, go fast or slow, backwards or forwards, just because a camera can do that. This results merely in a sensationalist, virtuoso exercise of skills and techniques. Cinematic form is more profound than that. It is a concept of the integration of techniques, a search for the meaning of a skill.

Cinema—and by this is understood the entire body of technique including camera, lighting, acting, editing, etc.—is a time-space art with a unique capacity for creating new temporal-spatial relationships and projecting them with an incontrovertible impact of reality—the reality of show-it-to-me. It emerges in a period marked, simultaneously, by the development of radio in communication, the airplane and the rocket-ship in transportation, and the theory of relativity in physics. To ignore the implications of this simultaneity, or to consider it a historical coincidence, would constitute not only a failure to understand the basic nature of these contributions to our civilization; it would also make us guilty of an even more profound failure, that of not recognizing the relationships of human ideology to material development.   [118–119]

The nazi concept of racial integrity, for instance, belongs to that period in which a mountain between two valleys served to localize the tribes of each. In such primitive civilization, subject to all sorts of natural disasters, rigidly localized by geographical and material restrictions, a philosophy which placed the unity of the tribe above all else was appropriate. The isolation gave reason to an absolutistic philosophy of time and space. The need for tribal unity gave reason to the concept of absolute authority in the state, religion and mores in general.

Today the airplane and the radio have created, in fact, a relativistic reality of time and space. They have introduced into our immediate reality a dimension which functions not as an added spatial location but which, being both temporal and spatial, relates to all the other dimensions with which we are familiar. There is not an object which does not require relocation in terms of this new frame of reference, and not least among these is the individual.

Imperceptibly, almost, this sense of relativism has begun to influence our thinking. In spatial terms, for example, the absolutistic differentiation between *here* and *there* loses meaning as *here* and *there,* being so mutually accessible, become, in effect, almost identical. In terms of time, the chronology of the past, present and future has also increasingly lost its meaning as we have come to understand the continuity of the past with the future—and, prodded on by the actual acceleration of historical processes, to deal with the present moment as an extension of the past into the future rather than as an independent temporal period.

Moreover, because of the quality of this new referential frame, validity is no longer a function of the object itself. It has become, instead, a function of the position of that object in the constellation of which it is part. The concept of absolute intrinsic values, whose stability must be maintained, gives way to the concept of relationships which ceaselessly are created, dissolved and recreated and which bestow value upon the part according to its functional relation to the whole. We face the problem of discovering the dynamics of maintaining an *unstable equilibrium.*

The individual, deprived of the absolutisms which moulded the moral pattern of his life, is faced with a critical, desperate need to discover in himself an integrity at once constant enough to constitute an identity and adjustable enough to relate to an apparently anarchic universe whose gravities, revolutions and constellations operate according to a logic which he has yet to discover. The solution does not rest in the infinite adjustments and revisions of a Ptolmeaic system of description.

Cinema, with its capacity to manipulate time and space seems eminently appropriate as an art form in which such problems can find expression. By manipulation of time and space I do not mean such established filmic [119–120] techniques as flash-backs, condensation of time, parallel actions etc. . . . these affect not the action itself, but the method of revealing it. In a flash-back there is no implication that the usual chronological integrity of the action itself is in any way affected by the process, however disrupted, of memory. The turning of spring into winter by one swift dissolve is a condensation of the presentation of the seasons, but does not affect the implication of customary seasonal rhythms. Parallel actions—as in a sequence when we see, alternately, the hero who rushes to the rescue and the heroine, whose situation becomes increasingly critical—is an omnipresence on the part of the camera as a witness of action, not as a creator of it.

When dislocations of reality occur in commercial films, they are inevitably presented as a quality, not of the reality itself, but of a distorted view of it. But the dislocations of modern life—are, precisely, dislocations of reality itself. And it is conceivable that an individual should be incapable of a distortion of vision which, designed to compliment and "correct" these dislocations of reality, results in an apparent "adjustment."

The external universe which we once considered, at least in our immediate locality, as the passive recipient of the manifestations of the individual will—the stage upon which the conflict of human wills was dramatically enacted—has been revealed as an active creative force. And again, cinema, with its capacity for animating the ostensibly inanimate, for re-relating the ostensibly immobile, is especially equipped to deal with such experiences.

The potentialities of cinema are rich and unexplored. It can relate two unrelated geographies by the continuous unity of an un-interrupted movement begun in one and concluded in the other. It can project as simultaneities, chronologically distant events. Slow motion, and the agony of its analysis, reveals in the most casual incident, a cosmic constellation. Yet no verbal description can convey the sense of a medium which is basically visual.

And here we return to the first considerations of this article, for such potentialities as the cinema contains for giving expression to these problems, will be developed only when cinema is treated as an independent art form, rather than as an instrument for the illustration of literary narrative. How little that is understood is evidenced by a recent article by the film critic of the New York *Times*. In a review of the "Best Film Plays of 1943–44" he applauds the fact that "the plays are presented—uncomplicated by the numerous camera directions which used to be the bane of the reader." When the day comes that the camera—the visual element—ceases to be thought of as an annoying complication by "film" writers who concern themselves with cinema not out of an appreciation of it as a medium, but because the film industry provides the most lucrative employment for "writers," cinema as an art form will begin to come of age.   [*120*]

1. What assumptions underlie Miss Deren's belief that cinema is not an art today?

2. Do you agree with Miss Deren's insistence that films should be made by one man? Make a list of the best films you've seen. How many of these were written, directed and edited by the same person?

3. Is Miss Deren correct in saying that the best-made American films deal with abnormal people or unusual events?

4. Is Miss Deren convincing in her arguments against those who believe that the documentary is the most authentic film form?

A NOTE ON THE MOVIES

Nicola Chiaromonte

What is your substance, whereof are you made,
That millions of strange shadows on you tend?
SHAKESPEARE, *Sonnet, 53*

No one can deny that there is a difference between reading a good novel and seeing a good movie.

A good novel tells us something while a good movie shows us something; or, to be more precise, a good movie *has shown* us something, since the emotional effect is over when the film is over, and can be recalled only verbally and in a peculiarly abstract fashion. For in spite of the way critics retell the plot of a film, a movie is not a narrative but a series of actions that seem to be occurring. And the emotion they give us is the emotion of the onlooker, not of the participant, which we are in the novel. What we remember about a novel is the *meaning* of the facts, which are always related from the point of view of the characters, who are pure possibilities of consciousness and not physical entities. Moreover, each one of its sections is a distinct, yet indivisible, part of the whole.

But our recollection of a film is quite different. Certain parts stand out distinctly, while the whole can be remembered only vaguely. Now it is interesting to note that we cannot recall the parts without changing their very essence, for we are forced to make static what was originally pure motion, and to translate into logi-

NICOLA CHIAROMONTE, a distinguished Italian drama and literary critic, is editor, with Ignazio Silone, of *Tempo Presente*.

This essay appeared in the March, 1960 issue of *Encounter*, pp. 58–61, and is reprinted by permission.

cal and figurative discourse what was originally cinematic. So that a film cannot really be retold, for example. And when a movie critic recounts the plot of a film he makes it sound like something it is not, namely, a narrative.

The cinema is the only art, with the partial exception of ballet and pantomime, that cannot be grasped by non-mechanical memory (that is, the memory of quality and meaning). Now, both ballet and pantomime are composed of allusive figures, each of which can be "stopped" by the mind, without their meaning being altered since they express the design and style of the whole. Nor do the movements of a pantomime or ballet attempt to be the equivalent of "real" actions, whose meaning resides entirely in their occurring.

But what about music, one might well retort? Isn't it true that as soon as the performance of a symphony is over and the sounds have died out the emotional effect cannot be recaptured unless the performance is repeated? Without entering into the qualitative difference between the experiences of a movie and a piece of music, one must point out that the analogy between a musical continuity and a sequence of images is false. A musical composition is not merely a succession of sounds; it is a rhythmical development and the creation of a completely qualitative duration of time. Even if the notes are forgotten the quality remains, so that when we say Mozart or Stravinsky we know exactly what unique *quality* we mean and what universe we are referring to.

At this point the cinema specialist will reply that when we say Eisenstein or John Ford we also know what we mean. In a sense this is true, since these directors have a way of putting together a film which is recognisable—a "style," if one wants to call it that. But "style" in the case of a movie is more like the difference between one brand of consumer's goods and another. In any case, it is far from the complete mastery of material which in the case of Giotto or Tolstoy makes style synonymous with meaning, and with the individual creator's own special vision of the universe.

The "style" of a movie may be the use of certain devices; it may be the tempo of the whole show; it may be the expressiveness of the acting; or it may be the way all these elements are held together by the tension of plot development. The point is that once the film is over what remains is a general effect, a certain excitement, a vague impression comparable to the one we are left with at the end of a sports event, rather than to the state of mind originated by the contemplation of a poetic, plastic, or musical [58–59] form. We have *consumed* something which seemed good or bad, clever or silly. But where is it now? And what was it exactly?

The cinema is universally fascinating because it is nothing but a passing show, resembling magically the actual experience of the passing of time. The peculiar pathos of film images lies in their evanescence. As soon as we try to arrest, fix, and capture them, or treat them as if they composed a stable form we destroy their magic, kill their essence, and obliterate whatever poetry they have. One might define the quintessence of cinema art as the giving of non-lasting form to what, in fact, does not last. The impossibility of the spectator's bringing back to memory the impact of cinematic action is an intrinsic quality of this means of expression. As no other medium does, the movies imitate in an overpowering way the flow of real time, charged as it is with events and expectation of events; and like real time, a film cannot be reversed or remembered, except in fragments.

After the most skilful and effective film, all we are left with are separate parts which we find peculiarly difficult to put together, plus a vague impression of the whole. We can, of course, visualise the scene in *Potemkin* when the sailor picks up a morsel of meat swarming with maggots, or the famous shot on the staircase; we can also recall the delicate romanticism of *Les Enfants du Paradis*. As we do this, however, we are immediately aware of the fact that we are not in possession of the complete image that evoked the original aesthetic emotion but fragments of it—scattered pieces, *disiecta membra*. It was the sequence of the impressions that we had when we first saw the film that gave rise to the original emotion, and now they have vanished. It is true that we can see the film again and repeat the feeling, but we cannot enrich it. It is nothing but a reiteration, and our only authentic experience of the film is the first one, no matter what we do.

Now this is never true of poetry, music, or painting. Of course one can read Canto XXVI of the *Inferno* a hundred times without feeling anything but cold admiration. However, the moment arrives when the verses come alive for us, and it is a *new* experience, the result of everything relevant to Dante's vision of Ulysses that we have experienced since the first reading.

As for a sonata or a painting, even when our recollection of these works is imperfect, and most details are present only faintly, we retain possession of the whole, because of the very nature of these objects. A few measures of Mozart are still Mozart, and a Van Gogh yellow *is* Van Gogh. Why? Because what counts in these works is always and solely their meaning; their sound and colour are important insofar as they send us back to the meaning. And it is the experience of *quality* which remains fixed in our memory.

Whereas what we remember in a movie are events that are put together in such a way that their meaning seems to be the same thing as their apparent motion. In fact, there cannot be two different executions of a movie. Pictures in a film do not have meaning, but direction, the irreversible direction of their happening. That is why memory cannot revive them. Just as it cannot revive the past events of real time until the miracle of Proustian resuscitation occurs, or we suddenly discover their meaning and value, the truth that lay hidden in them.

Such illuminations, metamorphoses, and conversions are the sign of what we call "spiritual life." And they are based, not on time as it is materially experienced, but on its very opposite, on that which transcends our "normal" experience of time, with its discontinuity, its errors, and its opacity. What captivates us in a film is the possibility of wallowing in an artificial time that is both extraordinarily similar to and more intense than "real" time. Yet, after the movie is over we are left with an insatiable desire for "real" time, which we can feel, enjoy, and move in. The catharsis of the real through the unreal, which up to now has characterised art, does not take place in the case of the movies.

It has been said that "the joy brought to us by the cinema is the revelation of the photogenic quality of the objects in movement."

Perhaps "excitement" rather than joy would be the right word to describe the impression left on us by the first picture of a locomotive racing into a station that we saw on the screen. Excitement at what? At the fact—which is as strange as it is everlasting and fundamentally childish—that there we saw action itself, pure movement abstracted from any context of reality, shown immediately and absolutely, as it can never be in actuality.

When we see movement in real life it is never movement alone that we see, except in moments of violent emotion as when a speeding car misses us by a few inches, or when a person invades our consciousness with frantic gestures. However, despite what is generally believed, movement is not the most important part of our experience of reality, and it becomes so only when the external world takes on a frantic aggressiveness and threatens or exalts us without leaving us time to think beyond the imminent danger or excitement.

What is remarkable is that such moments are distinguished from others by a feeling of great certainty in which the usual inertia of things [59–60] and the formlessness of ordinary time are overcome; the world is reduced to intense expectation and to a simple choice between grabbing or escaping whatever is speeding by; or just waiting feverishly for what is going to happen. The fascination of danger, gambling, and violent action lies in the great simplification of the world that they imply. And this fascination is connected with the instinct which makes the individual try to get hold of life as if it were an object whose meaning can be captured along with its material possession. There is no doubt but that the world is *also* what it seems to be in such moments of frenzy—totally present, totally hostile, or totally benign, and made up of a sequel of senseless events. This instinct can be exorcised by mind or heart; it can be hypnotised by collective emotion; or it can be appeased by the magic of machines; but it can never be suppressed. The cinema hypnotises it for a moment by offering it a temporary outlet in a world of moving shadows, and suggests that living is simply being involved in an indefinite series of events in a world devoid of any stable meaning.

. In real life movement is always subordinated to something else, and presented in a context of other signs and warnings that come to us from the external world: by itself, it means very little. When we look at people gesticulating and moving behind a window on the other side of the street their movements appear to be definite signs of something, yet they are so vague as to be enigmatic. Those gestures are the final outcome of feelings, intentions, and purposes of various kinds; and if we don't know what is behind them we don't know anything at all about them. Even if we succeeded in understanding their immediate significance we should still not know the deeper meaning they have in the story of the people's lives. Yet the spectacle is fascinating. The pantomime surely means something, since gestures are the clearest, least equivocal signs that a man can give of his immediate intentions and emotions—the final result of his inner life, as it were. Hence we cannot help speculating about that dumb agitation, that spectacle so pure it can have an almost infinite number of meanings, and yet seems to have but a single "right" one, exactly like a riddle. At the same time, however, we know that we can never go back from these incoherent gestures to exactly what they mean to those people, since we are ignorant of their actual context. From motive to act a stretch of time has flowed which cannot be reversed. Only when the gestures are extremely explicit can we put vague labels like "anger," "love," or the like on them. And only when the acts are frankly acts of violence do they become unequivocally indicative, even though the motives of violence remain obscure.

In real life, in a context of concrete experience, movements, actions, and the external aspect of things are not only what are most ambiguous, but what are least meaningful. What matters is that which precedes and follows these manifestations—their causes and their effects in the light of our knowledge of men, nature, and culture. In the movies (and their peculiar magic consists mainly, if not entirely, in this) the field of consciousness is completely occupied by gestures, actions, and other external signs; and these most fleeting aspects of the world are made to be not only supremely unambiguous but also the very locus of meaning. Everything that cannot be indicated by a gesture, or by a purely utilitarian verbal utterance in function of the gesture, is excluded from the screen. In spite of recurrent attempts to make films say more than they ever can say, a successful movie (that is, one that captures its audience because it manages to substitute the artificial time of its action for real time) is one where the pictures are made to follow each other according to their elementary logic and not according to complicated intentions and theories. The achievement is infinitely fascinating to the child in us.

In real life we love or we "love to love," as St. Augustine said; we think about love and we are never sure what it is and what it means. On the screen the hero and the heroine go through the motions of falling in love and that's that.

The eye of the camera is, indeed, the "eye of the world"—nobody's and everybody's eye. It gives us a kind of absolute perception which is impossible in reality, insofar as real perception is intrinsically complex, accompanied as it is by the richness and ambiguity of an individual consciousness. In reality we are never completely external to the world of persons and objects, but are always involved through our feelings and our thoughts. Photography, however, is a feat of mechanical magic by which we are made to stare at the world from the outside, so that we can actually look at it (for the first time, as it were) instead of just seeing it.

This strange privilege is what makes for the enormous importance and magnetic power of the camera as an instrument. But it is also the limit which can never be passed. Practically boundless, the magic of the camera is actually confined to the presentation of the physical appearance of things, *isolated from all the rest*. The language of physical appearance is the camera's own language, and it is the most elementary language we can conceive of, the least common denominator of all human expressions. It is, in fact, so elementary and so common [60–61] that it might be said that the camera is the idiom of the inarticulate itself in man. The idiom not of Caliban, the unhappy monster, but of a Caliban who has found perfect "adjustment" in a world made up entirely of fleeting acts and shadows, and cleared of all malicious spirits.

The photographs of disasters, famous men, and shapely women that we see in *Life* Magazine are supposed to "bring the world to us." But what these pictures actually accomplish is the inhuman feat of transforming real people and events into objects of sheer inspection, severed from all living context and meaning by the surgery of the camera. We can look without seeing, grasp without understanding, be excited without having any definite feeling. The density and slipperiness of real events with which we are connected by fears, expectations, desires, ideas, and conflicts of ideas are put out of action by the photographic image. Reduced to clear-cut appearances, things become infinitely more evident and infinitely more meaningless than they can ever be in reality. What we are left with is, indeed, the "film" of life. Instead of being brought *to* us, the world has been successfully "gotten out of our system."

The eye of the camera gives us that extraordinary phenomenon—the world disinfected of consciousness.   [*61*]

1. Can you think of any similarities that Mr. Chiaromonte overlooks in his contrast between reading a novel and seeing a film?

2. If Mr. Chiaromonte were right, film criticism would be impossible, because criticism involves contemplating experience for the purpose of evaluation. How can film critics cope with the evanescence of film? What kinds of permanence can they point to?

3. "Pictures in a film do not have meaning, but direction, the irreversible direction of their happening." This is the cornerstone of Mr. Chiaromonte's position. To what extent does it seem convincing?

THE FALL AND RISE OF THE FILM DIRECTOR

Andrew Sarris

Greta Garbo's creakiest vehicle of the Thirties was an opus entitled *Susan Lennox—Her Fall and Rise*. Film historians and archivists have repeatedly restored the classical cadence of "Rise and Fall" to the title in defiance of the plot line and the aggressively American optimism it represents. Film directors are comparable to sudsy Susan Lennox in that their tarnished professional image has regained its gloss after a long period of neglect and downright disrepute. In fact, the renewed awareness of the film director as a conscious artist is one of the more interesting cultural phenomena of the past decade. This renewal can be described as a rise only in the most relative terms. The director has risen no more than the sun rises. As the latter is a figure of speech describing the diurnal rotation of the earth from the point of view of the fallible human eye, the pre-eminence of the director has been a matter of public and critical fancy.

Like the sun, the director has always been out there on the set, and his turn to be worshiped has come full circle from the earliest days of his solitary pre-eminence behind primitive tripod cameras pointed at a world still visually virginal. This intimation of lost innocence is invoked in Billy Wilder's *Sunset Boulevard*

ANDREW SARRIS has written film essays and reviews, and has authored and edited numerous books on the subject. He is currently film critic of *The Village Voice*.

when Erich von Stroheim commands the newsreel cameras to turn on Gloria Swanson as she descends the staircase to utter madness. There is more than the numbing nostalgia for a burnt-out star in this sequence; there is also the evocation of an era when movie-making was more individual, less industrial. It is immaterial whether there ever was an era of directorial enlightenment. Many film historians have testified to the existence of a Golden Age in order to create a frame of reference. The gold may have turned to brass before 1925 or 1920 or 1915, but somewhere along the line, the legend persists, the film director lost all his freedom and integrity to some monstrous entity known as the motion picture industry—code name: Hollywood.

Confirmation of this legend of directorial decline and decadence has been provided by veteran Hollywood director George Stevens: "When the movie industry was young, the film-maker was its core and the men who handled the business details his partner . . . When [the director] finally looked around, he found his partner's name on the door. Thus the film-maker became the employee, and the man who had the time to attend to the business details became the head of the studio." [i–ii]

Studio head Samuel Goldwyn put the matter somewhat more brutally when a reporter had the temerity to begin a sentence with the statement: "When William Wyler made *Wuthering Heights* . . ." The reporter never passed beyond the premise. "*I* made *Wuthering Heights*," Goldwyn snapped. "Wyler only directed it."

"Only directed" is more precisely defined in the appendix of *The Film Till Now* by Paul Rotha and Richard Griffith: "Director—(a) In feature films the Director is usually the technician who directs the shooting of the film, that is, he tells the players what to do and the cameraman what to shoot, and usually supervises the editing. Most feature films are directed from scripts written by the script department or by an independent script-writer. The editing is carried out by a department under a supervising editor working in consultation with the director and producer. Sometimes a director will write his own shooting-script and do his own editing; thus the film will tend much more to carry his individual mark.

"(b) In documentary films the Director usually writes his own script after first-hand investigation of the subject, although sometimes he may employ a dialogue writer. He not only directs the action of the film, but controls it through all stages of editing, music, dubbing, etc. Wartime developments have tended to departmentalize documentary production as in story films."

The most interesting aspect of this duplex definition, devised during the Forties, is its ingrained bias in favor of the documentary director. Directors of "feature" or "story" films were presumably less artists than artisans not only because they were more closely supervised, but also because "feature" films were considered more frivolous than documentary films. Thus, most movie directors were doubly denigrated in the scholarly texts of the period. On the one hand, most directors were charged with having too little control over their movies, and on the other, their movies were not considered worth doing in the first place.

Not that scholarly texts had any appreciable influence on the motion picture industry. Like so many other products of capitalism, movies were designed for immediate consumption and rapid expendability. Once a movie became "old," it was returned to the vaults, never to be shown publicly again. Thus, even if there had been any interest in directorial careers, the necessary research materials were not available. To make matters worse, film history was split in two by the advent of sound in the late Twenties.

People who grew up in the Thirties were completely unaware of the cinema of the Twenties except for infrequent custard pie two-reelers or an occasional revival of the foreign repertory—from *Caligari* to *Potemkin*. By about 1934, censorship had placed many movies of the early Thirties out of bounds, a condition that existed until the Forties and Fifties when television gold made it lucrative for studios to open their vaults. We are still a long way from the day when scholars can obtain the films they need from film [*ii–iii*] libraries, but the proliferation of old films has had its effect on contemporary criticism. A greater awareness of the past, a sense of stylistic continuity in the works of individual directors, a cyclical pattern of period mannerisms—these are some of the dividends of the improved distribution of movies in the Sixties. The most hardheaded businessman in the movie industry must now be at least marginally concerned with the burgeoning scholarship in the medium. By the same token, the most serious-minded scholar cannot avoid taking movies more seriously than heretofore, particularly when it is now possible to trace links between the Marx Brothers and Ionesco, between Buster Keaton and Samuel Beckett.

Unfortunately, most scholarly works on the cinema are still written from a predominantly sociological viewpoint, and most directors are still subordinated to both the studio and the star system that allegedly enslave them. Indeed most directors have always been considered less as creators than as decorators of other people's scenarios. That most directors do not write their own scripts is enough to discredit these directors in the eyes of the literary establishment. Such discredit is often unjustified even on literary grounds simply because many directors decline to take credit for collaboration on the writing of their films.

Furthermore, screenwriting involves more than mere dialogue and plot. The choice between a close-up and a long-shot, for example, may quite often transcend the plot. If the story of Little Red Riding Hood is told with the Wolf in close-up and Little Red Riding Hood in long-shot, the director is concerned primarily with the emotional problems of a wolf with a compulsion to eat little girls. If Little Red Riding Hood is in close-up and the Wolf in long-shot, the emphasis is shifted to the emotional problems of vestigial virginity in a wicked world. Thus, two different stories are being told with the same basic anecdotal material. What is at stake in the two versions of Little Red Riding Hood are two contrasting directorial attitudes toward life. One director identifies more with the Wolf—the male, the compulsive, the corrupted, even evil itself. The second director identifies with the little girl—the innocence, the illusion, the ideal and hope of the race. Needless to say, few critics bother to make any distinction, proving perhaps that direction as creation is still only dimly understood.

As a consequence, contemporary film criticism has tended to diverge into two conflicting camps, the poor film director caught in the middle. First and foremost, we have the literary establishment, which relegates visual style to subordinate paragraphs in reviews. Then we have the visualists, who disdain plots and dialogues as literary impurities. Since most directors worthy of note work in the impure realm of the dramatic sound film, it is difficult to isolate their personal contributions to the cinema. The literary critics prefer to synopsize the plot, discuss the theme, if any, evaluate the performances, comment on the photography, editing, etc., and credit the director only for [*iii–iv*] "pacing," usually in the three speeds—fast, deliberate, and most often of all, too slow. Conversely, the visual critics concentrate on landscapes and abstractions as "pure" cinema, and castigate dramatic scenes as "talky," "stagey," "literary," etc. That is why the coming of sound was such a traumatic experience for serious film aestheticians of the late Twenties and early Thirties, and why much of what we call film history is actually the thinly disguised nostalgia of elderly film historians for the mute movies of their youth.

Through the haze of selective recollection, the silent film had apparently flown to an extraordinary elevation in the Twenties only to crash through the sound barrier with a screech and a squeak. It became fashionable to mourn the tragedy of talkies until well into the Forties, and after to talk about the cinema in terms of artistic decline until well into the Fifties.

The biographical pattern of almost every director went something like this: He started off very promisingly, but was soon corrupted by Hollywood (if he were foreign), or by big budgets (if he were American). His work became more and more "commercial," less and less "significant." Because distribution was so erratic, it was always reasonably safe to say that yesterday's movies were superior to today's.

On the whole, however, directors were penalized more by critical indifference than by critical captiousness . . . If the role of the director is now taken more seriously, it is because the cinema itself is taken more seriously. The director never really had any serious rival in the creative process. No one, least of all the serious scholar, was ever taken in by the pufferies of the producers. Selznick, Zanuck, Hughes, Goldwyn, and Thalberg did exercise great control over their productions, but few of their contributions were regarded as genuinely creative. Mostly, they maintained a certain level of technical quality in their productions, but production control without creative responsibility falls generally under the heading of interference.

The writer was even less serious a challenge to the director. Although the director was shackled to some extent by the studio system through the Thirties and Forties, the writer was virtually deprived of his identity. As far as studios were concerned, there was never a question of too many scribes spoiling the script. Quite to the contrary, most producers believed strongly in the safety of numbers, and the multiple writing credits on the screen made it difficult for screenwriters to be taken seriously as screen authors.

By contrast, directors almost invariably received sole credit for their efforts, however craven and controlled these efforts may have been considered. In addition, the director's credit always appeared last on the screen—or almost always—one contractual exception being the aforementioned Samuel Goldwyn, a producer with a passion for having his name follow the director's. Nevertheless, the director's position, even in Hollywood, has always [*iv–v*] been strategically superior to the writer's. In the early Forties, the Screenwriter's Guild felt obliged to agitate for greater critical recognition, and the conflict became so exaggerated that, at one point, Stephen Longstreet attacked Vincente Minnelli for distracting audiences from dialogue with fancy camera angles in the 1945 Judy Garland-Robert Walker romance, *The Clock*. Needless to say, no screenwriter today would dare make a comparable objection.

Even today, however, the film director faces massive obstacles to critical recognition. Writers, actors, producers, and technicians challenge him at every turn. Also, the analogous and yet anomalous relationship with stage directors tends to confuse the issue. It is fashionable to say that the screen is a director's medium and the stage a writer's medium, but it is difficult to demonstrate that a Broadway-to-Hollywood-and-back director like Elia Kazan is any less in command in one medium than in another. To some extent, of course, the role of the director, stage or screen, depends on the person playing it. Many, if not most, film directors are little more than glorified stage managers charged with maintaining a schedule for the execution of the preordained plans of the studio, the stars, the producer, the writer or writers, the technicians, the distributors, and even the vulgar public. At his least or his worst, the director is reduced to the level of a technician without the technician's pride in his craft. Such directors are like absolute despots compelled to act as constitutional monarchs, but lacking the style to conceal or circumvent their subservience.

At the other extreme, we have a new breed of film-makers who do not even call themselves "directors." These are the so-called independents, the "poets," the perpetual avant-garde of the cinema. They scorn or pretend to scorn the elaborate technical and industrial processes of movie production for the sake of a more individualized creation. They are descended, if only atavistically, from the first film-makers, the curious cameramen who were playing with a new toy. Ironically, the avant-garde has generally resisted the stylistic and technological innovations initiated by the so-called commercial movie-makers. Sound, color, music, variable screens were all developed by the film industry while the avant-garde was publishing manifestoes against them. The avant-garde has thus led the way not in form, but in content—anarchic, subversive, sacrilegious, scatological, and pornographic.

Through the years and decades, however, avant-garde attitudes in America have relied on the foreign "art film" for intellectual authority. The Germans and the Russians were particularly fashionable in the Twenties, before Hitler and Stalin stultified experimentation. Movies like *The Last Laugh* and *Variety* dramatized the expressive potentialities of the moving camera along with downbeat subjects considered too grim for Hollywood, but it was Sergei Eisenstein's *Potemkin* that galvanized a whole generation of intellectuals and aesthetes into wild enthusiasm over the creative possibilities of montage, a term that reverberated through the Twenties and Thirties the way *mise en scène* [v–vi] has reverberated through the Fifties and Sixties. Normally, montage is merely a fancy word for editing or cutting, but Eisenstein gave montage a mystique by linking it to the philosophical processes of dialectical materialism. As Eisenstein conceived of film-making, images equaled ideas, and the collision of two dynamically opposed images created a new idea. Eisenstein's montage theory was ideal for describing the collisions of the Russian Revolution, but there did not seem to be many other plots for which incessant montage was appropriate. The great majority of movies developed a dramatic style of expression to enhance audience identification with star personalities. Since in the world cinema the mystique of montage was thereafter honored more in the breach than in the observance, film histories turned sour with acid critiques of alleged betrayals of the medium. As the gap widened between what was popular and what was intellectually fashionable, Eisensteinian aesthetics were supplemented by Marxist politics. Movies were not merely vulgar; they were instruments of capitalism in the never-ending class struggle. Film directors were thus presented with two choices: fight the establishment, or "sell out."

It remained for the illustrious French film critic André Bazin to eliminate much of the confusion arising from Eisenstein's half-digested montage theories. Bazin pinpointed psychological and physical situations in which montage disrupted the unity of man with his environment. Indeed it was French criticism in the late Forties and early Fifties that introduced the mystique of *mise en scène* to counterbalance that of montage. The more extreme of Eisenstein disciples had reached a stage of absurdity in which what was actually on the screen was secondary to the "rhythm" of the film. The montage maniacs had thus enthroned punctuation at the expense of language. At times, it seemed that the camera was merely an excuse to get into the cutting room.

Ironically, the producers shared the highbrow enthusiasm over montage. "We'll save it in the cutting room" became one of the hackneyed slogans of bad producers. *Mise en scène,* with its connotation of design and decor, reintroduced pictorial values to a medium that had become obsessed with the musical rhythms of images flashing by to be slashed on the moviola.

Because French critics were less awed by montage, they tended to be more appreciative of Hollywood than their cultivated counterparts in America and England. Most Hollywood directors of the Thirties were disqualified from serious consideration because they did not supervise the final editing (montage) of their films, for editing was then considered, by the aestheticians, the supreme function of cinematic creation. With the collapse of the montage mystique, however, many directors of the Thirties have been rediscovered as undeniably personal artists. Not only do the best directors cut "in the mind" rather than in the cutting room, but montage is only one aspect of a directorial personality.

Nonetheless, the Hollywood director is still taken less seriously than his [vi–vii] foreign counterpart, and, in interviews, he generally regards himself with the same lack of seriousness. Part of his problem is the Hollywood ethos of the "team"; part is the tendency of Hollywood movies to conceal the inner workings for the sake of popular illusionism. Audiences are not supposed to be conscious that a movie is directed; the movie just happens by some mysterious conjunction of the players with their plot. Quite often, Hollywood directors have labored in obscurity to evolve an extraordinary economy of expression that escapes so-called highbrow critics in search of the obvious stylistic flourish. Consequently, there has been a tendency to overrate the European directors because of their relative articulateness about their artistic *angst,* and now a reaction has set in against some of the disproportionate pomposity that has ensued. Some of the recent cults for Ingmar Bergman, Federico Fellini, and Michelangelo Antonioni create the impression that the cinema was born sometime between 1950 and 1960. Not that European directors are entirely to blame for occasionally appearing pretentious. They are merely playing the role that is expected of them, just as Hollywood directors are conditioned to pretend that they are all hardheaded businessmen. But here, too, the gap is narrowing as Hollywood directors venture to be more explicit about their artistic intentions and European directors dare to be more candid about commercial and professional problems.

As film scholarship becomes more sophisticated, the facile distinctions between so-called "art" films and so-called "commercial" films become less meaningful. Out of the sifting and winnowing emerges a new division of good "art" and "commercial" films on one side and bad "art" and "commercial" films on the other. Not only do art and commerce intersect; they are intertwined with the muddled process of film-making. Even art films have to make money, and even commercial films have to make some statement. To put it another way, more and more critics are demanding that there should be more fun in art, and more art in fun. The post-Marxist pop and camp movements have perhaps overreacted to the socially conscious solemnity of the past, but the increasing skepticism about mere good intentions is a healthy sign of higher standards. Unfortunately, the pendulum has swung from the extreme of sobriety to the extreme of silliness. In the process, however, it has become possible to speak of Alfred Hitchcock and Michelangelo Antonioni in the same breath and with the same critical terminology. Amid the conflicting critical camps, both Rays, Nicholas and Satyajit, have gained a respectful hearing. Suddenly every director is entitled to equal time on the international critical scene in which critics are compelled to abandon many of their cherished prejudices and snobberies. In a more open-minded atmosphere of critical recognition, it is only natural that film directors should abandon some of their defensive attitudes toward their roles.

André Bazin has summed up the situation admirably: "There are, occasionally, [vii–viii] good directors, like René Clement or Lattuada, who profess a precise aesthetic consciousness and accept a discussion on this level, but most of their colleagues react to aesthetic analysis with an attitude ranging from astonishment to irritation. Moreover, the astonishment is perfectly sincere and comprehensible. As for the irritation, this often springs from an instinctive resistance to the dismantling of a mechanism whose purpose is to create an illusion, and only mediocrities gain, in effect, from malfunctioning mechanisms. The director's irritation springs also from his resentment at being placed in a position that is foreign to him. Thus, I have seen a director as intelligent (and conscious) as Jean Grémillon play the village idiot and sabotage our discussion of Lumière d'été evidently because he did not agree with me. And how can I say he is wrong? Is not this impasse reminiscent of Paul Valéry leaving the lecture hall where Gustave Cohen has presented his famous commentary on Cimitière Marin with a word of ironic admiration for the professor's imagination? Must we conclude therefore that Paul Valéry is only an intuitive artist betrayed by a pedant's textual analysis and that Cimitière Marin is merely automatic writing?

"As a matter of fact," Bazin declares, "this apparent contradiction between the critic and the author should not trouble us. It is in the natural order of things, both subjectively and objectively. Subjectively, because artistic creation—even with the most intellectual temperaments—is essentially intuitive and practical:

it is a matter of effects to attain and materials to conquer. Objectively, because a work of art escapes its creator and bypasses his conscious intentions, in direct proportion to its quality. The foundation of this objectivity also resides in the psychology of the creation to the inappreciable extent to which the artist does not really create but sets himself to crystallize, to order the sociological forces and the technical conditions into which he is thrust. This is particularly true of the American cinema in which you often find quasi-anonymous successes whose merit reflects, not on the director, but on the production system. But an objective criticism, methodically ignoring "intentions," is as applicable to the most personal work imaginable, like a poem or a painting, for example.

"This does not mean that knowing authors (auteurs) personally, or what they say about themselves and their work, may not clarify the critic's conception, and this is proven by taped interviews we have published in Cahiers du Cinema through the Fifties. These confidences, on the contrary, are infinitely precious, but they are not on the same plane as the criticism I am discussing; or, if you will, they constitute a pre-critical, unrefined documentation, and the critic still retains the liberty of interpretation."

Bazin's actual acceptance of the director as author or "auteur" is typical of the French critical orientation toward the director as the sole creative artist of consequence in the cinema. Although the personal and poetic artistry of Ingmar Bergman and Federico Fellini in their films of the early Fifties [viii–ix] helped encourage a resurgence of serious interest in the cinema, it was not until the nouvelle vague emerged that the role of the director became fully romanticized for young people around the world. Bergman and Fellini were, after all, mature artists and remote figures to most of their admirers. Truffaut and Godard were young men in their twenties without practical experience. They were critics and enthusiasts, and they obviously loved movies with none of the dead chill of professionals. They also admired many of their predecessors, artists as disparate as Jean Renoir and Alfred Hitchcock. Above all, they had resurrected many directors from the limbo of low regard and had popularized the Politique des Auteurs, a mystique for reviewing directorial careers rather than individual films.   [ix]

1. What does Mr. Sarris mean by the distinction between cutting "in the mind" and cutting in the cutting room? Does this support his argument that montage has been overemphasized in the past?

2. Compare all of the essays in this section on the subject of montage. What seem to be the central issues?

3. How convincing is Mr. Sarris in his argument that "art" and "commercial" films are too stringently separated?

THE WRITER
AND THE FILM

Dudley Nichols

Ours is the age of the specialist. In older times, before the Machine, men did specialize of course in the various arts and crafts—but those arts and crafts were not themselves subdivided into specialized functions. The man who painted did the whole job himself: he was a painter. So with the silversmith and the shoemaker and the sculptor. But the Machine changed all that. The painter today has his materials prepared by other people, by specialized craftsmen or tradesmen, and only wields those materials in the final function of creating pictures. The etcher buys his copper plates already prepared and seldom pulls his own prints. The sculptor models in clay and leaves to others the pouring of the mold or the work of the pointing machine. The writer no longer turns out beautiful manuscripts that may be passed from hand to hand: he pounds out a script on the typing machine and passes it on to his publisher's printing factories. In science and art we have become specialized, narrowing our fields of study and work because those fields have grown too enormous for the single mind to embrace. We are all specialized, for better or worse, and it is only natural that the one new art form which the Machine has produced should be the most highly specialized of all. For the motion picture *is* an art form, whether it be so regarded or not.

By rights this new art form should be controlled by individuals who include all functions in themselves. They should be film-makers. But the functions are too diversified and complex to be handled by the creative energy of one indi-

---

DUDLEY NICHOLS was one of America's most important screenwriters. Most famous are his filmscripts for John Ford: *The Informer* (1935), *Stagecoach* (1939), *The Long Voyage Home* (1940).

From *Great Film Plays* by John Gassner. © 1959 by Crown Publishers, Inc. Used by permission.

71

vidual. So we break them down into separate crafts—writing, directing, photography, scenic designing, optical printing and camera effects, cutting and assembly of film, composing music, recording, mixing and re-recording, the making of *dissolves* and *fades* and other transitions—into an immense field of works which require the closest and most harmonious collaboration to produce excellent results.

This in effect is a detriment to film as an art form and an obstacle to the development of artists who wish to work in film. It is too much the modern factory system—each man working on a different machine and never in an integrated crea-tion. It tends to destroy that individuality of style which is the mark of any superior work of art. Individual feeling gets lost in the complicated process, and standardized products come off the assembly line. I make these remarks by way of preface to point out that there is only one way to overcome the impediments—and that is to learn the whole process, to be a master craftsman within the factory system; to be, in [ix–x] short, a film-maker first and a writer or director or whatever-you-will after-wards.

Of course, this poses a dilemma: one cannot under our present system make films without first learning to make films: and the only way to learn film-mak-ing is by making films. Hence by subterfuge of one sort or another one must enter the field as a specialized apprentice and try to learn all the other specialized func-tions, so that the individual may return to his specialty with the full equipment of an artist. A screenwriter should have knowledge of direction, of cutting, of all the separate functions, before his imagination and talent can be geared effectively and skillfully to his chosen line of work. Unfortunately we are none of us so competent as we might be, if for no other reason than that Hollywood is too bent on turning out films to take the time to train its artisans to the top of their bent. As a result, there is always room for the interested new worker. A writer can find a place, even without knowing much about film-making, and if he has a secret star he may glitter into sud-den prominence even without knowing the slightest thing about film-making.

Hollywood is used to taking works of fiction in other forms and translating them into film; and for this and other reasons the talented writer does not feel.en-couraged to write directly for the screen. This is to be regretted because the screen-play might easily become a fascinating new form of literature, provided the studio heads acquired sufficient taste to recognize and desire literary quality. Yet there have been, there are, and there will continue to be written, screenplays of quality and sincerity—if only because of the dogged efforts of writers and directors who set themselves high goals and persist frequently against their own material interests.

There is one other circumstance which makes it difficult for the screen-play to be enjoyed as a literary form in itself: It is not and never can be a finished product. It is a step, the first and most important step, in the process of making a film. One might also say that a play is not a finished product for the theatre; yet a play relies entirely on the word; idea, character, and actions are projected by means of the word; and a skillful playreader can enjoy wonderful performances within the theatre of his own imagination. The screenplay is far less a completed thing than the play, for the skilled screenwriter is thinking continuously in terms of film as well as the word. The filmwriter must be a film-maker at heart, and a film-maker thinks and lives and works in film. That is the goal, the end result—eight or ten thousand feet of negative patched together to reproduce, upon its unreeling, an illusion of a particular kind and quality. It is that illusion which the film-maker—and in this instance the filmwriter—is pursuing when he begins to gather together his first nebulous conception.

The truth is that a motion picture undergoes a series of creations. First it is a novel, a short story, or a conception in the mind of the screenwriter. That is the point of departure. Next the filmwriter takes the first plunge toward the finished negative by building the story in screenplay form. This rough draft, at least in the case of the present writer, will undergo two or three revisions, each nearer to the peculiar demands of cinema. With luck the director, who must have an equal sympathy for the drama to be unfolded, will be near at hand during the groundwork, contributing cinematic ideas here and there, many of which will not appear in the script but will be remembered or recorded in other notes to be used when the time comes.

Ordinarily, when all ideas of cinematic treatment have been unearthed and the final draft completed, the writer's work is ended and the creation of the projected film moves on into the hands of the director and other specialists; this is most unfortunate for the writer, for his education ceases in the middle of an uncompleted process. Let us, however, follow along with the writer who is able to follow the progress toward film. The second creation of the film is in its casting, which can help or hinder the designed illusion. The novelist is a fortunate artist who creates his characters out of the flesh and spirit of his own imagination; they need never be distorted [x–xi] by being embodied by living beings who necessarily have other traits and characteristics. But the playwright and the filmwriter must have real people to present their characters—and identity is not to be found. There have been ideal casts, but even the most perfect will alter indefinably the shape and mood and meaning of an imagined drama. Now each of the actors chosen must create his part of the film; and the sum of their parts create another phase of the film. Implicated in this is the personality of the director, who creates the film by combining (in his own style, which may not be the style of the writer) the contributions of the writer and actors.

It is at this point that a peculiar thing occurs, which must be understood to discriminate between the stage and screen. I have never seen this pointed out before, even by film-workers, and it needs to be set down: Stage and screen are entirely different media because the audience participates in quite opposite ways. The theatre —and I use the term to embrace both stage and screen—demands an audience. It is not complete without its audience and even derives much of its power from its audience. Every stage actor knows this and has experienced it. The audience identifies itself with the actor, its collective emotions rush out in sympathy or buffet against him with antipathy like an unseen electric discharge—which increases the actor's potential, so to speak, permitting him to give back his feelings with increased power, which again returns to him, like the oscillating discharge of an electric machine. It is these heightened moments that create unforgettable experiences in the theatre when the drama is great both in its literary power and in its acting. Here the relationship between the actor and the audience is direct and the intelligent actor can grow by what he experiences, just as the audience does.

Now, curiously, this phenomenon does not exist at all in the cinema; but it does exist at the stage of cinema-making we are discussing. On the stage of a film studio the actor still has an audience, though a small one: the half-hundred people who comprise "the crew"—grips, juicers, cameramen, script girl, and all the familiar others. But if he acts in such a style as to affect this audience solely he is lost, for his actual audience is miles away and they will see him only through the uncaring single eye of the camera that looks on like a tripod man from Mars. The significant thing is that at this point there is an invisible transition taking place that will break all the rules of the stage and impose new ones of the screen.

The actors are creating a film, not a stageplay, even though it appears they are making a stageplay. We are not cameras, we are living beings, and we cannot see things with the detachment of a lens. In the early days of sound-film I observed many failures because this was not understood. The action seemed good on the sound-stage, but it did not come off on the screen.

The reason is that the audience, the film-theatre audience, participates in an entirely different way with the projected images of a film. This is not so strange if we remember that a motion-picture film will give just as good a performance in an empty theatre as in a full one. It will not, of course, be so moving or so amusing to a single spectator as it will to that same spectator in a crowded theatre: Members of an audience need each other to build up laughter, sorrow, and joy. But the film is unaffected; it does not in itself participate as do the actors on a stage. It is a complete illusion, as in a dream, and the power of identification (which you must have in any form of theatre) must be between audience and the visually projected re-actor.

Unthinking people speak of the motion picture as the medium of "action"; the truth is that the stage is the medium of action while the screen is the medium of reaction. It is through identification with the person *acted upon* on the screen, and not with the person acting, that the film builds up its oscillating power with an audience. This is understood instinctively by the expert film-makers, but to my knowledge it has never been formulated. At any emotional crisis in a [xi–xii] film, when a character is saying something which profoundly affects another, it is to this second character that the camera instinctively roves, perhaps in close-up; and it is then that the hearts of the audience quiver and open in release, or rock with laughter or shrink with pain, leap to the screen and back again in swift-growing vibrations. The great actors of the stage are actors; of the screen, re-actors.

If anyone doubts this, let him study his own emotions when viewing a good film; an experienced film-maker can do this automatically at the first showing of a film, but very likely others will have to go a second time, or check it over in mental review. I once did this with some lay friends after a showing of Noel Coward's *In Which We Serve,* and it was illuminating to find out that they had been most deeply moved by reactions, almost never by actions: the figure of a woman when she gets news her husband has been lost at sea, the face of an officer when told his wife has died. (And how cunningly Noel Coward had that officer writing a letter to his wife when the radioman entered with the news; the reaction then was continued to the point where the officer goes on deck and drops the letter into the sea, a reaction extended into action, so to speak.) In the same film one of the most affecting scenes was the final one where the captain bids good-by to the remainder of his crew; and while this appears to be action, the camera shrewdly presented it as reaction: It is the faces of the men, as they file past, that we watch, reaction to the whole experience even in their laconic voices in the weary figure of the captain.

It is because the film can, at any moment of high emotional tension, pull an entire audience close to the faces of the actors, that reaction exerts more powerful effects on the screen than on the stage. Thus, in the final climax of *The Bridge on the River Kwai* (to name a more recent film), we see the anguished bewilderment of the Colonel, played by Alec Guinness, as he realizes what is actually occurring; and this reaction goads him to the final enigmatic action which blows up the bridge. The intention behind this final act remains ambiguous, but the dramatic moment is the Colonel's realization of his terrible dilemma, which realization we read in his face. On the stage, this mental process would have to be projected in speech. On the screen, where nothing is so eloquent as the silent image, any utterance would be fatal.

Despite the importance of reaction in cinema, the film is regarded as a medium of action, or at least of motion, and we fail to perceive that *it is the audience which is in motion*. In the stage-theatre (the so-called legitimate theatre), each member of the audience sits in a fixed chair and is free to observe this character or that, or the ensemble; he is free to make his own montage or accumulation of impressions; in short, he sees through his own untrammeled eyes. But in the film-theatre, though he sits in a seemingly fixed chair, he can see only *through the roving eye of the camera* and must continually shift his position and point of view at the command of the camera.

Paradoxically, it is not so much the actors on the screen who are in motion as the viewer, comfortably seated and quite unaware of riding this witch's broom, which darts him in at one instant to peer into an actor's face or at some person or object at which the actor looks, the next instant jerking him far back to look at the ensemble, or racing him along in airplane, train, or car to watch the actions and reactions of actors and share their emotions and excitement. The viewer of a film is no longer an autonomous individual as in the stage-theatre. He can see only what the film-maker commands. It is this absolute control over the audience which makes the cinema essentially different from the traditional theatre and its plays. It is also, triumphantly, the very source of the art of the film.

This is not to say that the two theatre forms, stage and screen, are opposed. Stagecraft has borrowed many things (the flashback, for instance) from cinema, just as filmcraft has borrowed from the stage. And long before film was dreamed of, the Elizabethan stage, by leaving location and background to the imagination and continually shifting scene, [xii–xiii] anticipated aspects of the technique of film. In any case, bearing these fundamental principles of film-writing and direction in mind, we initiate a film, working first with the pen and next with the camera.

This brings us to the next phase in the making of a film, or next "creation" if you prefer. I have said that a film ensues from a series of consecutive creations, which were enumerated from the first stage of concept to the point where the first recording on film is made. The director, the actors, the art director, the cameraman, the whole crew in fact, have followed after a fashion (but with many inevitable departures in which the writer, if he is fortunate, has collaborated) the final draft of the screenplay. Now you have perhaps a hundred thousand feet of film, the negative of which is safely tucked away in the laboratory while you have for your study a "work print." Now the film is in the cutting room, in a thousand strips or rolls, some strips perhaps only a few feet long, some four or five hundred. Every foot-and-a-half is a second of time in the projection room, and you do not want your finished film to be one second longer than is determined by dramatic necessity. Every good artist, every good workman, has a passion for economy; if you can do a thing in one stroke, don't use two; if a certain mood or atmosphere is essential to the illusion you are after and it requires a hundred strokes, use them. By elimination and rough assembly the cutter patches together a work print, say, fourteen thousand feet long: two or three miles of strips of film, assembled consecutively on seventeen or eighteen reels. That is the first creation of the cutter.

Now another job begins, one of the most delicate and sensitive jobs of all. Rough cutting was determined by the screen-writer, but this did not and could not include the interior cutting of the director and cameraman. Since terminology is not yet standardized in film-making, I designate the cutting of the director on the set the "montage," using a word which the Russians apply for all cutting or editing. It is determined by the style of the director, his feeling for photographed images, the way he rests the eye of the audience or gives it sudden pleasures, moving in at different angles on his scenes and characters. Had the writer attempted to anticipate the director and set down all this montage on paper, his script would have become a useless mess, for this interior cutting cannot be determined precisely (though many attempt to do so) before arriving on the set. The manner of shooting and handling the camera must be guided by spontaneous feeling and by discoveries made on the set. I for one have no patience with the growing method of having every camera shot sketched beforehand so that director, cameraman, and actors can work by rote. It destroys that spontaneity of feeling which is the essence of film art; though of course so many films are so unimportant that it does not matter how they are shot: they never were alive at any moment.

To continue following our film through to its finish, you now have a rough assembly which is far overlength, the cutting of which was largely determined by the script and direction. But this is only a provisional arrangement. Everything depends on the final cutting, elimination, and rearrangement. And the only compass to guide you in this final orchestration of images is your own feeling. The final test is to project the film on the screen and see how the arrangement you have made affects you. By this time you have grown weary of every foot of the film but you doggedly keep your feeling fresh as the only touchstone, until you have wearily said, "That's the best we can make of it." And I promise you disappointment in every film, for it is far removed from the perfection of imagination, as is everything that is realized.

Yet you have not finished with this scratched and tattered work print, which now looks as tired as yourself. There are two final stages, sound and music recording, and finally the re-recording of the whole thing. Sound is a magic element, and part of your design as a screenwriter or director has been the effect of sound. In the case of *This Land Is Mine*, which [xiii–xiv] was directed by a great film-maker, Jean Renoir, one of the focal points of the drama was a railroad yard, and as we could not shoot the action in an actual railroad yard we determined to create it largely by sound. We spent endless days gathering sound tracks and trying to orchestrate our sounds as carefully as if they were music. And finally came the scoring of the music itself, not a great deal of it but every bar important: choosing Mendelssohn here, Méhul there, original composition for the rest, and getting it re-recorded in a harmonious whole.

At last you have, say, nine or ten thousand feet of image film and a split second of sound film of the same length synchronized to the split second. Every frame of both films is numbered, corresponding with the thousands of feet of negative in the laboratory. You send your final work prints to the laboratory, the negative is cut, the sound track printed alongside—and you receive your first composite print. And, if the composite print checks, your work is finished and the negative is shipped, ready for countless prints to be made and released through the theatres of the world. This is what you set out to make—or rather help to make—when you began writing your rough draft of a screenplay. And this is what you had to keep in mind all the wearisome while.   [xiv]

1. Test Dudley Nichols' principle ("the screen is the medium of reaction") as he advises: in some movie you liked, were you more impressed by the actions or by the reactions of the characters?

2. What are the analogies between making a film and writing a paper?

ON CINEMA ACTING

V. I. Pudovkin

All that has been said hitherto of the paramount importance and necessity of the actor's striving for wholeness in his image in the theatre applies, of course, with equal force to the work of the film actor. It might, indeed, be said that realism, that is, by implication, the lifelike unity of the image, is a problem more pertinent and urgent to the film actor than even to the actor in the theatre. It is characteristic of the stage that effective performance is, as a matter of fact, possible upon it on a basis of exaggeration of theatrical convention, performance having an abstractly aesthetic character maximally removed from direct reflection of reality, but the cinema is characteristically the art that gives the *utmost possibility* of approach to realistic reproduction of reality.

I emphasise here as elsewhere the word "possibility." This is in order that the reader shall not think our analyses of possibilities, or our recommendations, the attempt to fix a static complex of methods as sole law of expression for cinema once and for all. Certainly the cinema too is capable of production in conventionalised style, style abstracted from direct representation of reality; certainly the cinema also is capable of generalisation, can develop [249–250] it to any degree, even to the limit of the supreme antithesis black and white. But none the less, the cinema is par excellence the art form capable of maximum capture of living reality in direct representation.

The question of the degree of generalisation to be employed in any given specific instance in an art form—this is always a question of the sense of proportion of the skillful creative artist, and the measure of its rightness is ultimately the reaction felt by the spectator when the work of art is complete: either acceptance by the ex-

V. I. PUDOVKIN, the great Russian silent film director, taught at the state cinema school in Moscow. His films include *Mother* (1925), *End of St. Petersburg* (1927), and *Storm Over Asia* (1928).

From *Film Technique and Film Acting*. Revised Memorial Edition, Second Impression. London, 1968. Pp. 249–258, 266–270. Reprinted by permission; © Vision Press Ltd.

perience of a real emotion—always the highest valuation for a work of art—or else cold negation.

But in discussing possibilities, I endeavour to determine the general tendency of development of the specific given art form, which, after all, the creative artist must take into account, however personal his own solution.

In the cinema, exactly as in the theatre, we immediately come right up against the problem posed by the discontinuity of the actor's work being in direct contradiction with his need for a continuous creative "living-into" and embodiment of the image played.

Owing to the special methods used in filming, which we shall discuss later, this contradiction becomes in practice even more acute than in the theatre. If we assemble some of the stories that stage actors have to tell about their experiences on occasional film work, we shall find a whole host of [250–251] denunciations, protests, even indignant swear words, all inspired by the notorious and fantastically exaggerated discontinuity of the film actor's job.

Actors maintain that either they have to portray the image they play in extremely abstract manner, limited as they are in study to a superficial reading of the scenario, or, alternatively, they deliver themselves bound into the hands of the director and his assistants, becoming will-less automata, executing in obedience to a series of shouts and orders a mechanical task the purport of which is incomprehensible to them. Actors further hold that they lose every possibility of feeling the unity of the image, every possibility of preserving during the process of shooting a sense of live continuous individuality, owing to the fact that they act the end of their rôle to-day, the beginning to-morrow, and the middle the day after. The various bits are tangled, they are terribly short; from time to time somebody photographs a glance that relates to something the actor will be doing a month hence when somebody else has photographed a hand movement that has to do with the glance. The image created by the actor is split into minutest particles, only later to be gathered together, and, *horribile dictu,* this gathering is effected not by him but by the director, who, in the majority of cases, does not allow the actor to come anywhere near to or observe the process or even have the remotest connection with it. Such, on general lines, is the protest of the stage actor who has done work for the cinema.   [251–252]

But is it really true that the cinema, owing to its technical peculiarities, so inflexibly dictates an inevitable elimination of all possibility of the actor concretely feeling the wholeness of his rôle? Is it really inevitably necessary to make the actor work in such conditions, which, as creative artist, he is unable to accept? Of course not. We must recognise that the system of work with the actor hitherto in vogue with the majority of considerable directors is not only not perfect, but plainly and simply wrong. And it is our task to discover lines along which, just as in theatre (and we have already seen that discontinuity exists also in stage acting, but to a lesser degree), the actor can be furnished with working conditions enabling him to effect the essential process of living-into his rôle.

Let us state here in set terms that, however the solution be found, it will not be by avoidance of splitting up the acting of the actor during the process of shooting itself; for from this we not only shall not escape, but, in fact, must not escape if we are properly to appreciate the essence of the path along which the cinema's main development lies. We must not avoid this splitting up, but simply seek and find corresponding technical methods to aid the actor in struggling against and overcoming it, thereby re-establishing for him the possibility of internally creating and preserving a feeling of the sum total of the separate fragments of acting as a single image, organically livened by himself. The theatre helps the actor by development and particularisation [252–253] of the method of rehearsal. We in the cinema must find means of following the same path.

First for a moment let us understand whence derives this distorted degree of splitting up we have just admitted as characteristic for cinema. The discovery and establishment of the need to split up the actor's acting into *editing pieces* derives immediately from the methods, technical in the narrowest sense, found appropriate by directors and from the making of films as such. From the earliest moment of appearance of the cinema, those who most profoundly and seriously adopted it, whether consciously or otherwise, as an art form capable of development on independent lines were directors, and accordingly it is natural that the most important works first achieved in cinema were attained under the aegis of marked directorial control.

The directors sought, and indeed found, in cinema specific potentialities enabling them, by its means and its means alone, to exert an impression on the spectators not only powerful, but in certain instances more powerful than that which could have been achieved in any other medium.

It is the directors who discovered those special forms of composition for the at first wholly visual, subsequently compound (partly sound) images of film termed *montage* or constructive editing. Rhythmic composition of pieces of celluloid introduced the element of rhythmic composition indispensable for impression in any art. In providing the indispensable [253–254] basis for making the cinema an art at all, it at the same time made it an especially notable one, for it enabled also a wealth of embrace of the actual world impossible to any other art save perhaps literature.

The perception and realisation of the camera-microphone combination as an observer ideally mobile in space and time not only gave straightway to the film an epic sweep, it not unnaturally tended to distract the director and scenarist associated with him from proper recollection of the importance of bearing constantly in mind that a living human individual is an individuality of at least a given profundity and complexity of its own. The possibility of swinging the focus of attention of the technical recording apparatus to a boundless number of different points of interest, their combination in the cutting process, the possibility of eliminating action from a film at given intervals, as though contracting or expanding time itself, all these possibilities led to results that placed the cinema pre-eminent among the arts in its capacity for breadth of comprehension of material of the real world. At the same time, however, the distracting process of exploring these possibilities led directors at a given stage in the development of film to a point at which they began to use the living man, the actor, merely as one component in the film, side by side with and equivalent to other components, material of equal and undifferentiated value, ready to take its turn and place and submit as inanimately to editorial [254–255] composition in the closing stages of the creative work on the film.

The actor became, so to say, shuffled, sorted out, used, in effect, like an aeroplane, a motor-car, or a tree. Directors, in searching for the right methods of constructing a performance cinematographically, missed realising that to get fullest value in a performance, cinematographic or otherwise, by a living being, that living person must not only not be eliminated in the process, must not only be preserved, but must be brought out; and if this bringing out be not realistic, that is, not unified and alive, in the end the man in the film will be a great deal more lifeless than the aeroplane and the motor-car (which, it must be confessed, is precisely what has happened in the work of some of our directors). With the actor used as a machine, in a mechanical way, became associated a whole flood of theoretical outpourings based on a mechanical extension of the editorial methods of alternation in length of pieces in cutting into a methodology for the actor's work on the floor. These technical outpourings could, in fact, only unfairly be dignified with the name of theory, inasmuch as they were only justifications of an empiria based on experiments concerned with something quite different, the main problems of editorial composition in film.

Their trend, however, was roughly as follows. On the screen we have long-shots and close-ups. Therefore the actor must exactly adapt his behaviour in front of the camera to the requirements of these [255–256] various camera-angles. On the screen there exists an undoubted interaction of effect between two adjacent pieces of film, an interaction which obtains though the content of the first piece be acting by an actor and that of the second any phenomenon the director or scenarist may require, taking place at any point of space whatever, however far removed from the actor in actual fact. Therefore the actor must be able to act his short piece without beginning or end and in absence of that which eventually will influence the content of his acting by interaction with it on the screen.

On the screen we can move the actor in the action with lightning speed from any one point in time or space to another, which we cannot do in the actual shooting on the floor. Therefore the actor must be able to act separate bits separated from one another by any time interval and trust their combination entirely and solely to the director, the only person guided by fore-perception of the film in its already completed state.

This is the way in which some have imagined the sum total of technical activity demanded of the actor. This mechanical understanding lacks all appreciation of the main fact, which is that the creative process of the actor is and must remain the fight for the feeling of the living substance of that image any component separate action in the make-up of which, however far removed from its fellow, will none the less be connected with it within the actor. And, further, that the technique of this [256–257] process can and must be no more and no less than the methods of this fight. No help has ever been afforded the actor in this direction, and consequently, truth to tell, the technique of acting in the cinema has remained at a low level.

I must emphasise yet again that, in speaking of the unity of the image and divining a technique to help the actor to achieve it, I in no way renounce or repudiate the indispensability of making separate, relatively short pieces in the process of shooting. There is a tendency afoot to help the actor by transforming his work to longer pieces and longer shots. This tendency is really nothing but a step along the line of least resistance, squeezing back into the cinema by contraband route the specialties and technique of the stage. This tendency is one that ignores, or deliberately turns its back upon, precisely those potentialities of the cinema that have set it in a place distinct and apart from the other arts, a place, as I have already said, earned directly by the multitude, and therefore shortness, of the pieces composing a film. This path is open to anyone. The film Groza[1] must, from this point of view, be considered as definitely reactionary. At the same time it undoubtedly has an important instructive lesson for us, as it is one of the first in our cinema that has given the actor a chance to feel himself a live human being in the process of his acting on the floor.

Of course, it is not this road leading to the mere [257–258] bounding of cinematograph performance by stage limits of time and space that is the right road for the cinema. We must give battle on that general front that includes the uttermost wealth of possibilities the cinema can give, and whereon, as is the natural course, we shall consequently encounter the maximum number of obstacles.   [258]

*   *   *

Imagine an actor delivering an emotional speech in a large auditorium. The listening crowd reacts to the words of the orator. It applauds, it interrupts with isolated calls and shouts. Suppose we desire [266–267] to portray the crowd not as a thousand-headed faceless mass, but as a many-imaged unity, if we appreciate the fact that a mass is comprehended in its real content and significance only when are perceptible its component individual groups, and within these their component individuals. Then we shall be obliged to transfer the position of the camera rapidly from place to place, we shall be obliged, in the course of the oration, to change alternately from long shot embracing both orator and audience to separate closer shots, penetrating into the thick of the mass, and glimpsing a group or single listener reacting by shout or gesture. We shall inevitably have to split up the one speech of the orator into separate pieces, in order that they may be welded in the process of editing into a whole with the separate pieces of members of the audience reacting, and thereby derive unity from the multiplicity of many-imaged details.

It might be argued that, for the purpose of an editing construction of this type, it is unnecessary to break the whole speech of the orator into separate pieces in the shooting. It might suffice to shoot the speech as a whole and subsequently to chop it on the cutting bench into the necessary separate pieces interleaved with the given auditor pieces. But film directors who strive to exploit the cinema's possibilities to the full cannot follow this course. They use not only words out of the orator's speech. Realise what tremendous importance in the construction of the whole image of man in action have [267–268] his gestures and his pantomime connected with his utterances. This pantomime, at times of the most fine and complex order, plays a part no less important than the intonation of the voice.

Now, the culmination of the impression effected by an uttered word or sentence depends upon a movement of the hand; again, the closing of the eyes

[1] The Tempest, directed by Petrov, from the play by Ostrovsky.–Tr.

may add an unexpected touch of pathos to another word or phrase. Only the cinema, by virtue of the mobility of the camera, can so direct the excited attention of the audience that, at any given moment of his acting, the actor can, as it were, turn to the audience his most poignant, most expressive, side.

And it is this method of shoving the play of the actor right up under the nose of the audience that inevitably necessitates the splitting of the single process of the speech into separate pieces in the actual shooting.

At one moment we see the face of the orator with eyes tight shut. At another his whole body straining with arms held high. For an instant we catch his glance directed straight at us. A nervous movement of his hand behind his back may also serve as a definite and colourful characterisation of some moment.

Such material can only be obtained by shooting bits of the speech separately, with change of position of camera and microphone. Simultaneous shooting by several cameras at once, placed at separate points, will not give us an unhamperedly sharp and vivid editing treatment on the screen, [268–269] because a camera placed for a close-up would be bound to get in the way of a camera taking a long-shot at the same time. Separate, interrupted shooting is indispensable.

The question must be formulated simply in this way: should the immensely rich possibilities afforded by the cinema for the purpose of deepening the play of the actor be sacrificed to the natural desire of the actor to dwell in his acting image as wholly and uninterruptedly as possible, or should one search for means of helping him that none the less permit these possibilities to be maintained and exploited to maximum advantage?

The difficulty of solving this problem is, basically, the long and the short of the difficulty confronting the cinema actor, and the methods and ways of solving it are, in sum, the conditioning methods of his technique.

We have already seen that this difficulty exists also in the theatre. The break between two stage entrances of an actor does not differ materially from the break between two shots in the cinema.

The whole content of a stage play could, after all, take the form of a single continuous speech that one actor-speaker could utter without leaving the boards. In general, however, the theatre variegates its content, introducing action shared in by numerous dramatic personae, and portraying directly numerous deeds and events, not merely reporting them in speech. It splits the course of the play into acts, thereby eliminating chunks of time.   [269–270]

The actor could, really, remain on the stage throughout the duration of a whole act without for a second being switched from the action, but the theatre as a rule insists on taking him off into the wings, because realistic enlargement of the action demands the introduction of new characters, and these new characters must not only push various old ones temporarily into the background, but even from time to time squeeze them from the orbit of the audience's attention altogether. Whereupon the first actor must stand in the wings waiting for the moment when the development of the play's action will once more drag him front stage.

I repeat that this "split-life," this discontinuous animation, of the stage actor, does not differ organically from the "separate-shot-acting" of the film actor in the course of the shooting of a film.

The contradiction between the personality of the actor and his striving in the process of his acting to become a linked part of the whole circumstances environing the wide sweep of development of a realistic film, this contradiction, I repeat, exists not only in theatre and in cinema, but is analogous to the contradiction in creation general to all arts.

And, we must affirm once more, the solution of this contradiction will be achieved not by its elimination, but by proper understanding of the significance of the methods of acting technique, and consequently of the means legitimate to employ.   [270]

1. In attempting to minimize the difficulty of screen acting, Pudovkin uses an analogy to stage technique. Is the analogy convincing?

2. Does Pudovkin offer a reasonable solution to the problems of film acting?

3. Compare this discussion of film acting with Panofsky's brief remarks on the subject. Does Panofsky offer any solution to the problem?

HANDLING
THE CAMERA

Basil Wright

The cinema camera is a precision instrument, beautifully made. Its metal parts are intricately interrelated with perfect accuracy. They move unerringly at a speed which defeats the eye. Batteries of lenses, filters and other gadgets gleam with promises of new movements, new tricks, new means of expression. It is an object to be polished and cleaned continuously, to be transported with the care lavished on a new-born baby, to be guarded jealously against the hands of the incompetent and the careless, the destroyers of delicate machines. It is easy indeed to become so interested in camera-work that bad films are the result.

These notes are not written as a guide to the budding photographer. If they were, a cameraman would have been asked to write them. They are simply a brief attempt to consider some of the possibilities of the camera as a creative instrument in the making of films. In so short a space it will be necessary to omit much and to take much for granted.

In its early days the cinema was sufficiently miraculous in its presentation of photographed motion for the camera to be no more than a passive if vitally important agent. It never moved. It remained a good distance away from the scene. The technique of the stage, of the fixed view-point [37–38] of the spectator, was sufficient. The camera meekly recorded the self-sufficient actions before it.

One man freed it from this role. D. W. Griffith gave it creative power. He introduced the close-up. He introduced the trucking shot (used with vast effect in the ride of the Ku-Klux-Klan in *The Birth of a Nation*), and the panorama (again in

BASIL WRIGHT, the British director of documentary films, was an associate of John Grierson.

From *Footnotes to the Film,* edited by Charles Davy. London, 1937. Reprinted by permission of Peter Davies Ltd.

The Birth of a Nation, as when the camera moved inexorably from the group of weeping women to the battlefield in the plain below).

From Griffith's early films dates the use of the camera in its own right, as something which—equally with actors and cutters—can add a constructive element to the presentation of an idea in terms of film.

In Germany, during the lean times of the post-War inflation period, the limitations of apparatus and finance brought in a further advance, the use of so-called "camera-angles." A little later, the Russians, under very much the same influences, developed the same ideas, but added to their usefulness by a revolutionary technique of cutting.

Since then, apart from a temporary set-back when sound came in and glued the camera to the floor for a year, there have been no further great changes in the general technique of the camera. The handling of the camera, however—that is, the use of the technique referred to above—has in different hands become more and more interesting.

Let us first review what the camera can do; what are its possibilities, and what its limitations.

First and foremost we must remember that the camera does not see things in the same way as the [38–39] human eye. The brain behind your eye selects the points of emphasis in the scene before you. You can look at a crowd and see nothing but one umbrella, or you can look at an empty field and see millions of separate blades of grass. Or vice versa. Not so the camera. The lens soullessly records on a sensitised piece of celluloid simply the amount of light of differing values that passes through it. No amount of thinking on the part of the cameraman will achieve any other emphasis. Out of a wide landscape it will not pick out that certain tree. You, as a person, have got to interfere, to place the camera in such a way that the picture it records will somehow give the emphasis you require. Which is simply another way of stating the old adage that all arts exist by exploiting their own limitations.

The camera's main limitation is light. Light is also the camera's *raison d'être*—the core of its existence. All shots are merely the effect of light rays, and under the artificially conditioned circumstances of the film studio the term "camera-man" is probably less correct than the term "lighting expert." Be that as it may, the fundamental issue is that every shot in a film is the result of a period of organised threats, blandishments, and cajolery of light.

The realism of movie photography is in fact achieved by a constant interference with natural forces. A brief glance at the technique of the camera will reveal this—as well as getting this short essay another step towards its doubtful goal.

The average cameraman, then, has the following gadgets at his creative disposal.   [39–40]

He has interchangeable lenses of varying focal lengths. This means—to avoid technicalities—that without moving the camera itself he can take a number of different photographs of any object, ranging from the long-shot to the ultra close-up. For example, he sets up his camera opposite a church. With a one-inch lens he photographs the entire church and part of the surrounding landscape. With a two-inch lens he takes in the church only; with a four-inch lens he reveals only half of the church. With a six-inch lens he gives a close-up of part of the tower—and so on right down to the forty-inch lens which reveals no more than a notice pinned on the church door.

Now, as he could get exactly the same series of shots with, say, a solitary two-inch lens, by moving the camera itself nearer and nearer to the church, the battery of lenses might seem to be merely an encouragement to laziness, did we not remember that in many cases the camera cannot be placed near a given object (e.g., a ferocious wild elephant or a face at a window on the twelfth story).

But that by no means exhausts the value of a series of lenses. From the creative point of view, they can actually produce very important and varying effects. These are all distortions, in the sense that they endow the scene with spatial relationships different from those presented to the human eye.

The aspect given by the two-inch lens corresponds most nearly to the focussed area of the human eyesight.

Camera lenses of less than two-inch focal lenses distort scenes by exaggerating distances. A one-inch [40–41] lens can make a box-room look like a ballroom. It can also make a man's fist plunged at the audience look in such exaggerated perspective that it seems as big as his whole body. In fact, it extends space and enlarges distances.

Similarly, space can be reduced and concertina-ed by using lenses of more than two-inch focal lengths. In these, the longer the focal length, the closer together are brought the foreground and background of the picture, so that, in extreme cases, you can see people going through all the actions of running, but yet apparently—like the famous scene in "Through the Looking Glass"—staying in the same place. Scenes like this are frequently to be noted in news-reel shots of cricket matches.

Further interference with nature is possible by placing things to interfere with light before it reaches the lens—things such as coloured glass filters to accentuate or eliminate certain colour values; gauzes to soften the outlines of a scene; even smears of vaseline to distort the outlines. Also "masks," cut to give the effects of keyholes, binoculars, hearts, or what you will.

The normal cine-camera runs at a speed of twenty-four pictures a second. Film is invariably projected at this speed in the cinema. The cameraman can therefore get special effects by taking fewer or more pictures per second (the speed of projection remaining constant at twenty-four pictures a second). On the minus side he can even go so far as to take only one picture an hour or even a week. It is in this way that the plant-growths in *Secrets of Nature* films are [41–42] recorded. On the plus side, he can at present go as far as some 3,000 pictures a second, which will give you a slow-motion film of a bullet leaving a gun.

Between these two extremes are a great variety of possible effects. They are usually directed either to melodramatic, comic or scientific ends. The Hollywood motor-car chases, with their carefully calculated hairbreadth escapes, are a typical example of speeded-up motion, but on occasions these tricks of speed have been used in a more interesting manner. In *Zéro de Conduite,* for instance, Vigo shot a procession of boys during a dormitory riot entirely in slow motion. In *The General Line* Eisenstein used speeded-up office activities to indicate the urgency of the Five Year Plan.

Pudovkin has enumerated various plans for varying camera speed within a given sequence to increase the visual emphasis. He suggested, for example, that in filming a man wielding a scythe, the use of slow motion on some of the actions—such as the swathe of grass falling when the scythe has cut through, and the back stroke of the scythe itself—would produce a cinematic interpretation of the movements most closely akin to the emotions of a sympathetic spectator witnessing the actions in real life.

The cameraman can also make pictures fade-in and fade-out by the simple process of progressively diminishing or increasing the amount of light reaching the film. He can make "dissolves"—the gradual mingling of one picture into another—which are, to put it simply, the "fade-in" of one shot superimposed [42–43] on the "fade-out" of the previous shot. Superimpositions can be used in their own right to present the spectator with a double image. These are easily accomplished by winding back the exposed film and shooting a further image on the scene already imprinted on it.

It may be noted here that there is an increasing tendency to transfer these tricks to the optical sections of the processing laboratories—but as they are originally very much of the camera, they are mentioned here.

There are many other special effects still to be catalogued. Multiple-prism lenses can cover the screen with a mass of exact duplicate images of the object photographed. They are beloved of Busby Berkeley.

By means of various forms of back-projection, scenes played in the comparative peace of the studio can be combined with a background of Africa's wildest jungle, a raging Pacific, or the swiftly passing landscape seen from train or plane.

We can conclude by listing the use of cartoon, animated diagrams, and various colour systems, and so pass to yet another set of possibilities.

The camera must stand on a solid base, as the slightest rocking or vibration will be transferred, enormously intensified by enlargement, to the screen. So we must consider the tripod as a vital part of the camera. The top, or head, of the tripod, is usually made to move on a ball-bearing or gyroscopic principle which gives it a horizontal swing (or "pan") of 360 degrees and a vertical tilt (up and down) of [43–44] about 90 degrees. A single bar projecting from the tripod head operates both these movements, which can therefore take place simultaneously, and enable the cameraman to follow accurately such things as the erratic and unpredictable flight of a bird.

But the tripod can also be put on wheels, and travel forwards, backwards or sideways. Or the camera may be on a crane even more free in its movements. And while the truck or the crane is whisking the camera through space, it may also be performing the pans or tilts as explained in the previous paragraph.

Such are the powers at the disposal of a cameraman. With a little imagination you can visualise him as a small but omnipotent figure, standing beside the apparatus as a thousand-ton crane swings it up and forward through a vast hall lit by an incalculable amperage, while the camera itself in its dizzy flight is moved at his will horizontally and vertically on its own axis, shooting now in slow motion, and now with telescopic vision finally denying the genuineness of anything on earth.

Whereas, in point of fact the good cameraman is as sparing as possible in the use of elaborate stunts. After all, the technique of the camera has been evolved by the demands of men making films for their own specific purpose. The apparatus should be subservient to the idea.

There was an early talkie in which the obsession with camera tricks was so great that the hero could not speak to the heroine without the camera leaving his face, and, following as it were his winged words right round their luxurious apartment, finally coming [44–45] to rest on the heroine in time for her to reply. This was excessively tedious. Also, note you, it was shot by one of the best cameramen living.

This brings us to the vital point of the whole affair—the relationship of the camera to the other factors of equal or greater importance which go to make up the finished film.

If we are not careful, this will lead to an enormous disquisition on direction. The relation between cameraman and director therefore must be here considered in its narrowest sense, to avoid such an unwieldy digression. The essential point is that the camera is an instrument of expression and is there to do the director's will. The cameraman is, therefore, as it were, the Genie of the Lamp (and the Slave of the Director). His expert technical knowledge should be such that he can carry out the director's demands economically and expeditiously. This, however, is not necessarily to deny creative ability or creative personality to the cameraman. By his very knowledge of camera-work he may be able to carry into practice the vague desires of the director. "For God's sake make this wrinkled harridan look more like Manon," screams the director. With lenses, soft lighting, clever angles and what not, the cameraman achieves the miracle.

Any one who remembers the camera-work of, say, *Zoo in Budapest,* will realise this point (speaking generally, of course, and not about the heroine).

But camera-work is not all, and most people prefer bad camera-work plus good direction to good camera-work plus bad direction. It is interesting to note [45–46] that most cameramen famous for their artistic ability tend in the end to become directors themselves. And, in the solitary case of Robert Flaherty, you find a great director who has made of himself a great cameraman.

The ultimate need, in any case, is for a close sympathy to exist between director and cameraman. This teamwork aspect crops up again and again in all branches of cinema, and nowhere is it more vividly seen than in such partnerships as that of Eisenstein and Tissé, or Lang and Wagner. This give-and-take collaboration, in which the director, of course, always has the last word, is the ideal but all too rare state. The next best thing is for the cameraman to be supremely gifted as to technique, but without much artistic conscience of his own. In this case, the director evolves all the effects himself and is limited only by the competence of the cameraman or the physical possibilities at the disposal of a modern camera. In any case, a director seldom takes No for an answer.

Everything the director does is seen by his ultimate audience through the eye of the camera. He can operate only on what the lens sees. He must think of every scene, every action, in terms of the lens, in terms of what the camera can do. That is why so many directors can be seen with their eyes glued to the view-finder during a rehearsal—to make sure. In the same way, the impetus for camera movements or tricks of various sorts comes from the director via the shooting script.

This is no place to discourse on scenario and script [46–47] work, but it should be remembered that camera-movements are nearly always to be found indi-cated in the script. Sometimes, indeed, the result of the demands made by the script is the signing-up of a specialist in some particular field of camera-work.

Then, of course, there is the Art Director. His work means a lot to the cam-eraman, for on him rests the ultimate responsibility of lighting the completed set. It is absolutely essential for the designs to allow of the set being amply lit from above, for top-lighting supplies from three-quarters to two-thirds of the general illumination of a set. There must also be opportunities for side and front lighting. All this fre-quently makes it desirable for the set to be sectional, so that certain parts of it can be removed for special shots to allow the cameraman to re-arrange his lighting. It is, for instance, particularly important for the cameraman to keep *continuity of lighting* while shooting different shots on the same set. If the lighting effect is not the same in the close-up as it is in the long shot the cutting department will find itself in a jam and will rightly blame the cameraman. The studio electricians are, or should be, intimately acquainted with each cameraman's idiosyncrasies. The chief electrician frequently carries out the general illumination of a set before the cameraman arrives. This should not cause a dust-up. The relation between camera department and light-ing department must be as intimate and cordial as possible.

It is also necessary to remember that, in the studio at any rate, most shoot-ing is synchronous. The cameraman is therefore somewhat dependent on the [47–48] work of the Sound Department, which is in itself a branch of camera-work de-voted to the photography of sound waves. The Sound men demand as much freedom in the placing of their microphone as does the Picture man in the placing of his camera. And during the shooting, both Picture and Sound cameras are operated by a master switch. Here again the situation demands the maximum of co-operation and amiability.

These facts may indicate that the cameraman is not an Almighty God, but merely a member of a semi-democratic Olympus, presided over by a directorial Jupiter of uncertain temper. And behind it all moves the bony and relentless hand of Finance Omnipotent.

So much for technique and organisation. Next comes a more nebulous but also more interesting consideration—the artistic approach of the cameraman. The reference here is not a highbrow one, but an attempt to analyse the more per-sonal approach to the taking of any shot, in fact an analysis of camera-sense, or "a feeling for the subject."

This is more difficult, and is bound to some extent to be coloured by the personal feelings of the writer. It is, on the other hand, the most vital consideration in regard to the camera. It will be necessary in this case to consider the camera *per se*, and to forget about directorial control or the requirements of a script. The question is simply this: How does one approach the taking of a movie shot?

The number of positions from which a camera may take a shot of any given subject has to be regarded as unlimited. All points of the compass are available.

[*48–49*] Any degree of distance is possible. The camera may be poised in the heaven above or the pit below. From this illimitable field the most telling position (or positions) must be chosen. We are considering, in fact, the angle from which the object is to be photographed.

The first instinct, and the most natural, is to place the camera in the same position as the eyes of a spectator standing facing the object, at a distance which allows the object to be seen in its entirety. This could be regarded as the norm from which all variations proceed.

The first variation arises probably from the instinct to exploit the camera's genius for giving detail or intimacy. In other words, to approach more nearly to the object, either by moving in the camera itself or by using a longer focus lens from the same camera position. These alternatives—as has already been indicated—are not merely a matter of convenience, but also of the instinct of the cameraman. One man may prefer to use a lens of wide angle, with the camera near the object, in order either to emphasise the action by exaggerating the spatial relationships, or to retain a depth of focus as between the object and its background. Another— Flaherty is an example—may wish to achieve a greater spontaneity by taking a close-up of a person without the embarrassing presence of a camera right on top of him. For him, the telephoto-lens is the answer. Personal experience shows that there is seldom any hesitancy on the cameraman's part in making such a choice. His own instinct arrives at a foregone conclusion without his indulging in mental arguments of any kind.   [*49–50*]

He could also get another effect by "trucking" the camera in on its trolly so that the spectator witnessed every change of distance, from long shot to close-up. This he would probably do only if he wished to put heavy emphasis on the object to be seen in the final close-up position. Otherwise he would merely be using the apparatus for its own sake, with dreariness and waste of footage as an inevitable result.

The next step involves a change of angle as opposed to a mere change of distance. That is, the camera may be lower or higher than the norm we have already suggested. It may be put low down and tilted upwards, either for practical reasons (it may be the only way to show the size and extent of a tall building), or because the unusual view-point gives a special emphasis; for instance, a policeman shot from a low angle may look more impressive, more important, more monumental —especially if in addition to the camera position, the effect is increased by the use of a wide-angle lens.

It is pointless to elaborate too much on the actual possibilities of camera angles. The mere multiplication of examples is of no value. What is fundamentally important is to realise that where the camera is put must depend, not on an attempt to make the shot "striking" or "interesting" at all costs, but on the urgency of expression affecting the man behind the camera. By taking a movie shot the cameraman is not merely trying to reproduce something; he is trying also to comment on it, or to relate it to a specific idea, of which one shot may merely be an [*50–51*] item. But in cinema many items build up the coherent statement. If you like you can regard the standard long-shot of an object as the noun. Pans, changes of angle and distance, trick shots or what you will, these are the verbs, adjectives, adverbs, prepositions and so on which when put altogether make up a coherent sentence. In cinema, a flowery style is not an advantage. The more succinct the statement, the better. Two good shots, carefully chosen as regards distance and angle, are better than twenty taken either carelessly or with an eye only to the unusual.

In point of fact, if you ask any competent cameraman to take three shots of any occurrence, he will not go into any special huddle with himself. Experience has taught him the sort of position which will give him the best effects, and he will know within a foot or so the three most likely angles for his purpose. The *exact* angles are a matter for more care, and you may find him trying out various lenses and so on before he finally shoots.

There are certain fundamental points which still remain to be considered. They may be roughly grouped under one word—Composition.

It is vital to remember that the composition of a picture on the movie screen contains one element entirely denied to the art, say, of painting. Screen composition is fluid; it is perpetually in motion.

Now it is obviously the aim of any cameraman to achieve with each shot a balanced and good-looking composition (at the least). But if he tries to base his shooting entirely on the great painters, or for that [51–52] matter on the great still photographers, he will probably fail.

The movements of any persons or objects within the frame of the cinema screen are the prime factor of the composition. One may go further, and point out that even motionless objects may have a movement imparted to them by the panning, tilting or trucking of the camera. In other words, a movie shot of a group of statuary or a landscape may produce an aesthetic effect quite other than that possible in any other medium, arising simply from the carefully calculated movement of the camera itself.

Like most painters, good moviemen try for a composition which will get away as far as possible from the two-dimensional limitations of the screen. But they are not limited entirely to attempts to produce perspective by relationship of mass to mass within their composition.[1] They can also achieve it by the relationship of movement to movement, or of movement to mass, or both. That this is not mere theory can be easily proved by going to any cinema and analysing the effects by which good or bad composition is achieved, shot by shot, in the film which happens to be running. Various points will at once emerge. For instance, it will be seen that movements *to and from* the camera are more emphatic, and give a greater perspective, than movements *sideways or across* the camera. Or again, the use of some solid mass in the foreground of the picture will give point and emphasis to what otherwise would have been a [52–53] very uninteresting pictorial presentation. (The *reductio ad absurdum* of this last is to be found in certain cameramen on "interest" films, who used to carry a small branch of a tree around with them in order to get an artistic effect by placing it in the foreground as a frame or halo to any uninteresting village or church tower they had to shoot.)

These principles of composition are the subconscious stand-by of the cameraman, and they produce those idiosyncrasies which enable us to distinguish at a

[1] As yet, however, they lack one advantage which the painter exploits—controlled colour relationships.

glance between a shot by Flaherty and a shot by James Wong Howe. They are truly the fundamentals of the cameraman's art, and it is his sensibilities in this regard which make him either more or less of a genius in the manipulation of the apparatus at his disposal.

To these principles he subordinates his command over light—lenses, filters, fades, dissolves; his command over speed—fast motion or slow motion; his command over movement—pans, tilts, truck-shots, crane shots; in a word, his ability to use the intricate, difficult, but entirely fascinating reproductive mechanism which makes possible the art of cinema.   [53]

1. Compare this essay with the articles by Irving Pichel and George Bluestone. Are there any significant differences among their approaches to the fundamentals of film art?

2. Mr. Wright does not amplify one of the most important statements in his essay: "most people prefer bad camera-work plus good direction to good camera-work plus bad direction." What do you think accounts for this preference?

EDITING

George Bluestone

. . . "The first thing to be observed about the technique of editing," Lindgren observes, "is that it affords the film-maker a new field for his powers of selection." Since the complete action of any given scene is made up of a large number of moving components, the director must constantly choose which detail he will emphasize at a given moment. Selection, however, can go much farther than this. Through editing, the film-maker can eliminate meaningless intervals, concentrate on significant details, ordering his design in consonance with the central line of his narrative.

For example, Pudovkin poses the problem of presenting a man falling from a window five stories high. The director, in this case, would take one shot of a man falling from a window in such a way that the net (into which he safely falls) is not visible on the screen; then a shot of the same man falling from a slight height to the ground. Joined together, the shots would give the desired impression of continuous fall. It is precisely this technique that Griffith used in the Babylonian episode of *Intolerance,* which Pudovkin had seen and admired. The camera, it should be noted, has not followed nature. Instead, the director has selected two points in the process, leaving the intervening passage to be filled in by the mind of the spectator. This extraordinary power of suggestion is indeed unique in the dramatic arts. "It is not correct," Pudovkin warns us, "to call such a process a trick; it is a method of filmic representation exactly corresponding to the elimination of five years that divides a first from a second act upon the stage." The method corresponds roughly

GEORGE BLUESTONE, of the University of Washington, has published criticism and fiction in several magazines, as well as the book, *Novels into Film,* from which this excerpt is taken.

From *Novels into Film.* Baltimore, Johns Hopkins, 1957. Reprinted by University of California Press, 1961. Pp. 24–30. Used by permission of Johns Hopkins Press.

to the temporal gap between one [24–25] panel and another in Renaissance frescoes depicting the lives of saints, except that in the film the action seems continuous.

In cinematic terms, then, the method of connecting the film strips becomes the basic formative function. For the two strips, joined together, become a *tertium quid,* a third thing which neither of the strips has been independently. This is the essence of that much abused concept of Eisenstein's which we have come to know as montage.

Given the transition, the relationship between shots as the center of the creative process, a high degree of discipline must be exercised in the editing. Long shots must dovetail with close shots. There must be a logical connection between the shots, a kind of visual momentum, or transference. We see a man about to cross a street. In a close-up, we see his face twist in horror. We cut immediately to a scene in front of him. A car is bearing down on a small child. We accept the instantaneous shift because, interested as we are in the cause of the horror, we are propelled visually to the next significant detail. Different points of view must thus be carefully blended to suggest a continuous action.

Building his design out of individual strips, always thinking plastically, the film-maker may use almost endless spatial combinations. He may, for example, use contrast ironically. When Alec Guinness, in *The Promoter,* achieves a social triumph by dancing with the Countess of Chell, the film cuts to a shot of greasy sausage frying in a skillet. It is the next day and the "card's" mother is preparing his meal in their dingy kitchen. Or the director may use what the Feldman brothers call parallel editing.[1] A wife, to make her husband jealous, is seen flirting with a willing lover. We cut to an office where the husband is seen making advances to his secretary. The director may use symbolism. In *Strike,* the shooting down of workers is punctuated by shots of the slaughter of a steer in a stockyard. In *The Blue Angel,* birds are used with consummate artistry as a kind of leitmotif. In the opening scene, Professor Unrat coos at a caged canary. Later, having devoted himself to Lola, a music-hall singer, he watches pigeons flying up against a clock whose bronze figures ominously mark the passage [25–26] of time. And at the height of his degradation, the Professor crows like a cock. The possibility for plastic comments like these, as distinct from verbal renditions of the same effects, is unprecedented in the arts.

A new kind of relationship between animate and inanimate objects springs up, a relationship which becomes the key to plastic thinking. Pudovkin points out quite cogently that relationships between human beings are, for the most part, illumined by conversation, by words. No one carries on conversation with objects, and that is why an actor's relationship to objects is of special interest to the film technician.

Within the composition of the frame, the juxtaposition of man and object becomes crucial. "The performance of an actor linked with an object and built upon it will always be one of the most powerful methods of filmic construction."[2] We

---

[1] Joseph and Harry Feldman, *Dynamics of the Film* (New York, 1952), p. 86.

[2] Pudovkin, p. 115. A telling account of a familiar phenomenon appears in [Vachel] Lindsay, [*The Art of the Moving Picture,* New York, 1915] p. 15: " . . . There came to our town not long ago a film of a fight between Federals and Confederates, with the loss of many lives, all for the recapture of a steam-engine that took on more personality in the end than private or general on either side, alive or dead."

have only to think of Chaplin to see the principle in operation. The dancing rolls in *The Gold Rush,* the supple cane, the globe dance in *The Great Dictator,* the feeding machine in *Modern Times,* the flowers and drinks in *Monsieur Verdoux,* the flea skit in *Limelight*—these are only isolated examples of Chaplin's endless facility for inventing new relationships with objects. He leans on a doorman as on a lamppost, and the animate becomes inanimate. The spring of the watch in *The Pawnshop* comes alive, and the inanimate becomes animate. The confusion dynamizes the relationship, and the distinction between man and object is obliterated. Man and object become interchangeable, and the inanimate joins the animate as an actor. Certainly this accounts for a good part of Chaplin's filmic genius.

Not only has the film discovered new ways to render meanings by finding relationships between animate and inanimate objects, but the human physiognomy itself has been rediscovered. So pervasive has been the power of the close-up to convey emotion that in *"Der Sichtbare Mensch"* Béla Balázs places the film on [26–27] a par with the invention of the printing press. The method of conveying meaning by facial expression, a method which according to Balázs fell into desuetude with the advent of printing, has been revived by the "microphysiognomy" of the screen image. The face becomes another kind of object in space, a terrain on which may be enacted dramas broad as battles, and sometimes more intense. Physiognomy preëmpts the domain of nonverbal experience: "The gestures of visual man are not intended to convey concepts which can be expressed in words, but such inner experiences, such nonrational emotions which would still remain unexpressed when everything that can be told has been told."[3]

Just as words are not merely images expressing our thoughts and feelings, but in many cases their *a priori* limiting forms, the subtleties of the mobile face not only render hitherto unrecorded experiences but also create the conditions for new experiences to come into being. If, then, "the film increases the possibilities for expression, it will also widen the spirit it can express." If Balázs goes too far in calling for an "encyclopedia of comparative gesturology," he at least draws attention to the unprecedented possibilities of the human face. These possibilities have given rise to a wholly different kind of acting. The microdrama of the human countenance permits the reading of the greatest conflicts in the merest flicker of an eye. Understatement becomes the key to film characterization. The subtleties of Mme. Falconetti's face in Dreyer's *The Passion of Joan of Arc,* or of Giulietta Massina's in Fellini's *La Strada* would have been incomprehensible to anyone in the dramatic arts before 1900.

In a real sense, then, Pudovkin is right when he says, "In the discovered, deeply imbedded detail there lies an element of perception, the creative element that gives the event shown its final worth." By selecting and combining, by comparing and contrasting, by linking disparate spatial entities, photographed images of "the deeply imbedded detail" allow the film-maker, through editing, to achieve a uniquely cinematic equivalent of the literary trope.   [27–28]

---

[3] Béla Balázs, *Theory of the Film,* trans. Edith Bone (New York, 1953), p. 40.

SOUND IN EDITING

If the emphasis so far has been on spatial movement, I do not mean to overlook the function of sound in editing. I mean only to emphasize that sound is subsidiary to the moving image, that dialogue, music, aural effects take their place as separate lines in the ensemble which editing creates. Just as the first narrative films erred by imitating the fixed frame of the stage, the first sound films erred by imitating theatrical dialogue. Sound films, like the early silents, aroused curiosity as a toy and, in the process, were almost talked to death. Intelligent critics were quick to attack this fault, and some even argued against the sound track itself. An art, they said, thrives on the limitations of its materials and every gain in realism (like painting plaster of Paris figures in lifelike colors) must be accompanied by an aesthetic loss. But the aesthetic loss was temporary and the film learned the proper use of its new dimension. "One can imagine," writes Panofsky, "that, when the cave-men of Altamira began to paint their buffaloes in natural colors instead of merely incising the contours, the more conservative cave-men foretold the end of palaeolithic art. But palaeolithic art went on, and so will the movies."

A case in point is René Clair's initial resistance to sound. So repelled was he by the early dissonance that Clair for a time seriously considered abandoning the film for a career in fiction. Even after he resigned himself to the inevitablity of the soundtrack, as Georges Sadoul tells us, Clair satirized the medium. In *Sous les Toits de Paris,* "The glass-panel door that slams to before certain of the characters are about to speak is in this respect something of a symbol." Not until the recent *Les Belles de Nuit* does Clair seem to accept symbolically this entrenched nemesis of the silent film. Clair's poor composer reacts to a rash of discordant noise, aural representatives of a disordered world, by retreating into a world of dreams. In his dreamworld, the sounds—a bugle blast, the tenor-manager of an opera house accepting the young hero's opus, a seductive temptress singing her affections against exotic settings—fall more gently on the ear. But gradually the dreams become frantic and distasteful, the sounds more harsh than any in the hero's waking hours. And when he awakes, highly relieved to [28–29] escape the madness of his dream-world, he symbolically accepts the harsh acoustic world from which he had fled. With the discovery that sound could thus be integrated into the total film structure, Clair seems to have become reconciled to the aural dimension of motion pictures.

Yet in one sense the conservatives who objected to sound were right. Every filmic innovation from sound to 3-D and the wide-screen processes has been accompanied by a throwback to false theatrical conventions. But these throwbacks have been brought on less by the innovation than by a misunderstanding of its proper role in the film medium.

With sound, as with the subsequent innovation of color and stereoscopic film, came a new dimension and new possibilities for selection. But the proper role of sound became apparent only when the film, as in the work of René Clair, once again asserted its fundamental editing principles. Although Pudovkin's early notes are speculative rather than definitive, there is from the beginning, supplementing the *parallel* use of sound in dialogue and music, the guiding principle of counterpoint, a logical extension of the technique of editing. Pudovkin visualizes "a film in which sounds and human speech are wedded to the visual images on the screen in the same way in which two or more melodies can be combined by an orchestra. . . ." To urge the contrapuntal use of sound and image was to point up hidden resources that the filmist might easily overlook. But Pudovkin goes too far when he suggests that one must never show on the screen a man and reproduce his words exactly synchronized with the movement of his lips. To forego the right of synchronization is to forego another valuable and essentially contrapuntal device, namely the contrast between a line of dialogue and the speaker's face.

The classic statement on the aesthetic use of sound came as an articulate statement from the Russians after the Americans had presented the first commercially practical example. *The Jazz Singer* opened in October, 1927. In August of the following year, a statement by Eisenstein, Pudovkin, and Alexandrov appeared in a Leningrad magazine, arguing essentially for a strict use of "non-synchronization." The statement ignores, of course, the realistic tug of synchronized speech, just as an emphasis on editing [29–30] tends to overlook the photographic demands of the individual shot. If, however, we exempt dialogue from the onus of strict non-synchronization (Eisenstein violated his own credo by synchronizing speech and image in *Alexander Nevsky,* his first sound film), the statement can and has stood as a guide to most serious filmists. In *Alexander Nevsky,* the camera tracks along bleak wastes of ice. But the Prokofieff score, suggesting quiet, ominous preparations, adumbrates the coming Battle of the Ice. In *High Noon,* the theme of the ballad, introduced during the credit titles, is carried over into the marriage ceremony, suggesting the coming desertion, the lonely conflict. Thus sound is used to reinforce, comment on, anticipate the film's visual images.

That the final word on sound has not yet been pronounced is indicated when we contrast the aural work of various film directors. Discussing his scenario for *An American Tragedy* (which Paramount paid him for but never produced, substituting the melodramatic version directed by Josef von Sternberg in 1931), Eisenstein says flatly, "The true material of the sound film is, of course, the monologue." But such a recent tour de force as *The Thief,* which abandons dialogue entirely, seems to restate the case for movement, music, and nonverbal sound effects as the emblems of subjective moods. Between these extremes, is the combination which Laurence Olivier uses in the sound track of *Hamlet.* Sometimes Hamlet's voice is rendered in interior monologue; sometimes, when his emotions burst out naturally, in spoken soliloquy. At times, the words are synchronized with the speaker's lips; at other times they merely accompany the face of the listener. Suffice it to say that dialogue, interior monologue, sound effects, music are ultimately determined by and therefore subservient to the demands of the visual image. . . .   [*30*]

  1. Mr. Bluestone's discussion of sound editing is not as detailed as his discussion of visual editing. Are there any analogies that he does not state?

SEEING WITH THE CAMERA

Irving Pichel

I

It is typical of all forms of spectacle before the motion picture—the theater, the circus, the sports field—that the spectator remains in a fixed position at a determined distance from the action he sees. The spectator at a football game watches the movement of the two teams in relation to their respective goalposts. The goals remain at fixed distances from him. Only the players move. The spectator participates in their movement in so far as he turns his head to follow that movement. His mind participates in that movement as it estimates the distance of the moving players from the goal toward which they move. Knowing the rules of the game, this distance has significance for him. Assuming that he is concerned with the fortunes of one of the opposing teams, the lessening distance between the players and a goal induces excitement which may produce sympathetic movement on his part. He may jump to his feet, wave his arms, shout, cheer, or groan.

A newsreel photographer high above the field might photograph a game with so comprehensive a shot that both goals would be simultaneously visible. For parts of the game, as when the teams run the length of the field, only such a viewpoint is adequate to convey the significance of the play. However, from this distance the players appear so small that details of the action cannot be seen, players

IRVING PICHEL was an actor and director both on Broadway and in Hollywood. Among the films he directed are *The Moon is Down* (1943), *Tomorrow is Forever* (1945), and *Destination Moon* (1950).

© 1946 by The Regents of the University of California. Reprinted from *Hollywood Quarterly* (now *Film Quarterly*), Vol. I, No. 2, pp. 138–145, by permission of The Regents.

cannot be identified, and the ball is invisible. The cameraman, therefore, after a time, moves closer or changes the lens on his camera. More detail can now be seen, but his shot includes only half the field. Since the players are all at that end of the field, approaching one of the goals, this is a much more satisfactory viewpoint. In moving his camera he has, in effect, moved the spectator. When the newsreel is shown in the theater, the first comprehensive shot will be followed by the closer shot. Though the action will be continuous, the viewpoint of the spectator will change instantaneously. Then, as a player runs with the ball toward the far end of the field, the camera viewpoint will shift again to the more distant position so that the larger sweep of play can be seen and the significant relationship of players to distant goal be realized and measurable.

Changing the position of the camera during action to a closer position without any apparent interruption in the continuous flow of the spectacle was the first technical advance that was to make of motion pictures a new and unique form of visual experience. The fixed relationship between spectator and spectacle was broken down. The action could be brought closer or moved away, or, stated conversely, the spectator could have every sensation of moving closer except that of motility.

It will be noted that this instant change of viewpoint to one more advantageous [138–139] occurs, in a projected film, not in the action pictured, nor in the actual position of a person watching the film, but in the film itself. This is *movement,* though not action. As the screen play developed, this filmic movement was to take many forms: the abridged movement implied in the cuts from shot to shot—from long shot forward to medium shot, and still nearer to a close shot; the movement of point of view from one character in a group scene to another, and the much greater movements implied in cuts from one locale to another.

The convention which asked an audience to take for granted these instantaneous changes of viewpoint was easy to establish, since, first, it exploited in a larger sense fundamental film characteristics of movement, and, secondly, because it represented not too inaccurately the operation of the spectator's imagination. This structural motion in film objectifies fairly closely the manner in which the eye seeks out of any occurrence or spectacle the most interesting person or action and follows it to the exclusion of other elements presented at the same time. It operates as the mind does when one reads a story, visualizing with the author's account the actions now of one character and now of another, the events now in one place and now in another, the observing of large panoramas and then of minute details. It also objectifies magically, as no other medium can, the wish to be able to come closer, to see more clearly and intimately than life or the earlier forms of theater art have allowed.

Let us return for a moment to our football game. We shall assume that the cameraman is in the closer position, his lens covering only half the field. Through the finder he sees a player start with the ball on a run down the field to the farther goal. He swings his camera, following the runner, exactly as a spectator turns his head to watch the play. Instead of an *instantaneous* move to a viewpoint from which the action can be seen, there is a movement *simultaneous* with the action. The movement, timed with the action, occurs not in the film but in the seeing organ, the eye, the camera.

With the development of screen technique, camera movement has been elaborated. Mounted on wheels, the camera can precede or follow a character. Set on a crane, it can be lifted high above the action. It can recede from a detail to a full shot or, conversely, move from a full shot into a close-up of a single character selected out of the scene. Camera movement, it will be noted, takes place at a much slower tempo than filmic movement and has a different aim. Its rate is related either to that of the spectator's eye, or to that of a moving person or object as the spectator's eye follows that movement in the scene being filmed. Its aim likewise is twofold. It seeks either to imitate the eye movement the spectator would perform if he were present at the scene being photographed, as in most "pan" shots, or it undertakes to convey to the spectator the illusion that he himself shares the movement of the camera.

A person walking ha, the sense that he approaches a distant landmark which remains rooted at a definite place. The tree grows in one spot although its size and relationship to other objects in that landscape modify as the pedestrian draws nearer. Some part of [139–140] his own motility transfers itself to the tree. As he draws nearer, the focus of his eye changes, the tilt of his head is greater as he looks toward the tree's top. His approach causes him to bring into play a different set of muscles; to alter his relation to what he sees. He has the sense that, as he shortens the distance between himself and the tree, it is the tree that alters its aspect. He will say, "The tree grew taller" (as he approached), or "The tree loomed larger."

If he approaches a fixed object in a vehicle, an automobile let us say, in which his own physical effort is eliminated, he is likely to attribute the movement not to the vehicle or to himself, but to his surroundings. He will say, "The country flowed by," or "The house drew nearer."

Something equivalent occurs when the camera is moved while photographing action. The moving character or object is centered in the finder and remains virtually stationary on the screen, and the background becomes fluid. Landscape or buildings flow past and, on the assumption that the spectator identifies himself with the moving character, his relationship to the background is in flux while he himself is actually motionless.

In photographing a character in motion, it must be decided which is more important, the movement or the closeness of the point of view. Obviously, if the camera moves with a moving character, as in dolly shots, movement is negated, since, as has been noted above, the character remains centered on the screen and the background passes by.

II

Before attempting to make generalizations concerning the use of camera movement it is important to clarify the function of the camera. It is not enough to say that it is the machine by which a screen play is photographed. The chain of instrumentalities which begins with the camera and its negative film and passes through the developing machine and the printing machine, the development of the positive and the projection of the positive print on a screen, is too closely identified with an important human sense to be regarded simply as a mechanism. The camera, by which for brevity we mean the entire mechanism, is an eye. Like the microscope or the telescope or field glasses, it extends the capacity of the human eye. It is an eye that functions in a special way for a special purpose. Whose eye do we conceive the camera to be? And how is it to be used? The answer to the second question will be provided by our answer to the first. Most commonly, since the images photographed by the camera are to be viewed by a spectator, the camera is treated as an extension of the spectator's eye. It sees what the spectator could see if he were himself present at the events photographed. It reports as a newsreel does. It satisfies at each moment the spectator's wish or unconscious need to see now in general and now in particular the places, the people, their faces, their hands, their weapons, their actions toward each other, which compose into an organic dramatic or narrative whole. Through filmic movement it is endowed with selectivity. As a theater-goer with opera glasses will focus them now on one character and now on another, the camera, instantly eliding intervening [140–141] motion, goes from person to person, from image to image. Exhausting for the moment the interest of one locale and its characters it can go instantaneously to another group in another place to see how they are faring. It may accompany a character in an automobile or an airplane or go under the sea in a submarine. It may walk with sweethearts and overhear their most intimate conversation. It may accompany a criminal to the gallows. If the camera is used as a substitute for or an extension of the spectator's vision, it is limited only by the obligation to maintain at all times feasible human viewpoints.

If the camera is thought of, however, not as a projection of the spectator's viewpoint, but as the narrator's, it may move with greater freedom and latitude. Like the eye of a novelist, the camera then partakes of the character, personality, and approach of the narrator. It has, like a storyteller, omniscience and omnipresence, or, more exactly, the ability to see only what it wants to see and to be only where it needs to be in order to tell its particular fable. It has selectivity, seeing only those instants in the life of various images which add up to a continuity of time, spatial relationships and causative relationships which the natural eye is incapable of seeing. Conversely, it has the ability to avoid seeing everything in the lives of the fable's characters which is not germane to the telling of the fable. In this use of the camera a complete personality is created who, though not appearing before the audience's eyes, is yet real and definite and as highly personalized as the real storyteller, be he writer or director, who employs it. With this concept of the use of the camera the director can achieve personal style as definite as that of a writer. (The term director is here used generically, as the word camera is used generically. By director we mean the individual who creates or the group of individuals who collaborate in the conception, writing, directing, and editing of a film.) The camera will "see" the story as he sees it and will relate it to an audience through his eyes. It will select shots which for that director have acute expressiveness. Shot will be related to shot in a sequence which has special significance to him. If the camera moves, it will move where he wishes to direct the interest and attention of the spectator.

Attempts have been made also to personify the camera more subjectively by conceiving of it as a character of the story, a narrator using the first person; in other words, as the eyes of a participant in the events it describes. Rouben Mamoulian opened his film of *Dr. Jekyll and Mr. Hyde* with a long introductory sequence in which the camera represented the eyes of Dr. Jekyll. However, since the film play was not a story told by Dr. Jekyll, but a story about him, the device had to be abandoned after a few hundred feet.

In a film directed by the writer a few years ago, called *The Great Commandment,* the camera was used in two sequences in the first person, to represent the eyes of Jesus. Since the Nazarene appeared in only two short episodes, of which He was the focus, and since the story dealt not with Him but with a number of characters who encountered Him, the device accomplished two important results unobtainable in any other way. The first and less important was to avoid attempting to represent a Presence which could not [141–142] be visualized satisfactorily for a large proportion of the spectators, and the second, to enable the camera to see intimately and feel the effect of that Presence on the story's principal characters.

Certain limitations become immediately apparent when the camera is used in this manner as an actual participant. The fact that characters speaking to the character represented by the camera must look directly into the lens means that they look directly from the screen into the eyes of the spectator. Thus the spectator is identified with the character assumed by the camera. In the denouement of Hitchcock's *Spellbound* the camera becomes momentarily the eyes of Dr. Murchison. It follows Ingrid Bergman as she crosses the room to the door and hesitates under the camera in the exact center of the screen. Following her as she crosses, we see Murchison's hand holding the revolver. When the door closes behind her, the hand slowly turns the revolver away from the door, pauses, then turns it directly into the lens and shoots—the spectator. Such a twist may defeat the very aim of the device. Further, scenes must be played without cut in continuous action, and the point of view is unalterably that of an individual, and can be moved or changed only at the pace and within the range of the physical mobility of the individual represented by the camera. It is aware only of what he can see and know. Orson Welles had planned as his first picture in Hollywood the production of Joseph Conrad's *The Heart of Darkness,* to be told in the first person with the camera as the eyewitness and narrator, but the plan was defeated by some such considerations as these.

The camera may be used in another way. It is not conceived of as having a personality of its own, but as being simply an instrument in the hands of the director, capable of highly flexible expressiveness, as a violin is when played upon by a virtuoso. In this sense the camera is not so much an extension of the narrator's eye or mind as it is a wholly new kind of sight instrument, as fabulous as radar and free from most of the limitations that hedge about human sight. The director uses the camera, if this is his concept of its function, quite arbitrarily. It goes where no human eye could possibly go. It moves according to laws, if any, which apply not to the human eye or the human consciousness, but to itself. A number of directors use the camera with this virtuosity, achieving extraordinary effects. One recalls Von Sternberg's use of the camera in *The Scarlet Empress,* or that of Orson Welles in *Citizen Kane.* In the most skillful hands, virtuosity of the camera may enhance dramatic effect and produce a work as uniquely conditioned by the fact that it is transmitted through a camera as a violin concerto is conditioned by the fact that it is transmitted by a violin. The dangers attending this use of the camera are easy to define: it offers a constant temptation to place the camera arbitrarily, on the premise that a striking viewpoint or a striking composition is justification in itself, or that camera movement predicated wholly on the capacities of the machine requires no further motivation. To be sure, the end composition will have meaning which in the eyes of the director seems justification enough for the means employed to arrive at that end.

Such a purely cinematic use of the [142–143] camera is warranted in semiabstract treatments of nondramatic subjects or moments in dramatic films, as, for example, in the photography of musical or dance numbers. The camera movement may have a real or fancied relationship to the music or choreographic pattern, but often enough it simply employs an arbitrarily selected variety of angles and moves with no other object than constantly to refresh the spectator's interest in what he is seeing.

III

In actual directorial practice no compact is made with the spectator concerning the camera's function. He is not asked to recognize the camera either as his eye or the narrator's eye or that of a participant in the action, nor to identify himself with a participant in that action. Commonly, no principle in the use of the camera is constantly adhered to by the director. He uses the camera at one moment as though it were the spectator, at another to score a point of his own as the storyteller, or again, impersonally, as a tool for the achievement of an "effect." He justifies movement of the camera as the pursuit of "fluidity," or adheres to the idea that frequent change of angle gives "life" to the film or that sustained master scenes have a special value. These may all be warrantable generalizations under certain circumstances, but they ignore the fundamental that the camera acts as a living organ rather than as a tool.

For all that, the camera is governed by laws of optics as the eye is also. In function it partakes far more of the biological and psychological aspects of sight than of the purely mechanical physical aspect. Only a few directors exhibit a clear concept of a continuous understanding between themselves and the spectator concerning the function of the camera. Thus it would seem to the writer that John Ford uses the camera as the spectator's eye. He rarely causes the camera to move, thus permitting the spectator to orient himself in a stable world in which the people and not the landscape or the architecture are animate. There is a minimum use of close-ups, and close shots are achieved more often by causing the characters to approach the camera than by moving the camera closer to the characters. Ford holds that camera movement destroys reality, which is his recognition of the fact that the illusion of movement on the spectator's part cannot be supported by his physical experience as he watches the film. This gives to the rare shots in which he does cause the camera to move an uncommon effectiveness and meaning. In *The Grapes of Wrath* one recalls the wobbling progress of the camera through the Okie settlement when momentarily the camera took the point of view of the Joad family as its truck drove into the camp. Or the shot in *How Green Was My Valley* when, for a moment, Ford became the storyteller and moved the camera away from the faces of Mr. and Mrs.

Morgan to the street to the left of them to show the two sons leaving home. It is as though he were content to let the spectator see the story as an eyewitness, with occasional comment from the director—comment so infrequent that it gives pith and validity from the very detachment and objectivity with which the rest of the story is told. In Leo McCarey's *The Bells of St. Mary's* the camera is moved not more than half a dozen times—only when it is panned, as the spectator might follow with his eyes a character moving purposively from one part of the scene to another.

There are other directors whose camera technique is more fluid because they employ the camera as a storyteller employs words. The point of view is primarily their own. Although it is shared with the spectator, they seem to say, "Let me show you what I saw." They act as gentle guides leading the spectator from place to place, wittily or poignantly pointing to this or that character. Not infrequently their point of view is revealed with an element of surprise. The camera maintains a credible viewpoint but one somewhat superior to and in advance of the spectator's. It knows, although the spectator does not, where it is going and what it is going to reveal. It has a self-evident sense of plan and foresight. It tells a tale in which not even the accidents are accidental. To illustrate, a picture directed by Lubitsch is told consciously as a tale to amuse or to move the spectator, and the question of the reality or the occurrences shown is secondary. The aesthetic goal is not the illusion of immediacy, but the pleasure of an engaging tale.

IV

A skillful craftsman, regardless of his general philosophy concerning the use of the camera, will be governed by one fundamental consideration—that in every shot the content shall be more important than the manner in which it is transmitted. The story comes first, and every shot deals with characters and what they do. If what they do at a given moment is stated in terms of physical action, the camera will set up [143–144] space for the action and fixed points of reference. If the physical action is casual and secondary to what the character is saying or thinking, the camera will hold the character in the center of the screen whether he is moving or standing still. If his words or the intention that can be read in his face are important and interesting enough, the movement of the camera as it follows him will go unperceived. If, however, the character is stationary and the camera moves toward or away from him, the movement of the camera is bound to be perceived and must then have meaning in itself, saying, in effect, "Watch this man!" or, "We may now leave this person's thoughts and draw back to a place where we can observe his actions." If this preparation through movement or an act of attention on the spectator's part heightens dramatic effect, it is warranted. If it accomplishes merely mechanical readjustment of viewpoint, it draws attention to itself as movement and diminishes the importance of the content of the scene.

With the exception of pan shots which simulate the turn of the spectator's head, camera movement is of two sorts: either (1) the movement of the camera is motivated by and synchronized with the movement of a character or characters, or (2) the movement of the camera is not synchronized with movement on the screen.

It has already been pointed out that camera movement synchronized with physical movement is justified when it is more important to fix audience attention upon the moving character than upon his movement with relation to other characters or the background. Generally speaking, such movement does not change the initial distance relationship [144–145] between the spectator and the image on the screen.

In camera movement which is not physically motivated, a proper justification can be found only in the imitation or symbolic reproduction of movements taking place in the imagination either of the storyteller or of the spectator. Such movements may be classified roughly as follows: (1) movement from a longer to a closer angle, (2) movement from a closer angle to a longer one, (3) movement from a scene to a detail, (4) movement from a detail to a scene. If such movements have some correspondence with the emotional participation by the spectator in the action, drawing him closer to characters or retracting him to a fuller scene, directing his attention to an inserted detail or drawing his attention from a detail to the characters to whom the detail relates in some significant way, the movement may be justified. It may be observed, however, that these same alterations of viewpoint can be achieved filmically, that is, through direct cuts, more quickly and usually with less awareness of the move itself. Camera movement used in this fashion decreases the pace at which the film moves. The reduction in tempo may have emotional value in itself, though it should be noted that the primary emotional responses of an audience are to the content of the shot, and the enhancement of these responses through the addition of camera movement is achieved, if at all, at the cost of an arbitrary transferral of motion from the scene to the spectator's eye. Whatever value such movement may have in terms of rhythm or imagination, it must be observed that the effect attained depends not upon an imaginative adjustment of the spectator's point of view, as in the direct cut, but upon an adjustment which inevitably relates itself more closely to the spectator's capacity for physical movement. That is to say, the imaginary journey on which the spectator is taken proceeds at a pace of the body, not of the mind. When this is true, such arbitrary movement defeats the end for which it was planned. The tempi of screen action are set up in the scene itself. Filmic movement can accelerate these tempi; synchronous camera movement can retard or negate them. It is an open question whether camera movement not synchronized to physical movement on the screen or to a normal act of spectator attention adds effect to the screen play. Certainly, if the director doubts whether an effect can be better achieved by moving a camera or by letting it stand, he will let it stand.   [145]

1. In his discussion of *Spellbound*, Pichel points to a real problem in the use of the character-oriented camera. How else might a film director find external equivalents for subjective states?

2. Do you agree that content must always come before camera work? Can you think of any good films in which excellence is attributable more to camera work than to material?

PERSPECTIVES FOR CRITICISM

A CRITICAL CREDO

John Simon

The most important thing to remember about film criticism is that it is not fundamentally different from any other kind of criticism. But because criticism itself remains such a largely misunderstood and therefore feared and hated concept, it may be well to posit one's general critical credo before proceeding to film criticism proper. Now if there is anything the public avoids more than criticism, it is discussions and theories of criticism; yet these, consumed in moderation, could serve as useful energizers of both criticism and the audience, leading, I hesitate to say to better art, but at least to better conditions for art, which is not so very different a thing.

Matthew Arnold called poetry the criticism of life; it is not impossible to invert the formula and call criticism the poetry of life. For if I understand Arnold correctly, he means that poetry, by setting before man an ideal existence with thought and feeling performing to the utmost of their capacities, urges him to recognize the insufficiencies of the routine he calls living and directs him toward the heights. If this is so, then true criticism, which renders explicit the achievements and shortcomings of art—man's noblest aspiration—is in fact a kind of poetry, a poetry of hate for what is ugly or false, and of love for what is beautiful and true. I realize that it has become unfashionable in life—let alone in criticism—to use terms like "ugly" and "beautiful," but I accept the charge of being unfashionable with satisfaction and even, I confess, with pride.

The most common attacks on criticism (and especially on movie criticism, which, being as yet young and feeble, can least defend itself) are either that it is

JOHN SIMON writes regularly on film for *The New Leader,* on drama for *The Hudson Review* and *New York* magazine, and on literature for a wide variety of publications. He has also published two collections of criticism: *Acid Test* and *Private Screenings*.

unconstructive or that it is unnecessary. Unnecessary, apparently, because the public can think for itself: [1–2] if a book, a painting, a film is good, it will be accepted;
if it is bad, it will fail. What need, then, for critics? The most obvious answer is that
the world of art is full of works whose true worth or worthlessness took far too long
to be comprehended, and that even if time does sit in just and inexorable judgment,
its courts are apt to be as cruelly procrastinatory as those described by Dickens and
Kafka. To the extent that criticism can accelerate the verdict of the ages, it can speed
up the coming of pleasure and enlightenment, and, no less important, spare us the
waste of what as mortals we have the least of—time.

　　　Without criticism there would be no dialogue, and it is staggering to con-
template what would have been the history—if any—of government, education,
philosophy, psychiatry, and any other important discipline of learning or aspect of
life without dialectics, without the chance of both sides being heard and hearing
each other. Without criticism, the artist receives no serious answer; we must, on
solid empirical evidence, consider failure or success with the mass of one's contemporaries as nothing more than a snort from the crowd, to be interpreted however
one pleases. It is not important that the critical answer be that of an infallible oracle
—what oracle ever was that?—it matters merely that a critical answer be the best of
which a sensitive, experienced, eloquent, and honest mind and sensibility are capable. Thereby a purposeful issue is joined: the keen yet bloodless struggle for human
fulfillment, which it was once permissible to call the pursuit of truth and beauty.

　　　But what of "destructive" criticism, which is far and wide alleged to be
bad? The terms "constructive" and "destructive," as applied to criticism, have no
meaning whatever. There is only good and bad criticism. What indeed might "constructive" mean in reference to a critique? From the author in question, "Like me,
don't knock me!" which is an absurd request. From the pedagogue, "Show him or her
where and how the thing could be improved!" But any genuine artist would resent
the critic's offering to remake his work; only school compositions can so be treated
by teachers, and it may be that even they should not. I cannot write someone else's
book, play, or scenario for him; I can only point out where and why he lost me—
and that, I suppose, [2–3] would already be called "destructive" criticism. To the
casual layman, "constructive" criticism would be, "Go easy on him, he is doing
his best." But this is the worst fallacy of all: it assumes that art does not really matter.
If a surgeon's patients die on him, one after the other, does one excuse him by saying
he did his best? Can a statesman's, a military commander's, an educator's errors be
excused so cheaply? No; because those things *matter*. Whereas art, it would seem,
does not.

　　　But to the critic to whom art is important, sacred, and, ultimately, coex-
tensive with life itself, to produce bad art and to condone it—and thereby give rise to
further bad art and finally drive out the good—are the two most heinously dangerous
sins imaginable. And the most destructive. Still the temperate person will say, "All
right, forget about 'destructive' and 'constructive'—but couldn't you just be more
moderate in your dislikes?" Different evils need different modes of attack: from
Swiftian *saeva indignatio* to subtle puncturing, from "more in sorrow than in anger"
to *reductio ad absurdum,* one chooses whichever method is most suitable; or, if
one is less versatile, whichever method one is best suited to. The critic's words are

his tools, or weapons, and he would be foolish and incompetent if he did not use them to the utmost of his, and their, ability. If the critic is mistaken or too harsh, time eventually proves him wrong—much more quickly than it would a bad artist, because here it can rely on the enthusiastic help of the critic's colleagues. The genuine artist cannot be destroyed by words: It is not the *Quarterly*, "savage and tartarly," but consumption that killed John Keats. And the man who slings mud pies at the Venus de Milo hits only himself.

Good criticism and bad criticism, then; but what constitutes good criticism? Perhaps it is easiest to begin by defining the commonest kind of bad criticism, which is not criticism at all but reviewing. Reviewing is something that newspaper editors have invented: it stems from the notion that the critic is someone who must see with the eyes of the Average Man or Typical Reader (whoever that is) and predict for his fellows what their reaction will be. To this end, the newspapers carefully screen their reviewers to be representative common men, say, former obituary writers or mail-room clerks, anything but trained specialists. To [3–4] accept such a reviewer as critic and guide is like expecting school children to teach one another, or patients in a hospital ward to undertake one another's cure. A critic excites the public's curiosity, wonder, suspicion, rage, and enthusiasm; a reviewer elicits mostly one of two reactions: "Good! That's another one I don't have to see!" or "Great! I like it already." Both reactions stifle thought instead of encouraging the audience and, with luck, even the artist to grow.

Now the good critic is, first and foremost, a teacher. One problem, among many, with our education is that it ends. After a certain number of years, always too few, the last textbook is shut, the door closes on the last classroom, and we are free— free not only to desist from all further learning, but also to forget what we have learned so far. How many of us can pass up such a golden opportunity? This is where the critic comes in. With cogency, suasion, passion, charm he induces us to think, to widen our horizons, to open yet another book, to reconsider a snap judgment, to see something from a loftier vantage point, in historic prespective, and using more and truer touchstones. Good criticism of any kind—of movies, ballet, architecture, or whatever—makes us think, feel, respond; if we then agree or disagree is less important than the fact that our faculties have been engaged and stretched. Good criticism informs, interprets, and raises the ultimate questions, the unanswerable ones that everyone must try to answer none the less. This is teaching of the highest order.

Secondly, the true critic is an artist. "Criticism is a good thing, but poetry is a better," wrote Richard Le Gallienne. As a poet, he had every reason to preconize poetry; as a bad one, every reason to patronize criticism. But even the most enthusiastic practitioner of criticism, if he is not Oscar Wilde, would refrain from placing it above poetry; it would, however, be wrong to deny that a good piece of criticism must be as well written and shaped as, *mutatis mutandis,* a poem, a story, or a personal essay. It is, therefore, in its own way a work of art. As that remarkable but still underrated German playwright, poet, and novelist Frank Wedekind put it, "Without doubt, the systematic execution of a critique written with a sense of responsibility is a more difficult, worthy, and, even for art, more valuable task than the writing of mediocre [4–5] plays." And he went on, "Critic and author are . . . different stages

of development of the same calling. The two are collaborators on the same project."
The critic, as that enlightened poet Pierre Reverdy saw him, "fait, avec plus de
liberté, l'office du meilleur ami." But the artist will accept the friendship of the critic
only if he recognizes in him a fellow-artist: why should friendship become misal-
liance? In his occasionally outré but generally highly perceptive essay "The Critic as
Artist," Wilde observed, "the critic is he who exhibits to us a work of art in a form
different from that of the work itself, and the employment of a new material is a
critical as well as a creative element." Wilde called criticism "a creation within a
creation" and so the purest form of creativity, and indeed the piece of criticism that
cannot be read by a civilized and concerned person without knowledge of the work
or artist discussed is not a true critique. And that which can be so read is more
than a review; it is a work of the contemplative imagination, a work of art. So we can
read Longinus or Lessing, Sainte-Beuve or Hazlitt, without more than a general
awareness of the writers that were their points of departure. And in reading a drama
review of Shaw or Beerbohm it is scarcely necessary to have seen the production in
question to savor the matter and the manner of the review as literature. Of which
one of our film critics is this true? How many people now writing about movies are
worth reading even when the particular film is still fresh in our memories, and our
desire to discuss it still sovereign?

Thirdly, the critic is or should be a thinker. In an age when philosophy
has removed itself into theology or science or even, of all places, literary criticism,
it becomes incumbent on the critic to turn philosopher. To quote Wilde's essay once
more, "the highest Criticism . . . is the record of one's own soul." In other words,
the critic must have a world view, which, however one may wish to disguise it, is
a moral position. Nothing is more suspect in criticism nowadays than a moral position, and yet there can be no criticism without one. The moment something appears
to us better or worse than something else, we are being moralists—for aesthetics is
the morality of art, just as morality is the aesthetics of living. But if criticism cannot do
without morality, it can easily [5–6] remain unaware of its underlying morality, and
the penalty for such unawareness is inferior criticism. What form this morality will
take is comparatively unimportant; it may be—and I myself would wish it to be—
neither an established system nor the systematization of a yet unestablished one. It
should be, as nearly as I can describe it, a relevance to human life, an elegance of
spirit, a generosity and adventuresomeness of outlook, and above all, a concept or
intimation of what the ideal solution to an artistic problem would be, and the dogged
insistence on measuring every performance against the envisioned model. It should
never judge something, as is commonly done, on how well it fulfills its own aims,
for by that standard, if it sets out to be only junk, junk will have to be found excellent.
Essential too is an awareness of reconciled opposites: of the joy inherent in tragedy
and of the pathos no true comedy can be without.

But I am not trying to develop a whole critical philosophy here. I am
merely pleading for, or insisting on, the necessity of a realized philosophy translated
into artistic expression as the irreducible minimum of the true critic's equipment.
And it will be useful to bear always in mind the statement of the great sixteenth-
century Spanish Jesuit Baltasar Gracián: "Not only in words, but also in works is
lying practiced, and the latter form of lying is much the more dangerous."

With these general remarks out of the way, we may pass to considerations pertaining specifically to film criticism. The problem here is acute: Whereas the other arts seem to be blessed with more or less the critics they deserve—with modern music, painting, and sculpture receiving, as their just deserts, the most inept kind of criticism—film, which may well be the salient and vital art form of our day is getting hardly less incompetent criticism as a gratuitous insult. The main trouble is that most intellectuals, even if willing to concede that film is an art, would not consider criticizing it an art or even a serious occupation, perhaps because there are not enough serious film critics, or indeed serious films, around to get a meaningful dialogue started. A case in point is Kenneth Tynan, whose drama criticism was, whatever particulars one might cavil with, manifestly serious (and let me make clear, once and for all, that by serious I do not mean [6–7] long-faced), but whose film criticism, however much one may enjoy it, is patently frivolous. The fundamental problem, I suppose, is that film is being taken, ultimately, as an "entertainment" as opposed to a work of art, as if art and entertainment were mutually exclusive or, at least, separate entities, as form and content or meaning and style were once thought to be. While no one today would dare to think of form and content as separate or, except for purposes of classroom demonstration, separable, it still seems the most natural thing to erect a fence between the few films that "have something to say" and the many that are "merely amusements," and, apparently, come up with roughly equal endorsement for films in both groups, albeit by a double standard involving different scales.

Now I submit that the first responsibility of the film critic is to recognize that there is, to be sure, a superficial difference between comedy and tragedy, and a profound one between good and bad, but that to view and review *all* films as anything but an art is at best trivial and at worst stupid—always bearing in mind that I am talking of the serious critic. Suppose that I were speaking here as a literary critic, seriously and literarily (as opposed to banteringly or sociologically), and discussed the works of Herman Wouk or Leon Uris or James Michener. I should justly be considered, *ipso facto,* critically, if not indeed mentally, incompetent. But if, as a film critic, I were to present a rapturous tribute to the films of a Blake Edwards or Otto Preminger, or if I were to disgorge high-sounding effusions about the work of Godard or Chabrol (and, who knows, perhaps even that of Stan Brakhage or Jack Smith), I would be listened to with earnestness and deference, as if I were not dealing with men who are, in one case, hacks and charlatans, in the other, pretentious flounderers —and this despite the fact that one or the other of them may have stumbled on something useful, may have a certain facility, and may have even, *mirabile dictu,* turned out a passable film.

The point is that the critic—as distinguished from the historian, the sociologist, the collector, the faddist—has no business considering entertainment as an end in itself, any more than he may consider art, in film or elsewhere, as something dreary and [7–8] unentertaining. This does not mean, of course, that the critic should refuse to review a so-called entertainment film: we do not as yet have enough films that are art, or even aspiring to that condition, yet serious criticism must go on. To adapt a saying of Clémenceau's, the reviewing of films, such as they may be, is much too serious a matter to be left in the hands of mere reviewers. And it is crucial to remember that there is no genuine entertainment without artistry, just as there can be no art that is unabsorbing, i.e., boring. There is, however, this proviso: Artistry is not quite on the same level as art.*

A distinguished Polish film-maker and teacher remarked to me not long ago that we talk so much about film as art, yet there have been in the whole history of the cinema thus far no more than, at best, two works of indubitable art. I think that the number is higher, though not very much higher; I must also, in principle, agree. Hardly anyone writing about film today would maintain, for example, that D. W. Griffith was not an artist; yet, to me, he is the epitome of the nonartist, no matter how much he may have contributed to the *technique* of the film. I would say that Griffith is to the art of cinema what Achilles Tatius was to the art of the novel. Or that Griffith did for film what Sackville and Norton, the authors of *Gorboduc,* did for the English drama. And this, clearly, not because a film like *Birth of a Nation* is morally objectionable, but because it is artistically and intellectually insufficient.

This might begin to sound like support for all those potentially qualified film critics who prefer to abstain because of the grim prospect of bringing superior equipment to bear on nothing or next to nothing. It might be suggested here that Aristotle was able to write extraordinarily fine dramatic criticism at a time when there were only a half dozen dramatists worth considering. But the position of the film critic today is truly anomalous: It is to be confronted with an art that, even though it has done remarkably [8–9] well in the short span of six decades, has not had anywhere near enough time to develop fully; and to confront it with a critical discipline that, even if only in related fields, has acquired a vast tradition and imposing expertise and sophistication. The main thing the critic can do while waiting for the day when it will be possible to limit oneself to writing serious criticism about serious films for serious publications is, with every means at his command, to help bring about that day.

The age is eminently ripe for film to become a true art. For this is only possible when something newer and more profitable exists to syphon off the most irresponsible, inartistic, greedy elements from an older art. "It is unimaginable," wrote Friedrich Dürrenmatt, "what would have to be played on the stage nowadays if film had not been invented and the screenwriters were turning out stage plays." This statement can now be revised: It is inconceivable what trash would be put on film these days if television had not been invented, and the TV writers were functioning as scenarists. As it is, far too many of them are.

The next responsibility of the critic is to recognize the difficulties inherent in the form of film. There are simple and complex arts. Fiction, for example, is a simple art, based on the word. So too is painting, based—until recently, anyway—on the image. Conversely, ballet, opera, film are complex arts. Although this is not a value judgment, implying that complex arts are superior to simple ones, or vice versa, writing good criticism of a complex art presents a multiplicity of problems. Now, to make things a little easier for the critic, one aspect of a complex art usually

* Allowances must, I suppose, be made for such a category as "failed art." *Paradise Regained,* or most of Blake's prophetic books, for example, are art in intention, and do not make the compromises of pseudoart. But works which intelligent readers (except, perhaps, contemporaries struck by their timeliness) will read only under duress might as well be considered failed or nonart.

far surpasses the others in importance. Ballet is perfectly possible without costumes and sets, and even music has been dropped in some recent experiments. Opera could do without words, using nonsense syllables, which most librettos quite successfully approximate already. Modern composers, like Stravinsky, have tended to use the voice purely as an instrument; and even the best texts are likely to be of little avail: What the elaborate orchestration does not swallow, the singer's diction certainly will.

But film is the one complex art in which two main components are equally important: text and cinematography, that is, word and image. The youthful critic, contemptuous of words [9–10] and proud, like the young film-maker, of "thinking in film"—which means, I suppose, perceiving the whole work as images—should beware: Words are no less important than pictures. But the old-school critic should also be wary: Pictures are no less important than words. A film that is all image and poor words is like a beautiful woman who, the moment she opens her mouth, offends us. We cannot love her. But neither can we love a brilliantly eloquent woman who is ugly as sin. In any case, the relation between image and word is much more intimate than some people realize: Even in silent or near-silent films the mind tends to translate seen actions into words—so that the word, excluded, creeps in by the back door.

Now because film is such a complex—perhaps, indeed, a total—art, the ideal film critic would have to be conversant with cinematography, literature, acting techniques, painting and sculpture (form and composition), music, dance (film musicals), and in view of the generally poor subtitles, as many foreign languages as possible. Can one encompass all this? I dare say that when T. S. Eliot gave as *the* requirement for a critic that he be "very intelligent," he was not thinking of the film critic. Otherwise, I suspect, he would have had to say "very, very intelligent." But ironically, as we shall see, it is precisely some of the least intelligent people who wander into film criticism.

We have now reached the point where it is appropriate to indicate some of the things a film critic should not be. Film criticism, like film-making, is a field that attracts the anti-intellectual—whether he be an intellectual turned sour, or a bona fide anti-intellectual of long standing. Now, whereas film-making does not require a rational basis, film criticism does. Yet it is all too readily conceived of as some kind of game, if not, indeed, a con-game, or even a form of public defiance—something withal that enjoys enough of a vogue to make it look like work. Thus, for example, the people who evolved and practice the *auteur* theory were playing a faddist in-game, which does not begin to hold up under rational scrutiny, yet they were able to corner a large part of the critical market. (I use the unsavory metaphor advisedly.) But film criticism, again like film, has particular appeal for an even worse crowd, the lunatic fringe, because it [10–11] offers a perfect substitute world. The fact that film, of all arts, comes closest to looking both like life and like dreams, both like palpable reality and like wish-fulfillments made manifest, makes it the preferred medium for escape: it has neither the arrant artifices and inescapable limitations of the theatre, nor the crippling self-censorship and disintoxicating commercials of television to cope with. Thus it invites us on a voyage where all is *luxe, calme et volupté,* or, if we would rather, *luxe, frénésie et volupté,* and the seekers of artificial paradises flock right in. Consider the so-called Underground Cinema with its party fun and games that become films, and its film screenings that turn into fun and game parties in an uninterrupted daisy chain, non-world without end. And, in due time, the lunatic fringe evolves its own critics, even while it gradually wears down the resistance of those reviewers initially opposed to it.

And even when it is not the fanatical movie buff who turns critic, the temptation is great for the critic to become a movie buff, which is the exact opposite of being a critic. Because the history of film is short and because film comes at one automatically, the way a book, for instance, does not, the critic may be seduced into trying to see as nearly every film as possible. Only, though the history of film may indeed be short, it is also extremely wide: the output is tremendous. What self-respecting literary critic would try to keep up with every novel, or even every slightly better novel, that comes along, to say nothing of all the other literary genres? That way lies madness. So, if our man is not already a madman when he becomes a film critic, he stands an excellent chance of ending up as one.

Yet, heaven knows, the film critic needs every bit of lucidity and resourcefulness to do justice to a job in which mountains of difficulty insist on mistaking him for Mohammed. It is part of the critic's responsibility to be unremittingly aware of the almost insuperable problems that face him the moment he wishes to be more than the reviewer of a specific film that happens to come his way, or, given that situation, to write something that will have widespread and lasting value.

A book can be read slowly and reread. The painting usually, though nowadays not always, stands still; it is also available in [11–12] reproduction. Music places score, text (if there is one), and recordings into one's hands. Even the ballet critic has the advantage of viewing and reviewing certain ballets over and over again, and thus knowing at least some of the staples of the repertoire practically by heart. In film, even where a printed script is obtainable, the critic depends on a few notes—often, because they have to be scribbled in haste and darkness, illegible— and on his evanescent memory of a fleeting experience.

And even if a cinematheque is at the critic's disposal—but how many of us are so privileged?—he still cannot take the film home with him and ponder it at leisure. True, some film lending libraries are beginning to be heard of, but they are as yet only little more than a tantalizing promise, a drop in the bucket, and the problems surrounding lending libraries being what they are, it is doubtful that this bucket will ever quench anyone's thirst. To be sure, new inventions may come along, but I am not trying to practice Utopian criticism here. In any case, the critic will eventually need to have his own film library, just as today's literary critic and scholar has his own essential books. But even that is not the end of our problems. However much access the critic may have to films, his readers will most likely not have it. In this way it becomes, in the large number of cases, hard or impossible for the reader to verify the critic's contentions. But, worst of all, there is no way of accurately *quoting* film: Still photographs can barely do justice to stationary objects of art; dialogue conveys only a fragment of what happens in a film. Verbal evocation also has a hard time of it: If you use technical terminology to explain shots and camera movements, you may very well lose your reader, and will certainly end up boring him; if you use impressionistic, imaged prose, unless you are very skillful indeed, you may wander far afield. Thus a genuine understanding, let alone a dialogue, between critic and reader is almost impossible.

As if all this were not enough, the film critic is also up against a space problem, though, unlike greater powers with such problems, he is not asking for the moon, merely for enough space in a paper or magazine to develop his ideas and impressions. But the space accorded him is usually quite insufficient, precisely because [12–13] film, as we said before, has so many components. Consequently it is the rarest thing to find a review that can begin to do justice to the manifold achievements and lacks of the film it deals with.

And there is apt to be yet a further obstacle. Because film represents such a large financial investment for the producers, the honestly outspoken critic, if he is working for an influential publication, becomes a threat to Hollywood. As a result, many are the tales of critics losing their jobs, or not even getting them, because of pressure—direct or indirect, actual or merely anticipated—from the big film companies.

If one contemplates the obstacles I have just enumerated, one might well consider undertaking to write film criticism an act of singular, if not suicidal, desperation. And yet, more than ever, good film criticism is needed.   [13]

1.   In what way can criticism lead to "better conditions for art?"

2.   Do you think the terms "ugly" and "beautiful" are unfashionable? What do you mean when you use them? How does one determine when language is fashionable?

3.   In deriding "constructive criticism," Mr. Simon uses the analogy of school grading. From your own experience, would you agree with him? In any case, do you think his point well-taken?

4.   Mr. Simon makes much of good writing or style in criticism. Analyze and evaluate his writing. Is he a good example of his own principles?

5.   In view of the problems of quoting and verifying that Simon describes, how can film critics produce evidence for their views?

THE CRITICAL QUESTION

Penelope Houston

"The English critic, always protesting that the drama should not be didactic, and yet always complaining if the dramatist does not find sermons in stones and good in everything . . ."—*Bernard Shaw*

Was Shaw right, and has the English critic a constant, if concealed, longing for the right-minded work, the play or film or novel with its moral lessons as firmly and unambiguously stitched in as those of a nineteenth-century sampler? Sometimes it seems so, when the nanny instinct that lurks somewhere in most critical consciences rises to the surface and the reader is warned off the cruel or the depressing in entertainment as though being counselled against taking sweets from strange men. (Only nanny, who has never had much of a sense of humour, could so signally have failed to see the joke of *Psycho*.) On the whole, though, nanny knows her place. The governing characteristic of English critical writing, rather, seems to be its empiricism, its innate distrust of theory and reluctance to draw demarcation lines. The aspiring critic naïve enough to ask advice is likely to be given it succinctly. His job: to make up his mind about what the artist was trying to do; then to consider how well he has done it. The third question is the dangerous one: was it really worth doing in the first place? To ask it implies that the critic is judging the work not "on its own merits" (that favourite, elusive English phrase) but according to some system of values; that, in fact, he has a theory.

One of England's most important film critics, PENELOPE HOUSTON edits *Sight and Sound* for The British Film Institute.

Reprinted from *Sight and Sound,* Vol. XXX, Autumn 1960. Copyright © The British Film Institute.

Exactly four years ago, Lindsay Anderson's article "Stand Up! Stand Up!" was published in this magazine. In some quarters it was greeted as a significant statement of principle, its insistence that the dangerous third question could not be evaded being accepted as a statement of something self-evidently true although too often neglected. In other areas, Mr. Anderson was welcomed rather like a bowler caught throwing in a test match. The method might take a wicket or two, but wasn't he trying to impose his own reading of the rules of the game? In any case, the argument about commitment was on; and it has been with us ever since. The commitment question still remains central to any discussion of a critical theory. But there has been so much misunderstanding and confusion about just what the expression ought to mean, more particularly about how Lindsay Anderson interpreted it and where people thought this interpretation was leading that a certain restatement is still necessary.

QUESTIONS OF COMMITMENT

"Stand Up! Stand Up!" called into question the not uncommon idea that a critic should somehow be able to separate the analytical, appreciative, professional side of his personality from the rest of his attitudes to life. In itself, of course, the idea is an illusion: there is no such thing as entirely objective, unbiased criticism; there is only critical writing (and not a great deal of it at that) which aspires to this condition. But the critic who will gaily admit his personal quirks of taste just because these help to build up his image, his personality as it addresses itself to the reader, will keep tactfully quiet about where he stands on the larger issues. He will make moral judgments (on films like *Peeping Tom*) more easily than social ones (on films like *The Angry Silence*). He will attack what he feels to be dangerously vicious while tolerantly letting pass what he knows to be as insidiously damaging in its encouragement of snap reactions and slipshod thinking.

Lindsay Anderson is not an Englishman, and he has none of the English respect for words like "fair" and "balanced" and "impartial." With all a Scot's distrust of compromise, he took the critical writing of four years ago to task for its undefined liberalism and asked it to declare its principles: he [160–161] wanted values to be openly admitted. Some of the misunderstanding began here. How, he was asked, could he properly review a film such as the Nazi *Triumph of the Will* or the Catholic *Journal d'un Curé de Campagne*? These films' quality was in their "use of the medium"; and wasn't a critic's expressed dislike of the ideologies they reflected going to cloud his perception? This sort of question in itself shows a striking lack of appreciation of how the disciplines of criticism operate. The critic does not have to agree with a case to know whether it is being well or badly stated; he does not have to find the Bernanos-Bresson ethos, with its masochistic self-questioning, a sympathetic one (he may even find it repellent) to appreciate that *Journal d'un Curé* is a masterpiece of resolute conviction. He can admire without agreeing and agree without admiring. And although this ought to be self-evident, apparently it has not been.

The belief—more often it looks like a pretence—that one can somehow write a sounder review of a film by keeping to style and method, by not bothering to work out what its motive force may be, is surprisingly influential. *Triumph of the Will* is the kind of film brought up as an example; and if ever an example boomeranged against those who introduce it, then this is the one. No critic can overlook the film's brilliance, its electric authority. Anyone who feels that it should be reviewed *primarily* in terms of technique rather than for its unique value as a document of Nazism triumphant has somehow failed to establish contact with the century in which he is living. Maybe there are those who prefer it that way.

There is no point in discussing here the arguments for committed criticism. They ought to be familiar enough by now. And Lindsay Anderson's article, in any case, was not only—was not perhaps even primarily—an attempt to elucidate a theory. It was also a call to arms, an appeal to the critics to stand up and be counted. Mr. Anderson made no secret of his own commitments, which are Left Wing, though in the humane rather than the actively political sense; and, by implication, he has since made it apparent that he is not greatly concerned with other people's commitments unless they coincide more or less with his own.

Although the critical profession traditionally occupies a position somewhat left of centre, the critics as a whole did not relish being told that they ought to be radicals. In all the arts, in the eyes of its upholders and in those of its opponents, committed criticism effectively means Left Wing criticism. If you say that you are committed, you are also saying (or are thought to be saying) that you are a socialist; and this makes it impossible to consider the critical problem without relating it to some of the wider issues of life in this country.

"Stand Up! Stand Up!" was not simply an isolated article: it was part of an atmosphere which may be evoked through the names of half a dozen groups and organisations: the Royal Court Theatre, Joan Littlewood's Theatre Workshop, Free Cinema, *Universities and Left Review* (now the *New Left Review*), *Encore*, *Tribune*, the Aldermaston marches. During the last half of the Fifties, most of the creative and energetic thinking directed to that point where politics and culture meet has been orientated towards the Left. There has been nothing that could precisely be defined as a movement, but there has been constant interaction. Meanwhile, socialism in the country at large has steadily been losing ground. The 1959 election was a turning point; and the *New Statesman's* election-eve comment that, whatever the result, the campaign would prove to have been a triumph for Labour, only underlined the distance between illusion and reality. Since the election, all the divisions within the Labour Party have been paraded before the electorate; a split of which rather less has been made is that [161–162] between the young, radical, socially critical faction (who have their allies also on the Right) and the politicians of the Left. The gap between political practice and quasi-political thinking can seldom have been wider: the Young Left, which has found its Osbornes and Weskers, its Bergers and Tynans, has yet to find its politicians.

This is hardly the climate of optimism, which means that a brave, essentially hopeful gesture such as Arnold Wesker's attempt to interest the unions in the arts seems all the more encouraging. What Wesker is attempting may not work, and he knows it, but the effort itself is magnificently positive. But Wesker gives the impression of having some of the confidence that moves mountains; and there is not a great deal of that around. Rather, there is an air of disillusionment, a soured, disapproving frustration, which is the mood least helpful not only to creative endeavour but to good writing of any kind. The critic who appears a congenital nagger and disapprover, who tries to bully and hector art into following the path he would like it to take, is more of a liability than a help to his cause.

The worst enemy, it sometimes seems, of commitment in criticism is the writing of some of those who carry its banner. There is, for instance, the lunatic theory, occasionally paraded, that art *only* becomes meaningful if it has something directly to say to the ordinary man. Many writers, in this magazine and elsewhere, have appealed for a cinema and theatre more closely related to life as we are currently experiencing it, an appreciation of the ordinary as subject matter. But the idea that art cannot also afford to be difficult, esoteric, private, would take us into the sphere of the cultural *gauleiters*. Then there is the theatre critic who will lambast a depressingly bad drawing-room comedy one week, because this is decadent bourgeois entertainment, and will find virtue next week in a no less pitiful farce because this, at least, has the "honest vulgarity" that the man in the street enjoys. This is the special pleading of criticism, the setting up of a double standard.

In the cinema, opponents of the committed approach claim that the double standard again operates. Technique, they say, is dangerously devalued: a badly made film is forgiven its faults if its approach is found sympathetic. This is difficult territory and one can only make a personal comment. Should the critic write a selling notice of a work which he believes deserves encouragement, or should he be stringent in pointing out its weaknesses? My own belief: enthusiasm is essential to the critic, and where he feels it he must communicate it. Incompetence deserves no quarter, but when the promise is unmistakable, and the effort to grapple with a subject not merely in terms of technique but of trying to understand the truth about it, then the time to start making a major issue of what went wrong is with the artist's second or third film.

LIVING IN THE DARK

Changes in critical attitudes are not merely inevitable but absolutely necessary, since art keeps alive through a constant process of re-evaluation and reassessment. It is through this process that criticism ought to stimulate creation; and it is through it that the "masterpieces" that take a clique or a critical group or a whole generation by storm are revalued for the future. There should be no final judgments in criticism.

If a new generation is emerging in film criticism in this country, some of its first stirrings may be visible in an undergraduate magazine, *Oxford Opinion* (it is now twelve years since *Sequence* came out of Oxford), in the letters that reach *Sight and Sound* from young writers or would-be writers, in more or less vague hints and indications. As might be expected, by the natural process of reaction, the new mood is directly opposed to the one that preceded it. Its allegiance is solely to the cinema; its heroes are directors also greatly admired by the younger generation of French critics (Nicholas Ray, Samuel Fuller, Douglas Sirk, Frank Tashlin); its concern is essentially with the cinema as a director's medium. The general attitudes are extremely close to those of the French critics, which are discussed in detail elsewhere in this issue; but some brief statement of them is necessary here.

Insisting that criticism as generally practised pays overmuch attention to script, story, acting performances, subject generally, they have themselves swung to the opposite extreme. All this is irrelevant, something cinema shares with [162–163] the other arts: what must be isolated is the special, elusive quality that is the cinema's own, and that can be found in the way a sequence is lit, the way space is manipulated, the way a mood can be transmitted through the choice of camera angles and the pacing of a scene.

So far, so good. Here is *Oxford Opinion* on Samuel Fuller, director of the current cult "masterpiece" *The Crimson Kimono*: "Fuller is at his best, i.e. most beautiful, when his ideas are at their least inspired—in Steel Helmet, the most exciting images came when he was producing total nonsense." On *Comanche Station*, a B-Western very favourably reviewed: "*Comanche Station* does not use its structure as a framework for ideas. In fact it has almost nothing to say . . ." On Nicholas Ray's sense of composition: "In *Party Girl* there is a shot of a girl lying with her hands dangling in a bath full of water which is red from the blood of her slashed wrists. Even by Ray standards it is outstandingly beautiful." On Anthony Mann: "He seems to me to be far worthier of a cult than John Ford; at least Mann never made a *dull* movie." And, not unexpectedly, on *Sight and Sound*: "It is only a pretty typical product of an approach to films that is fundamentally perverted . . ."

Perverted, perhaps, but not blind to what the new critical school—if that is not too pompous a phrase for it—are after. There are no good or bad subjects; affirmation is a word for boy scouts; social significance is a bore; don't expect a film to present you with sympathetic characters; don't even, if one takes it far enough, look for character; don't have any truck with anything that smacks of literature. Cinema, by this definition, means first and foremost the visual image; and the critic's response is to the excitement it can communicate.

A lot of this comes from *Cahiers du Cinéma,* along with the list of admired directors. And it is this list itself, as much as the way in which the films are discussed —don't look to these reviews for analysis, but rather for a series of slightly breathless statements—that underlines fundamental divergences of viewpoint. A letter from Ian Jarvie, one of the more articulate of the younger writers although not attached to the Oxford group, gave us a hint two years ago: "The young take odd, isolated, almost idiosyncratic lines like: preferring later Hitchcock to the pre-war vintage, enjoying the fast, tough (perhaps sadistic?) gangster film, rhapsodising over Nazi films, being bored with neo-realism and Free Cinema . . ." Nicholas Ray or Satyajit Ray? Samuel Fuller or John Ford?

Here, we are reaching the main area of disagreement. Methods of criticism are not the most significant point, since no one, however resolutely disinterested in subject matter, can avoid coming to grips sooner or later with the question of what a film is about. The limitation of the aesthetic approach, finally, is that it simply won't work: reviewing a film in terms of half a dozen striking shots, and of what their emotional impact and technical brilliance meant to you, is like walking in a fog without a torch. The mist of images swirls around, landmarks are obscured, without realising it one progresses in a series of circles. Cinema is about the human situation, not about "spatial relationships."

What the young critics mainly admire, however, are films whose relation to the business of living is in itself somewhat precarious. You cannot write, for instance, about a film like *Pather Panchali* (or *Les Quatre Cents Coups,* or *The Tokyo Story*) without concerning yourself with the way in which certain truths about the relationships between people, and the place of these people in their society, are defined on the screen. The film is not enclosed within its circumference; it is not retreating behind any protective hedge of "art." *The Crimson Kimono,* however, which is pulp literature with (oddly enough) some stabs at a social conscience, is a film which can only be admired in terms of its immediate impact. We would be a prim and dismal lot if we denied admiration to this kind of cinema, though I would not myself choose *Crimson Kimono* as an example. But we all have a way of constructing general theories on the basis of particular admirations; and a theory of criticism constructed around an appreciation of *Crimson Kimono,* or *Party Girl,* or *Written on the Wind,* seems to me a distinctly barren one.

Extreme skill, working on subject matter of whatever banality, can produce an intoxicating excitement of its own; and because the conditions of film-making are such that almost no creative worker in the cinema can be a full-time artist, we are all used to finding some of our excitement in part-time art—in seeing, that is, what the first-rate talent can do with the third-rate subject, even in watching how he can work against the subject to communicate something of his own. In the American cinema, especially, the big subject often intimidates; it is the casual glances at reality which are more telling. To pass from this, however, to a belief that the subject itself is always irrelevant is to make a preposterous leap. And, in this context, one suspects that the subjects are not as irrelevant as all that. "Run out and get yourself a positive affirmation and cinematically you're made," says one of *Oxford Opinion's* contributors about *The Grapes of Wrath.* "Fine, but don't ask me to sit through it." Well, of course, one wouldn't. But one might ask whether it is the accretion of critical opinion that has built up around *Grapes of Wrath* or the film itself that is being denigrated; whether the mistrust is of committed criticism or committed cinema.

Attitudes of this kind are, one suspects, fairly widespread. And they are understandable enough. To the generation which has grown up during the last few years, art is seen as something for kicks: films which stab at the nerves and the emotions; jazz, and the excitements surrounding it; Method acting, with its carefully sustained illusion of spontaneity. Violence on the screen is accepted as a stimulant and anything which can be labelled as slow or sentimental is suspect. Conversely, though, there does not seem to be much appreciation for the consciously cynical and sophisticated. The attitude is far from being one of disillusionment or defeat:it is more [163–164] simply a disinterest in art which does not work on one's own terms, and an inevitable belief that those terms are the only valid ones.

The gap between my own Oxford generation, the initiators of *Sequence,* and the present group of Oxford critics is only twelve years or so. But those of us who grew up during the war, when violence was perhaps too close to be also a handy stimulant, and whose attitudes to the cinema were being formulated at the time of the neo-realist experiment, of the general outburst of wartime and post-war realism, are not easily inclined to divorce art and morality or art and society in our minds. At the same time, this is the generation that made the critical discovery of Nicholas Ray, helping to get his first film, *They Live By Night,* its London screening, and that admired the "black" Hollywood cinema of the post-war years. We liked (and still like) *The Big Sleep* and *Sunset Boulevard* and *Mildred Pierce*; and not for their qualities of affirmation.

These, in any case, are the skirmishing grounds of criticism; the real battle-field is elsewhere. Criticism ought to be a perpetual questioning of values, a sub-jection of opinions and standards to pressure. And the weakness of the *Cahiers du Cinéma* school, both in its own country and among its exponents here, seems to be that it barely admits of experience which does not take place in the cinema. Its criticism too easily becomes shop talk for the initiated; its enthusiasms are self-limiting; it turns inward upon itself, so that a film's validity is assessed not in relation to the society from which it draws its material but in relation to other cinematic experiences. It is all a bit hermetic, as though its practitioners had chosen to live in the dark, emerging to blink, mole-like, at the cruel light, to sniff the chilly air, before ducking back into the darkness of another cinema.

LOOKING FOR A THEORY

"The so-called commitment argument, by forcing the antagonists to take up ex-treme and impossible positions, has confused the real issues. These are not whether the social or moral standpoint of the artist or aesthetic values are more important, but whether the cinema can find its own mode of expressing essential truth."— *Film Journal,* Melbourne.

"What we mean by 'standards' is surely nothing that can be tabulated, but rather a general approach, a willingness to assess in detail the social and moral content of a film by analysing the impact it makes upon us. And such analysis presupposes a clear conception of the way the film medium works—i.e., an aesthetic."—*Defi-nition,* London.

"The impasse in film-making and in film criticism is essentially the same as the impasse in radical thought. In both, old traditions have run their course . . . In both, vague and unsystematic new stirrings have begun."—*Film Quarterly,* San Francisco.

These three quotations, taken from recent issues of film journals published in three continents, all reflect the same dissatisfaction. Film criticism is in search of an aesthetic, which will not be found in the narrower issues of committed versus anti-committed attitudes; and, as *Film Journal* says, this debate ceases to be illumi-nating when both sides are forced into taking up extremist positions. The unattractive truth, of course, is that there is plenty of reviewing and not nearly enough criticism (and a magazine such as this one must accept its share of the guilt); that the film, because it cannot be taken home and studied like a novel or a play, invites reactions and impressions rather than sustained analysis; that there has never really been an aesthetic of the sound cinema, and that most of the standard text books are useful only for those who still believe that cinema history virtually stops with *Blackmail* and *The Blue Angel*.

The contemporary cinema is moving, and moving fairly rapidly, in half a dozen directions at once: a state of affairs which increases the bewilderment of the critic who would like to hang on to an aesthetic like a life-belt in a stormy sea. An aesthetic that can encompass Resnais' constantly moving camera and Ozu's stationary one; the anti-dramatic cinema of Zavattini and the anti-dramatic cinema of Bresson; the intellectual refinements of a film by Antonioni and the sensuous impact of one by Renoir; the stripped down cinema of Buñuel and the dressed up cinema of Bergman . . . this is a tall order. I do not believe, in any case, that the elusive, will o' the wisp "aesthetic of cinema" is suddenly going to emerge; and I can't believe that it greatly matters.

In the long run, the critic is still on his own, confronted with the work of art. His tools: his sensibility, his knowledge, his judgment, and his apparatus of values. There are fifty different ways of being a good critic, and again I do not believe it really matters—as the editors of *Definition* apparently do—that two critics "who might be expected to share certain basic values" can arrive at judgments almost diametrically opposed. "What are the differences in attitude, in presuppositions, in general view of life which can elicit conflicting responses to a single film?" enquires *Definition*. One might almost as profitably ask why two witnesses disagree about what really happened in a traffic accident.

Any theory one can formulate is of general value only in so far as it illuminates the general problem. And the main duty of criticism at present, as I see it, has little to do with the argument about form versus content, aesthetic values versus values of subject. If the film makes an impact, it does so through its style, using style here to mean the full force of the artist's personality as revealed in his work: there can be no argument here. Primarily, though, I would suggest that the critical duty is to examine the cinema in terms of its ideas, to submit these to the test of comment and discussion. That the cinema is an art is no longer in question; that battle is over and won. But if it is an art on the same plane as literature and the theatre, then it is the use of its special techniques for the expression of ideas that must make it so.

One is not asking here for an intellectual cinema, though some corrective to the present mistrust of intellect and overemphasis on emotional content might not be a bad thing. And the content of a film in terms of ideas, naturally, is as much [164–165] a matter of its attitude as its subject, since if there is no attitude there can be no idea worth speaking of. Beyond this, and beyond art, assumptions and ideas about the entertainment film are constantly changing; and the critic has here a responsibility to keep the entertainment cinema clearly in focus, to put assumptions to the challenge of analysis.

If these are the critic's jobs, what of his principles? Commitment, clearly, is inescapable, but commitment precisely to what? I find much contemporary "committed" writing needlessly didactic, too readily prepared to lay down the law and to accept, unconsidered, such Brechtian dicta as the one that the only questions which can usefully be asked are those which can be answered.

Art has an inescapable relationship to politics, but the committed critic, in practice, tries too often to narrow it down: art must be related to *his* politics, and the relationship must be recognisable. There is a suspicion of the complexities of the artistic process and a preference for the subject which lays its cards on the table. Lionel Trilling, in his book *The Liberal Imagination,* writes of "the dark and bloody crossroads where literature and politics meet. One does not go there gladly," he adds, "but nowadays it is not exactly a matter of free choice whether one does or does not go." And he proceeds to an analysis of American critical attitudes to Henry James and Theodore Dreiser, of the "fear of the intellect" which inhibited American critical responses to the complexities of James and the indulgence extended to Dreiser because "his books have the awkwardness, the chaos, the heaviness which we associate with 'reality'". Over-simplification of the kind Trilling attacks is the ambush awaiting the critic who does not question his own commitments as severely as he does those of other people.

If cinema is the art we think it is, then it is entitled to the kind of critical analysis that has traditionally been devoted to the theatre and the novel: and the principles which seem most likely to be constructively useful remain the liberal ones. The socialist may argue that liberalism is not so much a commitment as a refuge from commitment; which is to say that the liberal label has been the excuse for any amount of escape from thought. On the level at which ideas are formulated, however, both about society and about art, I believe there is at present rather more conflict and disagreement about means than about ends; and liberalism, which ought to mean allegiance to principles but a certain flexibility of mind about assumptions, a readiness to subject them to the pressure of thought, is more valuable here than the rigidity of mind which believes that once the end is agreed on the means must be predetermined. Again, one might profitably turn to Trilling: "The job of criticism would seem to be to recall liberalism to its first essential awareness of variousness and possibility, which implies the awareness of complexity and difficulty." The awareness of complexity; or the readiness, perhaps, to investigate the questions an artist chooses to ask rather than to expect him to answer those we would put to him.

In terms of our own medium: *Hiroshima mon Amour, L'Avventura, Nazarin* are concerned with questions; *Les Quatre Cents Coups,* or *The World of Apu,* have more to do with the answers. The recurring question: the difficulty of loving and the problem of communication. It would be entirely profitless to discuss which of these films is the "best"; and hardly more useful to discuss whose approach is the most valid. But a tradition of criticism—and I believe it would necessarily be a liberal one—which looked to the cinema to extend our range of ideas rather than to confirm pre-conceived assumptions, could find some of its material here. We might not be able to pull down a film aesthetic out of the clouds, but we should be able to get closer to defining the cinema's place in the world we live in. And, while we are about it, we might try to rescue the word "liberal" from its present implications of indecision and inertia.   [*165*]

    1.   Do you agree with Miss Houston that it is possible for a critic to judge whether or not a point of view is well-expressed even when he doesn't like it?

2. What should the place of commitment be, according to Miss Houston? Do you agree?

3. Is Miss Houston convincing in her argument against totally aesthetic criticism?

4. How clear and satisfactory is the position that Miss Houston takes?

THE NEW HOLLYWOOD: MYTH AND ANTI-MYTH

Robert Brustein

It must now be apparent even to the most indifferent movie-goer that something unusual has recently been happening on the screen. Although for years he has been accustomed to suspending his cares in the soft black impersonal lap of his neighborhood auditorium, the spectator is now more frequently jolted than caressed by many of the films he sees—they seem especially designed to disturb his tranquility. The celluloid is losing its sharpness of focus and assuming the murkier tones hitherto associated with European realism. The settings are changing from plushy modern apartments atop imposing skyscrapers to shanty-town slums in rotting southern or northern towns. The costumes, apparently acquired no longer from Mainbocher but from the surplus stores of the Salvation Army, hang on the actors as dashingly as skivvies on a scarecrow.

At the same time, the glamor queen is unpinning her hair, exposing her faulty skin and puffy eyes, and reverting to the untutored accents of her original speech; the matinee idol is yielding before a tousled, scratching, stammering, frequently unhandsome average Joe as distinguished as you or I; and the extras are

Currently Dean of the Yale Drama School, ROBERT BRUSTEIN was for many years drama critic for *The New Republic*. He has published three books: *Seasons of Discontent, The Theatre of Revolt,* and *The Third Theatre*.

being recruited not from Central Casting but from taverns and corner drugstores. The heyday of Hollywood glamor is drawing to a close, hastened by catcalls from the wings. Behind the scenes one can almost hear the fading tread of the cosmeticians, the speech teachers, and the beauty consultants—that vast army of unfamiliar names inscribed on a film's opening credits—who have hitherto played so large a part in creating "screen magic."

It would seem, then, that Hollywood is making room among its old formulas for radical new developments; it would seem also that the film-makers are beginning to assume attitudes toward their products which, twenty years ago, they would have considered visionary and impractical. Certainly, pictures like *On the Waterfront, A Hatful of Rain, Wild Is the Wind, The Goddess, Come Back Little Sheba, Baby Doll, The Rose Tattoo, The Long Hot Summer, Hot Spell* (and countless others) embody, whatever their actual merits, a conscious artiness at which producers would formerly have shivered.

Is it possible that our celebrated dream factory has abandoned its artificial merchandise for the complex stuff of life? Is the industry undertaking to agitate the populace with harsh truths rather than lull them asleep with comforting fantasies? Is Hollywood, in short, now prepared to subsidize works of art? In order to answer these questions, it is necessary to recall the conditions that brought these new films into being.

After the war, of course, television absconded with a large portion of the audience the movies once held captive. Since millions of Americans, sitting in a drugged stupor before their sets, became deaf to the call of the box office, the movie moguls began to conclude that the old formulas were no longer sufficient. Only two classes of movie-goers remained faithful, and even these were beginning to desert: the teen-agers, who used the balconies of movie theaters as trysting places, and the inveterate celluloid-eaters, who preferred foreign films and the occasional [23–24] art movie. The first attempt to woo back the deserters was the technique of the giant screen. CinemaScope, VistaVision, Todd-AO, Cinerama, and stereophonic sound were originally designed to awaken the spectator to the limitations of TV's constricted universe. The giant screen tried to demonstrate that the price the spectator paid for entertainment in his own home was to be eternally trapped in his own domestic troubles. This was a discerning judgment. At the time that the new movie techniques were introduced, the predominant video form was the domestic drama, only a cut above soap opera. The prophet of the new drama was Paddy Chayefsky, and its new heroes were middle-aged men in quest of romance, loveless butchers, nervous white-collar workers, and dissatisfied wives. Even the "adult western" soon developed into a family drama where a hero in a cowboy suit set about solving a minor domestic crisis not too far removed from the problems of the viewer.

The giant screen, on the other hand, emphasized the boundless dimensions available to Hollywood. Besides exulting in their leisurely tempo, the movies could stretch themselves in limitless space. While the TV viewer sweated and gasped for air in sympathy with a quiz contestant in a coffin-like isolation booth (the authentic symbol of TV's world), Todd-AO took the movie-goer for a three-hour trip around the world.

But rather than offer anything new in the way of material, the giant screen attempted primarily to preserve and enhance the old formulas. The movie-makers were trying to feed a traditional public appetite that to a large extent no longer existed: the craving for colossal screen glamor. The old matinee idols, despite their graying hair and sagging jowls, were still expected to attract admiration from the spectator through the time-worn methods: their extraordinary good looks, their superhuman deeds, and their freedom from petty human complaints. On the assumption that few would dispute the heroic proportions of a man over thirty feet tall, these qualities were now exaggerated by the hero's enormous size. On the giant screen, Gary Cooper grew lankier, Jayne Mansfield bosomier, and Richard Widmark meaner, while the cleft in Kirk Douglas' chin enlarged into a minor Grand Canyon. It was Hollywood's last attempt to exploit America's old hunger for giantism: Paul Bunyan was breaking the plains on a horse as big as a mountain, its hoofbeats magnified a thousandfold by the magic of stereophonic sound.

Although the giant screen had a few big successes and recaptured a few of the deserters, it could not hold them past the initial novelty. The public, preferring claustrophobia to agorophobia, remained largely apathetic, still immobilized before their sets. What is worse, even the faithful began to desert. The teen-age girls might identify with Audrey Hepburn as Gary Cooper made [24–25] love to her under a table, but the teen-age boys were finding it hard to identify with a hero who looked old enough to be their grandfather. Similarly, the more discerning film-goers were generally cold, in some cases positively antagonistic, to the lure of the giant screen. The movie-makers decided to surrender their claim to the confirmed TV addicts and try to consolidate their position with the audience that still remained. They cast around for a new form which might be acceptable to all their patrons, and discovered—"realism."

It was, of course, an extremely belated discovery; realism, in various guises, had been flourishing on European and American stages for over a hundred years. But, considering Hollywood's traditional reluctance to agitate anybody, it was inevitable that the movie-makers would turn to the most inoffensive type. Rather than the Ibsenite form which rigorously exposed the cant, hypocrisy, fraud, and humbug beneath the respectable appearance, Hollywood's realism was to become more akin to Zola naturalism—dedicated to a purely surface authenticity.

The postwar Italian movies of deSica and Rossellini, concerned with poverty-stricken characters of the lower class and focusing on the unpleasant physical conditions of Italian city life, had caught the eye of the critics and collected a vigorous following among intelligent film-goers. When Paddy Chayefsky turned an inexpensive film like *Marty* into a surprising commercial success by reproducing the atmosphere (and junking the moral concerns) of Italian movies, Hollywood had to conclude that television had conditioned the American public to commonplace reality. It was becoming clear that the aimless and boring lives of people like Bronx drugstore cowboys could—if seasoned generously enough with sentimentality—attract box-office gold. Hollywood, in consequence, ever alert to changes in mass taste, began to retool in preparation for the new form.

The first move was a radical change in personnel: Hollywood went on an exhaustive quest for new experts. Zola realism, for a number of years, has been the artistic domain of the New York theater, so it was inevitably to the New York theater artist that the industry turned. Directors especially were in great demand. Elia Kazan was provided by Warner Brothers with his own production unit and absolute freedom in choosing his subjects, casts, and associates; Sidney Lumet and Delbert Mann were kidnaped from TV; Joshua Logan was periodically imported to energize such films as *Bus Stop* and *Sayonara*; even fledgling directors like Martin Ritt (*Edge of the City, The Long Hot Summer*) and Daniel Mann (*Come Back Little Sheba, Hot Spell*), with only a few Broadway shows to their credit, were whisked to Hollywood, where they are now afforded a respect they never enjoyed in New York.

Along with the directors came their collaborators—Broadway dramatists, television writers, and novelists. The plays of Tennessee Williams, William Inge, Robert Anderson, and Michael Gazzo, for example, are finding their way to the screen, sometimes transferred by the author, sometimes by an able adapter, frequently with surprising fidelity. In mounting competition over literary material, studios are purchasing off-Broadway plays, TV scripts, and even as yet unpublished novels. If, in the 'thirties and 'forties, William Faulkner and Aldous Huxley could write films in complete anonymity, today Tennessee Williams and Paddy Chayefsky draw almost as large an audience as the star.

Inevitably, a whole new crop of young stars was introduced as well, many of them [25–26] trained in New York naturalistic theater schools like the Actors Studio and already familiar to Broadway and television audiences. Marlon Brando, Anthony Perkins, Paul Newman, Ernest Borgnine, Anthony Quinn, Anthony Franciosa, Don Murray, Steven Hill, and Ben Gazzara have become the matinee idols of the 'fifties, with actresses like Eva Marie Saint, Julie Harris, Barbara Bel Geddes, Anna Magnani, Shirley Booth, Kim Stanley, and Carroll Baker as their romantic counterparts. Few of these people are notable for their outstanding good looks, for there is an increasing tendency to deglamorize the Hollywood star. The new actors attract attention by their intensity of feeling, rather than by physical attractiveness, and have developed a style of acting which even some of the older stars are beginning to adopt.

In other words, New Yorkers have begun to infiltrate the film industry and to influence it with many of the convictions of the Broadway stage, including a traditional distaste for the old Hollywood products. In the past, Broadway's antagonism toward Hollywood took the form of moralistic condemnations and satiric attacks. The Group Theatre, that dynamic production unit which flourished in the 'thirties and which reluctantly fed so many of its associates into the films, always regarded Hollywood as Inferno and the Hollywood producer as a vulgar Mephistopheles who purchased the soul of the serious artist and degraded his talent with attractive offers of money, fame, swimming pools, and the love of beautiful women. Elia Kazan attacked, in an article, the "manufactured entertainment" of the movies, while Clifford Odets took his revenge on the film colony for enticing him from the stage with a venomous play (*The Big Knife*) exposing Hollywood's corruption, artificiality, and acquisitiveness. To Broadway, Hollywood has traditionally been a land of phony dreams created of tinsel and cotton candy where the real questions of existence are generally ignored.   [26–27]

Today, however, instead of overtly attacking the industry, the Broadway people are covertly attempting to reform it from the inside. They now constitute a highly influential unit within the larger circle of Hollywood movie-making. Such is

Hollywood's desperation over declining receipts that the studios (and banks) are willing to subsidize the new artist, provide them with independent companies, and distribute their pictures. The result is that Hollywood has been underwriting the destruction of its old forms. Most of the conventions of the realistic film seem to have been created almost in purposeful contrast to the conventions of the traditional Hollywood romance. Consistent with their own tradition ("real," in the Broadway lexicon, has generally been a synonym for "seamy"), the realistic film-makers are dedicating themselves to the exposure of the unsavory truth behind the manufactured dream.

With suggestions of incest in *Desire Under the Elms,* sadism in *Baby Doll,* adultery in *God's Little Acre,* and homosexuality in *The Strange One,* the realistic movie works manifold variations on conventional sexual themes. Similarly, violence becomes more open and frequent. A brawny hero in a Hollywood epic by John Ford might batter another for hours with chairs, sticks, stones, and broken bottles and emerge from the melee with no more than an attractive little bruise on the cheek. When Marlon Brando is beaten up by labor racketeers in *On the Waterfront,* he streams cascades of blood from open wounds, loses a few of his teeth, and suffers visibly from broken bones.

Not only does the realistic film stand in purposeful contrast to romantic films, but it sometimes even derives its effects by playing on the spectator's memory of the old Hollywood myths. Marilyn Monroe's performance in *Bus Stop,* for example, in which she played a dissipated, anemic, peroxide-blonde "chantoosy," has significance primarily if one remembers her in more well-groomed roles—say, as the glamorous idiot of *Gentlemen Prefer Blondes.* Similarly, the dilapidated, weather-stained Mississippi mansion used in *Baby Doll* calls to mind, and even comments on, the movie magnificence of Tara's enormous halls and curving staircases in *Gone With the Wind.* The dirt and the cobwebs, and the sex and the violence, of the realistic film serve a partial debunking function. They expose the glittering and hyperbolic lies of Hollywood glamor.

This is further emphasized by the techniques of the genre. In contrast to the technical virtuosity of the CinemaScope epic, the realistic film is singular for the modesty of its presentational devices. It is frequently shot in black and white and designed for projection on the smaller, conventional screen. The director, furthermore, prefers to work in actual locales rather than on the more artificial studio lots—many movie actors today spend more time in Arkansas, Mississippi, and New York than they do in Hollywood. Similarly, like the realistic play the realistic film employs interiors more often than exteriors. Despite the hypothetical advantage of the movies over the stage in its flexibility of locale, the new film is generally content to keep its hero fixed in and around the four walls of his house.

The character of the hero undergoes a corresponding change. The old matinee idols were groomed as romantic leading men, at pains to exhibit their charms in the most attractive possible manner; the new idols are less concerned with their persons than with their agonized spirits. If Clark Gable and Cary Grant could set a million female hearts aflutter merely by exposing their teeth, Anthony Quinn and Ben Gazzara struggle—lest they violate some secret agreement [27–28]—never to smile. Glowering, slumping, and scowling, the new actors exert their appeal not through graceful dash but through sullen bad humor. Furthermore, if the hero of the romantic film is accustomed to performing mighty deeds, usually in an open-air setting, the realistic hero is more often victimized by the confining world in which he lives. And he is trapped not only in the interior of his world but in the interior of his soul. Rather than holding an enemy at bay with a couple of loaded pistols, he is himself held at bay by the power of his neurosis. . . .   [28]

And yet, one must ask just how close to the average spectator's situation the material of these films really is. Undoubtedly, a drug addict and a nymphomaniac seem more "real" to us than a cowboy, a big game hunter, or a ballroom dancer; but why, when America has the largest middle-class population in the world (when, in one sense, it sees itself as entirely middle class), are its predominant movie heroes dock workers, motorcyclists, juvenile delinquents, prostitutes, butchers, Southern farmers, seamen, and drifters, the economically and the emotionally dispossessed?

For the adult audience, I think, these heroes are interesting precisely because of their *distance* from everyday life. Americans can now afford to be indulgent toward grubbiness and poverty because they have been enjoying over the past ten years a prosperity unparalleled in their history. Having achieved what Hollywood once presented as the comfortable illusion—the well-stocked refrigerator, the well-furnished apartment, and the gleaming new car—the great middle of the American population can now regard the torn T-shirt, the dirty fingernails, and the cluttered sink as the "truth about existence." What once was immediate and painful can now be viewed with cheerful equanimity because, although it *seems* close and real, it is becoming remote from our experience. For the adult audience, in other words, the anti-myth is in the process of becoming the myth, its images almost as exotic as Hollywood's old close-ups of spotless clothes and faultless features.

For the adolescent audience, on the other hand, the appeal of the realistic film is immediate and direct. It is no accident that, although movie heroes like Humphrey Bogart and Jimmy Stewart never seemed to have any families and were remote even from their women, the heroes of the realistic film are invariably involved in conflicts with their parents and hang on to their girls for dear life. (Even films like *A Hatful of Rain* and *The Goddess,* with supposedly "adult" content, derive their action and motivation from parent-child conflicts.) For his relations with his parents provide the crucial dilemma of the adolescent's life. It is hardly [30–31] a coincidence that actors like Marlon Brando, Jimmy Dean, and Anthony Perkins— the mainstays of the realistic film—have become the central heroes of adolescent culture, or that teen-age images like Natalie Wood, Julie Harris, and Susan Strasberg (rather than mature women of the type represented by, say Norma Shearer and Greta Garbo) are generally the new heroines. The huge blow-up of Carroll Baker in *Baby Doll* lying in a crib and sucking her thumb is a more articulate symbol of the new genre than its creators know.

What has happened is that Hollywood, resigned to the fact that the majority of its audience is now composed of people between the ages of fifteen and twenty, has yielded to the teen-ager's demand to see himself and his problems depicted. Sometimes this results in an amalgamation of realism and adolescent drama —Andy Hardy is provided with a switchblade. Films like *Rebel Without a Cause,*

East of Eden, The Blackboard Jungle, The Wild One, and *High School Confidential* employ realistic techniques to depict the delinquent adolescent's troubled relations with his parents, his girl, or his gang. But Zola realism, whether directly aimed at adolescents or not, is admirably suited to mirror the problems of the young because it offers a youthful, rather than a mature, picture of the world. Like the hero of the realistic film, the adolescent feels himself a victim of forces beyond his control. Like this hero, he feels manipulated against his will into situations he does not desire and traumatized by a world he never made. In limiting its world to the domestic scene, the realistic movie provides the adolescent with scenes that he can recognize. In centering on delinquents, addicts, and escapists, it gives him a perfect expression for his own feelings of rebellion and isolation.

Needless to say, such a form has no more claim to art than a comic book— realism has become another peg on which Hollywood hangs its commercial hat. Although its traditions are auspicious enough, the realistic film has now settled into rigid formulas, no more true to life than the formulas of the Western and a good deal more restricting to the imagination. The Broadway people who come to Hollywood are simply swapping their own conventions for the conventions of the romantic film. And though these conventions are more sophisticated and in some cases (the films of Elia Kazan) more expertly controlled, they are really as ingratiating, as false, and as far removed from the moral concerns of art as the old. Films of high quality do occasionally emerge from Hollywood: John Huston's early films were first-rate and Stanley Kubrick promises to be an authentic movie talent if his anger holds out. But such films are infrequent, seldom box-office successes, and never written to formulas. For films of quality proceed not from the demands of a mass audience but from the painful prodding of an artist's conscience. They do not creep along the surface of the skin, but journey deep into the recesses of the soul.   [*31*]

1. Mr. Brustein's article was written about films of the 50's. How well do his generalizations apply to the 60's?

2. Mr. Brustein asks why middle-class viewers like films about "the economically and the emotionally dispossessed." Do you agree with his answers?

3. Who seem to have replaced Brando, James Dean, and Natalie Wood as teen heroes? What shift in audience values is suggested by these replacements?

4. Compare this article with the essay by Prof. Panofsky. Which audience expectations, listed by Panofsky, does Brustein find unfulfilled in contemporary films? What can you infer from this about today's audiences, contemporary Hollywood, the relationship between film and society?

5. How does this essay relate to *The Graduate? Bonnie and Clyde? Blow-Up?*

THE GANGSTER
AS TRAGIC HERO

Robert Warshow

America, as a social and political organization, is committed to a cheerful view of life. It could not be otherwise. The sense of tragedy is a luxury of aristocratic societies, where the fate of the individual is not conceived of as having a direct and legitimate political importance, being determined by a fixed and supra-political—that is, non-controversial—moral order or fate. Modern equalitarian societies, however, whether democratic or authoritarian in their political forms, always base themselves on the claim that they are making life happier; the avowed function of the modern state, at least in its ultimate terms, is not only to regulate social relations, but also to determine the quality and the possibilities of human life in general. Happiness thus becomes the chief political issue—in a sense, the only political issue—and for that reason it can never be treated as an issue at all. If an American or a Russian is unhappy, it implies a certain reprobation of his society, and therefore, by a logic of which we can all recognize the necessity, it becomes an obligation of citizenship to be cheerful; if the authorities find it necessary, the citizen may even be compelled to make a public display of his cheerfulness on important [127–128] occasions, just as he may be conscripted into the army in time of war.

Naturally, this civic responsibility rests most strongly upon the organs of mass culture. The individual citizen may still be permitted his private unhappiness so long as it does not take on political significance, the extent of this tolerance being determined by how large an area of private life the society can accommodate. But every production of mass culture is a public act and must conform with accepted

At his early death in 1955, ROBERT WARSHOW was widely regarded as one of America's most talented film critics. He was an editor of *Commentary,* to which he contributed pieces on books and film.

From *The Immediate Experience.* New York, 1962. Reprinted by permission of Paul Warshow.

notions of the public good. Nobody seriously questions the principle that it is the function of mass culture to maintain public morale, and certainly nobody in the mass audience objects to having his morale maintained.[1] At a time when the normal condition of the citizen is a state of anxiety, euphoria spreads over our culture like the broad smile of an idiot. In terms of attitudes towards life, there is very little difference between a "happy" movie like *Good News*, which ignores death and suffering, and a "sad" movie like *A Tree Grows in Brooklyn*, which uses death and suffering as incidents in the service of a higher optimism.

But, whatever its effectiveness as a source of consolation and a means of pressure for maintaining "positive" social attitudes, this optimism is fundamentally satisfying to no one, not even to those who would be most disoriented without its support. Even within the area of mass culture, there always exists a current of opposition, seeking to express by whatever [128–129] means are available to it that sense of desperation and inevitable failure which optimism itself helps to create. Most often, this opposition is confined to rudimentary or semi-literate forms: in mob politics and journalism, for example, or in certain kinds of religious enthusiasm. When it does enter the field of art, it is likely to be disguised or attenuated: in an unspecific form of expression like jazz, in the basically harmless nihilism of the Marx Brothers, in the continually reasserted strain of hopelessness that often seems to be the real meaning of the soap opera. The gangster film is remarkable in that it fills the need for disguise (though not sufficiently to avoid arousing uneasiness) without requiring any serious distortion. From its beginnings, it has been a consistent and astonishingly complete presentation of the modern sense of tragedy.[2]

In its initial character, the gangster film is simply one example of the movies' constant tendency to create fixed dramatic patterns that can be repeated indefinitely with a reasonable expectation of profit. One gangster film follows another as one musical or one Western follows another. But this rigidity is not necessarily opposed to the requirements of art. There have been very successful types of art in the past which developed such specific and detailed conventions as almost to make individual examples of the type interchangeable. This is true, for example, of Elizabethan revenge tragedy and Restoration comedy.

For such a type to be successful means that its conventions [129–130] have imposed themselves upon the general consciousness and become the accepted vehicles of a particular set of attitudes and a particular aesthetic effect. One goes to any individual example of the type with very definite expectations, and originality is to be welcomed only in the degree that it intensifies the expected experience without fundamentally altering it. Moreover, the relationship between the conven-

---

[1] In her testimony before the House Committee on Un-American Activities, Mrs. Leila Rogers said that the movie *None But the Lonely Heart* was un-American because it was gloomy. Like so much else that was said during the unhappy investigation of Hollywood, this statement was at once stupid and illuminating. One knew immediately what Mrs. Rogers was talking about; she had simply been insensitive enough to carry her philistinism to its conclusion.

[2] Efforts have been made from time to time to bring the gangster film into line with the prevailing opitimism and social constructiveness of our culture; *Kiss of Death* is a recent example. These efforts are usually unsuccessful; the reasons for their lack of success are interesting in themselves, but I shall not be able to discuss them here.

tions which go to make up such a type and the real experience of its audience or the real facts of whatever situation it pretends to describe is of only secondary importance and does not determine its aesthetic force. It is only in an ultimate sense that the type appeals to its audience's experience of reality; much more immediately, it appeals to previous experience of the type itself: it creates its own field of reference.

Thus the importance of the gangster film, and the nature and intensity of its emotional and aesthetic impact, cannot be measured in terms of the place of the gangster himself or the importance of the problem of crime in American life. Those European movie-goers who think there is a gangster on every corner in New York are certainly deceived, but defenders of the "positive" side of American culture are equally deceived if they think it relevant to point out that most Americans have never seen a gangster. What matters is that the experience of the gangster *as an experience of art* is universal to Americans. There is almost nothing we understand better or react to more readily or with quicker intelligence. The Western film, though it seems never to diminish in popularity, is for most of us no more than the folklore of the past, familiar and understandable only because it has been repeated so often. The gangster film comes much closer. In ways that we do not easily or willingly define, the gangster speaks for us, expressing that part of the American psyche which rejects the qualities and the demands of modern life, which rejects "Americanism" itself.   [130–131]

The gangster is the man of the city, with the city's language and knowledge, with its queer and dishonest skills and its terrible daring, carrying his life in his hands like a placard, like a club. For everyone else, there is at least the theoretical possibility of another world—in that happier American culture which the gangster denies, the city does not really exist; it is only a more crowded and more brightly lit country—but for the gangster there is only the city; he must inhabit it in order to personify it: not the real city, but that dangerous and sad city of the imagination which is so much more important, which is the modern world. And the gangster—though there are real gangsters—is also, and primarily, a creature of the imagination. The real city, one might say, produces only criminals; the imaginary city produces the gangster: he is what we want to be and what we are afraid we may become.

Thrown into the crowd without background or advantages, with only those ambiguous skills which the rest of us—the real people of the real city—can only pretend to have, the gangster is required to make his way, to make his life and impose it on others. Usually, when we come upon him, he has already made his choice or the choice has already been made for him, it doesn't matter which: we are not permitted to ask whether at some point he could have chosen to be something else than what he is.

The gangster's activity is actually a form of rational enterprise, involving fairly definite goals and various techniques for achieving them. But this rationality is usually no more than a vague background; we know, perhaps, that the gangster sells liquor or that he operates a numbers racket; often we are not given even that much information. So his activity becomes a kind of pure criminality: he hurts people. Certainly our response to the gangster film is most consistently and most universally a response to sadism; we gain the double satisfaction of participating vicariously in the gangster's [131-132] sadism and then seeing it turned against the gangster himself.

But on another level the quality of irrational brutality and the quality of rational enterprise become one. Since we do not see the rational and routine aspects of the gangster's behavior, the practice of brutality—the quality of unmixed criminality—becomes the totality of his career. At the same time, we are always conscious that the whole meaning of this career is a drive for success: the typical gangster film presents a steady upward progress followed by a very precipitate fall. Thus brutality itself becomes at once the means to success and the content of success—a success that is defined in its most general terms, not as accomplishment or specific gain, but simply as the unlimited possibility of aggression. (In the same way, film presentations of businessmen tend to make it appear that they achieve their success by talking on the telephone and holding conferences and that success *is* talking on the telephone and holding conferences.)

From this point of view, the initial contact between the film and its audience is an agreed conception of human life: that man is a being with the possibilities of success or failure. This principle, too, belongs to the city; one must emerge from the crowd or else one is nothing. On that basis the necessity of the action is established, and it progresses by inalterable paths to the point where the gangster lies dead and the principle has been modified: there is really only one possibility—failure. The final meaning of the city is anonymity and death.

In the opening scene of *Scarface,* we are shown a successful man; we know he is successful because he has just given a party of opulent proportions and because he is called Big Louie. Through some monstrous lack of caution, he permits himself to be alone for a few moments. We understand from this immediately that he is about to be killed. No convention [132-133] of the gangster film is more strongly established than this: it is dangerous to be alone. And yet the very conditions of success make it impossible not to be alone, for success is always the establishment of an *individual* pre-eminence that must be imposed on others, in whom it automatically arouses hatred; the successful man is an outlaw. The gangster's whole life is an effort to assert himself as an individual, to draw himself out of the crowd, and he always dies *because* he is an individual; the final bullet thrusts him back, makes him, after all, a failure. "Mother of God," says the dying Little Caesar, "is this the end of Rico?"—speaking of himself thus in the third person because what has been brought low is not the undifferentiated *man,* but the individual with a name, the gangster, the success; even to himself he is a creature of the imagination. (T. S. Eliot has pointed out that a number of Shakespeare's tragic heroes have this trick of looking at themselves dramatically; their true identity, the thing that is destroyed when they die, is something outside themselves—not a man, but a style of life, a kind of meaning.)

At bottom, the gangster is doomed because he is under the obligation to succeed, not because the means he employs are unlawful. In the deeper layers of the modern consciousness, *all* means are unlawful, every attempt to succeed is an act of aggression, leaving one alone and guilty and defenseless among enemies: one is *punished* for success. This is our intolerable dilemma: that failure is a kind of death and success is evil and dangerous, is—ultimately—impossible. The effect of the gangster film is to embody this dilemma in the person of the gangster and resolve it by his death. The dilemma is resolved because it is *his* death, not ours. We are safe; for the moment, we can acquiesce in our failure, we can choose to fail.   [*133*]

1. Do you agree with Warshow's opening generalizations? What qualifications would you make?

2. Warshow's essay was originally published in 1948. Do you think his analysis of the relationship between mass culture and private life is still accurate?

THEORY APPLIED

THE GRADUATE

CUM LAUDE

Stanley Kauffmann

Happy news. Mike Nichols' second film, *The Graduate,* proves that he is a genuine film director—one to be admired and concerned about. It also marks the screen debut, in the title role, of Dustin Hoffman, a young actor already known in the theatre as an exceptional talent, who here increases his reputation. Also, after many months of prattle about the "new" American film (mostly occasioned by the overrated *Bonnie and Clyde*), *The Graduate* gives substance to the contention that American films are coming of age—of our age.

The screenplay, based on a novel by Charles Webb, was written by Calder Willingham and Buck Henry. The latter, like Nichols, is an experienced satiric performer. (Henry appears in the picture as a hotel clerk.) The dialogue is sharp, hip without rupturing itself in the effort, often moving, and frequently funny except for a few obtrusive gag lines. The story is about a young cop-out who—for well-dramatized reasons—cops at least partially in again.

Ben is a bright college graduate who returns to his wealthy parents' Hollywood home and flops—on his bed, on the rubber raft in the pool. Politely and dispassionately, he declines the options thrust at him by barbecue-pit society. The bored wife of his father's law partner seduces him. Ben is increasingly uncomfortable in the continuing affair, for moral reasons of an unpuritanical kind. (The bedroom scene in which Ben tries to get her to *talk* to him is a jewel.) The woman's daughter comes home from college, and against the mother's wishes, Ben takes her out. He falls in love with the girl—which is predictable but entirely credible. He is

STANLEY KAUFFMANN is film critic and Associate Literary Editor for *The New Republic*. He has also been drama critic for *The New York Times* and a visiting professor at Yale. He publishes literary criticism in a variety of magazines and has collected his film criticism in *A World on Film*.

From *The New Republic,* December 23, 1967. Reprinted by permission of *The New Republic,* © 1967, Harrison-Blaine of New Jersey, Inc.

blackmailed into telling her about his affair with her mother and, in revulsion, the girl flees—back to Berkeley. Ben follows, hangs about the campus, almost gets her to marry him, loses her (through her father's interference), pursues her, and finally gets her. For once, a happy ending makes *us* feel happy.

To dispose at once of the tedious subject of frankness, I note that some of the language and bedroom details push that frontier (in American films) considerably ahead, but it is all so appropriate that it never has the slightest smack of daring, let alone opportunism. What is truly daring, and therefore refreshing, is the film's moral stance. Its acceptance of the fact that a young man might have an affair with a woman and still marry her daughter (a situation not exactly unheard of in America although not previously seen in American films) is part of the film's fundamental insistence: that life, today, in our world, is not worth living unless one can *prove* it day-by-day, by values that ring true day-by-day. Moral attitudes, far from relaxing, are getting stricter and stricter, and many of the shoddy moralistic acceptances that dictated mindless actions for decades are now being fiercely questioned. Ben is neither a laggard nor a lecher; he is, in the healthiest sense, a moralist—he wants to know the value of what he is doing. He does not rush into the affair with the mother out of any social rote of "scoring" any more than he avoids the daughter—because he has slept with her mother—out of any social rote of taboo. (In fact, although he is male and eventually succumbs, he sees the older woman's advances as a syndrome of a suspect society.) And the sexual dynamics of the story propels Ben past the sexual sphere; it forces him to assess and locate himself in *every* aspect.

Sheerly in terms of moral revolution, all this will seem pretty commonplace to readers of contemporary American fiction. But we are dealing here with an art form that, because of its inescapable broad-based appeal, follows well behind the front lines of moral exploration. In America it follows less closely than in some other countries, not because American audiences are necessarily less sophisticated than others (although they *are* less sophisticated than, say, Swedish audiences) but because the great expense of American production encourages a producer to cast the widest net possible. None of this is an apology for the film medium, it is a fact of the film's existence; one might as sensibly apologize for painting because it cannot be seen simultaneously by millions the way a film can. Thus the arrival of *The Graduate* can be viewed two ways. First, it is an index of moral change in a substantial segment of the American public, at least of an awakening of some doubts about past acceptances. Second, it is irrelevant that these changes are arriving in film a decade or two decades or a half century after the other arts, because their statement in film makes them intrinsically new and unique. If arts have textural differences and are not simply different envelopes for the same contents, then the *way* in which *The Graduate* affects us makes it quite a different work from the original novel (which I have not read) and from all the dozens of novels of moral disruption and exploration in recent years. Recently an Italian literary critic and teacher deplored to me the adulation of young people for films, saying that the "messages" they get from Bergman and Antonioni and Godard were stated by the novel and even the drama thirty or forty years ago. I tried (unsuccessfully) to point out that this is not really true: that if art as art has any validity at all, then the film's peculiar sensory avenues were giving those "old" insights a being they could not otherwise have.

This brings us to the central artist of this enterprise, Mike Nichols. In his first picture *Who's Afraid of Virginia Woolf?*, Nichols was shackled by a famous play and by the two powerhouse stars of our time; but considering these handicaps, he did a creditable job, particularly with his actors. In *The Graduate*, uninhibited by the need to reproduce a Broadway hit and with freedom to select his cast, he has moved fully into film. He is perceptive, imaginative, witty; he has a shrewd eye, both for beauty and for visual comment; he knows how to compose and to juxtapose; he has an innate sense of the manifold ways in which film can be better than *he* is and therefore how good he can be *through* it—including the powers of expansion and ellipsis.

From the very first moment, Nichols sets the key. We see Ben's face, large and absolutely alone. The camera pulls back, we see that he is in an airliner and a voice tells us that it is approaching Los Angeles; but Ben has been set for us as *alone*. We follow him through the air terminal, and he seems just as completely, even comfortably isolated in the crowd as he does later, in a scuba suit at the bottom of his family's swimming-pool, when he is huddling contentedly in an underwater corner while his twenty-first birthday party is being bulled along by his father up above.

Nichols understands sound. The device of overlapping is somewhat overused (beginning the dialogue of the next scene under the end of the present scene), but in general this effect adds to the dissolution of clock time, creating a more subjective time. Nichols' use of non-verbal sound (something like Antonioni's) does a good deal to fix subliminally the cultural locus. For instance, a jet plane swooshes overhead—unremarked—as the married woman first invites Ben into her house. [22]

In *Virginia Woolf* I thought I saw some influence of Kurosawa; I think so again here, particularly in such sequences as Ben's welcome-home party where the camera keeps close to Ben, panning with him as he weaves through the crowd, moving to another face only when Ben encounters it, as if Ben's attention controlled the camera's. As with Kurosawa, the effect is balletic; it seeks out quintessential rhythms in commonplace actions.

On the negative side, I disliked Nichols' recurrent affection for the splatter of headlights and sunspots on his lens; and his hang-up with a slightly heavy Godardian irony through objects. (The camera holds on a third-rate painting of a clown after the mistress walks out of the shot. When the girl leaves Ben in front of the monkey cage at the San Francisco zoo, the camera, too luckily, catches the sign on the cage: Do Not Tease.) And a couple of times Nichols puts his camera in places that merely make us aware of his cleverness in putting it there: inside the scuba helmet, inside an empty hotel-room closet looking past the hangers.

But the influences I have cited (there are others) only show that Nichols is alive, hungry, properly ambitious; the defects only show that he is not yet entirely sure of himself. Together, these matters show him still feeling his way toward a whole style of his own. What is important is his extraordinary basic talent: humane, deft, exuberant. And I want to make much of his ability to direct actors, a factor generally overlooked in appraising film directors. (Some famous directors—Hitchcock, for example—can do nothing with actors. They get what the actor can supply on his own. Sometimes—again like Hitchcock—these directors are not even aware of bad performances.) He has helped Anne Bancroft to a quiet, strong portrayal of the mistress, bitter and pitiful. With acuteness he has cast Elizabeth Wilson, a sensitive comedienne, as Ben's mother. From the very pretty Katharine Ross, Ben's girl, Nichols has got a performance of sweetness, dignity, and a compassion that is simply engulfing. Only William Daniels, as Ben's father, made me a bit uneasy. His WASP caricature (he did a younger version in *Two for the Road*) is already becoming a staple item.

In the leading role, Nichols had the sense and the courage to cast Dustin Hoffman, unknown (to the screen) and unhandsome. Hoffman's face in itself is a proof of change in American films; it is hard to imagine him in leading roles a decade ago. How unimportant, how *interesting* this quickly becomes, because Hoffman is one of the best actors of his generation, subtle, vital, and accurate. Certainly he is the best American film comedian since Jack Lemmon, and, as theatregoers know, he has a much wider range than Lemmon. (For instance, he was fine as a crabby, fortyish, 19th-century Russian clerk in Ronald Ribman's play *Journey of the Fifth Horse*.)

With tact and lovely understanding, Nichols and Hoffman and Miss Ross—all three—show us how this boy and girl fall into a new kind of love; a love based on recognition of identical loneliness on their side of a generational gap, a gap which —never mind how sillily it is often exploited in politics and pop culture—irrefutably exists. When her father is, understandably, enraged at the news of his wife's affair with his prospective son-in-law and hustles the girl off into another marriage, Ben's almost insane refusal to let her go is his refusal to let go of the one reality he has found in a world that otherwise exists behind a pane of glass. The cinema metaphors of the chase after the girl—the endless driving, the jumping in and out of his sports car, even his eventual running [37–38] out of gas—have perhaps too much Keaton about them; they make the film rise too close to the surface of mere physicality; but at least the urgency never flags. At the wedding, when he finds it—and of course it is in an ultra-modern church—there is a dubious hint of crucifixion as Ben flings his outspread arms against the (literal) pane of glass that separates him from life (the girl); but this is redeemed a minute later when, with the girl, he grabs a large cross, swings it savagely to stave off pursuers, then jams it through the handles of the front doors to lock the crowd in behind them.

The pair jump on to a passing bus (she in her wedding dress still) and sit in the back. The aged, uncomprehending passengers turn and stare at them. (One last reminder!—of Lester's old-folks chorus in *The Knack*.) Ben and his girl sit next to each other, breathing hard, not even laughing, just happy. Nothing is solved— none of the things that bother Ben—by the fact of their being together; but, for him, nothing would be worth solving without her. We know that and she knows that, and all of us feel very, very good. The chase and the last-minute rescue (just after the ceremony is finished) are contrivances, but they are contrivances tending toward truth, not falsity, which may be one definition of good art.

Paul Simon has written rock songs for the film, sung by Simon and Garfunkel, and as in many rock songs, these lyrics deal easily with such matters as God, *Angst,* the "sound of silence," and social revision. But they *are* typical of the musical environment in which this boy and girl live.

Some elements of slickness and shininess in this wide-screen, color film are disturbing. But despite them, despite the evident influences and defects, the picture bears the imprint of a man, a whole man, warts and all: which is a very different imprint from that of many of Nichols' highly praised, cagy, compromised American contemporaries. *All* the talents involved in *The Graduate* make it soar brightly above its shortcomings and, for reasons given, make it a milestone in American film history. Milestones do not guarantee that everything after them will be better, still they are ineradicable.   [*38*]

Postscript*

Doesn't the film split in half? This is the recurrent question in a number of letters about *The Graduate*—although almost all correspondents start by saying they enjoyed it! I have now seen it again and have read the novel by Charles Webb on which it is based, and some further comment seems in order.

I like what I liked in the film even more, but now, having read the original, I can see a paradox about its shortcomings. (Many of which were noted in my review.) Besides the fact that a great deal of Webb's good dialogue is used in the screenplay, the structure of the first two-thirds of his book—until Benjamin goes to Berkeley—is more or less the structure of the film. The longest scene in the picture —the one in which Benjamin tries to get his mistress to talk to him—is taken almost intact from the book. But Mike Nichols and his screenwriters rightly sensed that the last third of the book bogged down in a series of discussions, that Webb's device for Benjamin's finding the place of Elaine's [20] wedding was not only mechanical but visually sterile, and that in general this last third had to be both compressed and heightened. In reaction to the novel's weaknesses, they devised a conclusion that has weaknesses of its own. But there is a vast difference between weakness and compromise.

Benjamin does *not* change, in my view, from the hero of a serious comedy about a frustrated youth to the hero of a glossy romance; he changes *as Benjamin*. It is the difference between the women in his life that changes him. Being the person he is, he could not have been assured with Mrs. Robinson any more than he could have been ridiculous and uncommanding with Elaine. We can actually see the change happen—the scene with Elaine at the hamburger joint where he puts up the top of the car, closes the windows, and talks. *Talks*—for the first time in the film. Those who insist that Mrs. Robinson's Benjamin should be the same as Elaine's Benjamin are denying the effect of love—particularly its effect on Benjamin, to whom it is not only joy but escape from the nullity of his affair and the impending nullity of himself.

There is even a cinematic hint early in the picture of the change that is to come. Our first glimpse of Mrs. Robinson's nudity is a reflection in the glass covering her daughter's portrait.

* From *The New Republic*, February 10, 1968. Reprinted by permission of *The New Republic*, © 1968, Harrison-Blaine of New Jersey, Inc.

In character and in moral focus the film does not split, but there is a fundamental weakness in the novel which the film tries, not quite successfully, to escape. The pivot of action shifts, after the story goes to Berkeley, from Benjamin to Elaine. From then on, he knows what he wants; it is she who has to work through an internal crisis. It was Nichols' job to dramatize this crisis without abandoning his protagonist, to show the girl adjusting to the shocking fact of Benjamin's affair with her mother, and to show it with, so to speak, only a series of visits by her to the picture. To make it worse, the environment—of the conventional campus romantic comedy—works against the seriousness of the material. The library, the quad, the college corridor have to be *overcome,* in a sense. Nichols never lets up his pressure on what he feels the film is about, but the obliqueness of the action and the associative drawbacks of the locale never quite cease to be difficulties. And, as I noted, the final chase—though well done—does get thin.

But I think that, with some viewers, Nichols also suffers from his virtues. He has played to his strength, which is comedy; for, with all its touching moments and its essential seriousness, this is a very funny picture. A comedy about a young man and his father's partner's wife immediately seems adventurous; a comedy about a young man and a girl automatically gets shoved into a pigeonhole. This latter derogation seems to me unjust. We have only to remember (and to me it is unforgettable) that what is separating these young lovers is not a broken date or a trivial quarrel but a deep taboo in our society. For me, the end proof of the picture's genuine depth is the climax in the church, with Dustin Hoffman (even more moving the second time I saw him) screaming the girl's name from behind the glass wall. A light romance? That is a naked, last cry to the girl to free herself of the meaningless taboo, to join him in trying to find some possible new truth.

Yes, there are weaknesses. Yes, there are some really egregious gags. ("Are you looking for an affair?" the hotel clerk asks the confused Benjamin in the lobby.) But in cinematic skill, in intent, in sheer connection with us, *The Graduate* is, if I may repeat it, a milestone in American film history.   [37]

1. Is Mr. Kauffmann correct about Benjamin's presumed discomfort with the affair? What is the evidence?

2. Why does Mr. Kauffmann approve of the film's moral stance? Has he defined it correctly? Do you agree with his evaluation?

3. In his postscript Mr. Kauffmann answers some of the criticisms made of *The Graduate* by others. How convincing is he in defending the movie against such objections?

4. Though his review is basically favorable, Mr. Kauffmann points out numerous flaws in *The Graduate.* Do you think he gives appropriate emphasis to both flaws and virtues?

CALLING DOCTOR SPOCK!

Edgar Z. Friedenberg

Twice, in Mike Nichols's motion picture, *The Graduate,* its young and fashionably unheroic central character, Benjamin, is shown driving to Berkeley across the familiar, still magnificent Bay Bridge. As most readers will know by now Benjamin, who has just graduated from an Eastern college, lives in one of the more expensive neighborhoods of the Los Angeles area; and the transition to Northern California is treated in the film as if it were a passage from a region of unalloyed cruelty and egocentric sham to one of ambiguous but decisively human beauty. Northern California is shown as more real even though not always nice—a little like Paris in old René Clair movies. Accordingly, Benjamin soars toward Berkeley on the upper deck of the bridge in his graduation present; a little red sports car, gay and promising against the superb blue sky and the distant skyline.

Unfortunately for Mr. Nichols's purposes each deck of the Bay Bridge is one-way; and, in fact, traffic to Berkeley travels on the prosaic lower deck from which no picturesque view is possible. They don't close the Bay Bridge to facilitate such Southern Californian activities as movie-making. The distant, alluring skyline Benjamin is driving toward proves, on scrutiny, to be not that of the East Bay but the industrial skyline of San Francisco south of the bridge—the familiar landmarks like Telegraph Hill and Alcatraz that might have given the trick away are all north of it and out of sight. Benjamin, of course, is presented throughout the movie

Member of the Sociology Department at the State University of New York in Buffalo, EDGAR Z. FRIEDENBERG is a frequent contributor to leading periodicals. He is the author of *The Vanishing Adolescent* and *Coming of Age in America.*

as a disoriented youth with confused goals, and it would be quite in character for him to try to drive to Berkeley on the top deck; after the initial shock I thought this was going to turn out to be the point and prepared myself for a Keystone-type chase. But no, this is just a bit of artistic license for the sake of the scenery. Benjamin has no trouble on the bridge; it is about the only place in the whole film where he knows how to handle himself. He gets to Berkeley both times, though he has trouble enough *there.*

In a more obviously conventional picture this little gimmick would not be worth mentioning, and would in any case be well within the director's rights as a way of establishing place, mood, and atmosphere. But from the very beginning *The Graduate* is cutely literal and pseudo-documentary. The picture opens with a scene in the coach-cabin of a westbound jet in which the Captain is announcing, in the conventional liturgy, that the aircraft is beginning its descent into the Los Angeles area. Then the idiosyncratic details are thrust on the viewer: as the credits are shown, Benjamin rides through the tunnel on an underground sidewalk linking the satellites where aircraft land in Los Angeles to the central baggage area—a feature, fortunately, shared by no other airport. There is a closeup of the baggage tag LAX; and when he finally comes out of the terminal building there is heard the familiar recorded chant warning drivers that parking in this area is limited to three minutes and not to leave their cars unattended. It is all designed to give a thrill of recognition and to assure [25–26] the viewer that he is *there;* and this mood is so well sustained that the business with the bridge seems a breach of the director's self-imposed rules.

This literalness is the film's most striking feature; it provides some unforgettable scenes as well as a plethora of sight gags. Nichols, working in widescreen and color, goes far beyond the character touches that used to distinguish Bolting Brothers comedies, with their picturesque British faces and snatches of gaggy dialogue. *The Graduate* is not very subtle, but it certainly portrays what it wants to portray. In one great scene, a group of a dozen or so rich old people push Benjamin aside as they stream into the lobby of an old-fashioned luxury hotel in which he is trying to work up the courage to make arrangements for the affair which Mrs. Robinson, the wife of his father's business partner and old enough, though not otherwise qualified, to be his mother, has forced him into. These old Birchers come on like the very essence of senile corruption; Nichols says as much in this one scene as Wilde did in the whole of *Dorian Gray*—not, to be sure, a story of great moral complexity. They constitute not a sight gag but a tragic epigram without words. Other scenes, more contrived, are equally telling. Benjamin, imprisoned in a black rubber wet-suit with complete scuba apparatus and spear gun, for his parents to show off in their swimming pool, is quite unbelievable but by no means irrelevant, as the film shows the grimacing aggression of his parents through his face mask behind which they are, finally, inaudible.

The good but ineffectual young man, who is portrayed by Dustin Hoffman as small, dark, and homely, in this scene looks like Gregor Samsa, after his metamorphosis—a water beetle. In sharp contrast, a later scene in the Berkeley fraternity house Benjamin visits searching for the blonde beast Mrs. Robinson's daughter is about to marry instead of him is just as striking. It takes place in a shower-

room full of handsome, exuberant giants any one of whom might have been nick-
named Apuleius by his friends had Berkeley given a more classical education. They
are not good guys, and are callous and rude to Benjamin when he tries to find out
from them where the wedding is being held; for they mistakenly assume that he
shares their vicarious and lewd anticipation of their brother's sexual triumphs. But
they tell him; and, barely restraining himself from responding to their insults, he
rushes off to Santa Barbara—400 miles south again in his little red car—to interrupt
the wedding. He is seconds too late, in a scene whose Chaplinesque tragicomedy
was marred for me by the knowledge that it takes seven or eight hours to drive from
Berkeley to Santa Barbara and about an hour to fly, which is cheaper. Two airlines,
United and Pacific, provide frequent service.

   This scene in the fraternity house comes, of course, near the end of the
movie, which closes as Benjamin and his girl—now, awkwardly, just married to
his rival—flee from the church in which he has managed to imprison the wedding
guests by wedging a crucifix in the door. I had been watching the film with mounting
but uncomprehending dissatisfaction until the scene between Benjamin and the
boys in the shower-room; and, at that point, I began to understand my dissatisfaction.
The difficulties stem, I think, from the fact that *The Graduate* is so realistic in its
detail—not just its visual detail but bits of characterization as well—that the falsity
and frivolity of its premises become more annoying than they would be in a less
brilliant movie.

   The central relationship of the movie is that between Benjamin and the
middle-aged Mrs. Robinson, whom Anne Bancroft portrays as a more sophisticated,
bitchier Medea. This begins when Mrs. Robinson comes into his bedroom where he
is trying to hide away from the noisy, demanding guests his parents have invited to
celebrate his graduation. She tricks him into driving her home and tries to seduce
him without even really trying to deceive him as to her purpose; her candor and open
sexual aggression are shown, explicitly, as forms of contempt. But the first attempt
fails because his dithering delays the action till the sounds of Mr. Robinson returning
home are heard. Benjamin rushes downstairs in time to avoid detection—Mr. Robinson is too uninterested in his wife to require that he avoid suspicion—and the scene
is aborted into a maudlin conversation between the two men. Later, bored and op-
pressed by his silly and domineering parents, Benjamin telephones her and reopens
the situation. The central crisis of the movie occurs when the Robinson's daughter
comes home from Berkeley and Mrs. Robinson demands, and receives, a promise
that Benjamin will have nothing to do with her. At this point, not unpredictably,
Medea takes on overtones of *Oedipus Rex* and *Romeo and Juliet,* done in contemporary style by the San Francisco Mime Troupe.

   Mrs. Robinson is portrayed throughout as cruel, exigent, openly contemptuous of everyone she knows but especially of Benjamin and herself, and incapable
of the least concern for the welfare of any human being. She is also ugly and, though
suave, quite without dignity. Benjamin's involvement with her is therefore explicable
only as an expression of his own self-hatred and contempt; and on this basis the picture makes a great deal of sense. But on this basis the broad comedy style also becomes incongruous; *The Graduate* cannot be, simultaneously, a realistic study of

a young man who is so sick that he cannot say no to save his life and a wacky, homely satire about the emptiness of life among the managerial class in Beverly Hills.

Benjamin, as an individual, is a pathetic figure who would be tragic if he had any *hubris* at all. He becomes comical only if taken as general, as every-middle-class-boy; and this, I infer, is the conventional response to the film. Benjamin's lack of pride and selfhood on which to mount his feelings is just the point; middle-class life in America—and Southern California is America, America, is it not?—makes us all like those loveless people and their pathetic victims, surely. So Simon and Garfunkel inform us in the movie's sound track; "The Sounds of Silence" reminds us over and over that people talking without speaking, people hearing without listening, are Benjamin's problem, and ours.

Indeed, yes; and besides, movies are meant to entertain, and what is more enjoyable than elegant self-mockery? But here Mr. Nichols's love for realistic detail —Benjamin even drinks a West Coast brand of beer—betrays his intention to generalize. In a nightclub or TV sketch, telling detail helps the viewer to fill in the character for himself. But—as McLuhan suggests—in a movie, so much detail particularizes and rigidifies the scenes and characters; they become so specific that the viewer may find that they no longer yield anything to his experience. Never having known anybody like Mrs. Robinson, I was able to go along with Benjamin's acceptance of her evil dominion over him because I am familiar with the American convention that sexual attraction, like Communism, is omnipotent and transcendent, even in situations in which it is obvious to all those involved that it can lead only to ruin and slavery—I hadn't expected *The Graduate* to be so much like *Dr. Zhivago,* but it was naïve of me not to.

The moment of truth came for me as I watched the scene in the fraternity shower-room. The big, golden boys were presented as vicious, hostile, and aggressive, too; only poor, ineffectual Benjamin was accorded any real human feeling. But they looked so real frolicking in the steam that they reminded me that I already knew what they were like, just as I knew from personal experience which way traffic moves on the Bay Bridge, and that they were just not so bad as this. Such young men, typically—they vary, too—are very narcissistic and often exploitive, yes. They do, indeed, think they're God's gift to women—as they may well be—Who else could have made them, and for what other purpose? But they are also usually very good-humored about it; they mean no blasphemy and admire and respect His taste and His handiwork, which is more than Benjamin does.

This scene also reminded me how different Mrs. Robinson would have looked if Renoir had painted her among his *Baigneuses.* Her costume is not the issue; Nichols shows her bare enough in several scenes. But he uses her in the film as the embodiment of empty and exploitive evil. She is too inhuman even to talk about herself, as Benjamin occasionally tries to make her do; his efforts to reach her only arouse her contempt. Miss Bancroft tries to show by her facial expression that inwardly Mrs. Robinson is ravaged by guilt and despair, but it doesn't go with what she says and does. I could as easily believe it of Chancellor Roger Heyns; but Mrs. Robinson is not supposed to be an administrative official. She is just a mother. Except for the [26–27] young couple, all the characters in the movie are shown as empty ruins incapable even of ambivalence. And this raises a question about why they are all so bad.

   The Graduate presents itself as chic, comic social commentary. The social commentary is expressed as it would be in a nightclub sketch, almost entirely through exaggerated characterization. This works very well for the short bits. Benjamin's landlord in Berkeley, for example, is a classic cartoon of a paranoid, lower-middle-class type which, in this particular form at least, seems to be California's peculiar nemesis. He is suspicious that Benjamin, who admits when questioned that he is not a student, is "one of those outside agitators"; and turns viciously hostile after a visit by a furious Mr. Robinson convinces him that Benjamin is a "degenerate." Nichols tapes him perfectly; but he, like Mr. Robinson, comes off simply as one of the Furies who pursue Benjamin. They *are* the social commentary; there is no hint in the movie of why they are like that, or that they are factors in any social conflict occurring in California. This simplicity makes the landlord a stroke of genius; but it hardly suffices for the Robinsons or Benjamin's parents, whom we spend enough time with to become curious about, especially since they are done in such detail.

   But it is waxwork detail which the audience is expected to admire and marvel at. And a waxwork is precisely *not* social commentary because the realism is supposed to take the place of historical or political insight; it is enough to say "it must have looked exactly like that" instead of asking what is really happening. This is why, even though it captures the look and sound of much of the contemporary California scene so skillfully, *The Graduate* seems to me basically a copout.

   All the symptoms of alienation on which this movie dwells with such *Schadenfreude* are, after all, expressions of a social and political dynamic that leads people to behave as they do, partly by affecting their personality—this is what *The Graduate* implies—but also by affecting their consciousness, their choices, and their relationship to the market and the supermarket. I am not suggesting that Mr. Turman had any obligation to produce a political tract or even a genuine documentary; he didn't. But an honest movie about human disaster—even a comedy—must place that disaster in its cultural setting as well as make witty comments about it. Benjamin is not a solitary victim; and his problems are as much a consequence of his objective place in society as they are of his feeble personality. He keeps muttering inarticulately that he is "worried about his future"; but nobody in the picture mentions the draft or the war; dissent in Berkeley is symbolized only by a hippy-looking couple leaving a jewelry store and by the landlord's hostility. These are enough to show that *The Graduate* is an "in" movie; but the realism doesn't extend to burning draft cards or smoldering police. In this movie there are no issues, only scenes.

   But the scene in California is full of issues and completely different in mood from what *The Graduate* suggests: wilder, angrier, more uncertain, less decadent. The plastic is a lot tougher than the movie admits; but there is real blood under it. Mr. Nichols is not obliged to put this in his picture; but he ought, at least, to have indicated the space where it might have been—and, in fact, is. Alienation is not Benjamin's only possible future. With a little more gumption and resourcefulness, he could be indicted.   [*27*]

1. How convincingly does Mr. Friedenberg use the film's literal errors to expose deeper artistic and conceptual flaws?

2. Is Mrs. Robinson what Mr. Friedenberg says she is throughout the film? Compare his views with discussions of her character in the following reviews.

3. At a key point, Mr. Friedenberg faults the film's accuracy not on inarguable facts (like the structure of the Bay Bridge) but on judgment (of the fraternity boys). Is this a legitimate critical strategy? In any case, what is your opinion of such people, and how did it affect your response to the film?

4. Do you agree that the film is poor because it provides no causal explanation for the characters' behavior?

THE GRADUATE

Stephen Farber & Estelle Changas

Mike Nichols's name is so magical today that even if *The Graduate* had been the worst movie of the year, people would be buzzing reverently about it. As it is, *The Graduate* is only the most cleverly fashionable and confused movie of the year—and the responses, from critics and customers alike, have been ecstatic. We expected a lot—we're young, and so is Nichols; in addition to youth, he has money, talent, intelligence, irreverence. And after lots of quickie exploitation films about teenyboppers and acidheads, *The Graduate* might have been the first movie about todays' youth to tell it like it is. But Nichols has too much at stake to risk involving us. He's adored because he's hip and safe at the same time; his audiences know that he won't go too far.

The Graduate opens promisingly enough. Ben, a successful young Eastern college graduate, is returning home to Los Angeles, and Nichols immediately and effectively conveys his isolation by focusing exclusively on Dustin Hoffman's apprehensive face moving through the crowded LA airport. Nichols has said that he chose the thirty-year-old Hoffman (a talented comedian—to get that out of the way) to play his callow young hero because he had a face that suggested suffering. Hoffman himself thought there was something strange about the choice; he felt he wasn't suited to the part, which he described as "a young, conventional, squarejawed *Time* Magazine Man of the Year type." Hoffman was right of course. We soon learn that Ben, for all of his credentials and in spite of his vulnerable face, is clean-cut and stupid. He's supposed to be a champion college debater, but he can hardly form a sentence. In the first scenes he's thrown into his rich parents' cocktail and poolside parties; it's easy enough to caricature suburban phoniness, and [37–38] we see quickly—Nichols provides a slick, superficial summary of anti-bourgeois satire of

STEPHEN FARBER and ESTELLE CHANGAS are graduate students at UCLA.

© 1968 by The Regents of the University of California. Reprinted from *Film Quarterly,* Vol. XXI, No. 3, pp. 37–41, by permission of The Regents.

the last decade—everything that's wrong with LA society. But what does Ben see? He gapes a lot, but he never looks more than bewildered by what's going on. He certainly can't articulate any sort of protest. All he knows is that he wants his future to be "well . . . different. . . ." He really sweats to get that word out, but he doesn't seem capable of going further. When he's troubled, he stares into his bedroom aquarium.

Of course we're supposed to like Ben because he's victimized by all of those nasty, aging country clubbers. In the face of their boozing and their twaddle, he has a chunky innocence that is to endear him to us. Nothing is going on in his head, but because he's "mixed up," as he says at one point, and abused by his parents, audiences cluck over him and rush to give him credit for understanding anxieties that are actually beyond his grasp.

Nichols does use a few fine Simon and Garfunkel songs (written long before the film was conceived) to pump poetic and intellectual content into *The Graduate*. Because the songs, especially "The Sounds of Silence," are so concise, lyrical, eloquent, we're tempted to believe that the film contains their insights and that Ben understands them. We're supposed to assume that Ben shares Paul Simon's perceptions of "people talking without speaking, people hearing without listening" in a world whose "words of the prophet are written on the subway walls," but in truth Ben couldn't *begin* putting the world in that kind of order. He's only a beer-drinking *Time* magazine type, as Hoffman recognized, rather harmlessly stupid and awkward, but tricked up with a suffering face and an *Angst*-ridden song intent on persuading us that he's an alienated generational hero. And audiences eager to believe that all young people are sensitive and alienated and that all old people are sell-outs or monsters gratefully permit Hoffman's mannerisms and Paul Simon's poetry to convince them of a depth in Ben that the part, as written, simply does not contain.

The film's best scenes are the early ones in which Ben is seduced by the wife of his father's partner (superbly played by Anne Bancroft—her performance is reason enough to see the film). Bancroft, a young man's deliciously provocative sexual fantasy come to life, makes us aware that there *is* something to be said for women over thirty. When she's on, Ben might just as well roll over and play dead. Bancroft is engagingly wicked as Mrs. Robinson; she is at once supremely confident of her sexual power and mercilessly casual in the face of Ben's adolescent fear of her. Alone with him in her house, she takes calm delight in exposing her legs, while he ejaculates moral misgivings. Her sophistication enables her to see through his repeated protests: "You *want* me to seduce you, is that what you're trying to tell me, Benjamin?" she chants in poker-faced style. And finally, having trapped him in her daughter's bedroom, she remains utterly cool, while her daring flirtatious assault, comically caught by rapid cuts from bare bosom to Ben's anguished face, leaves him helplessly gasping, "Jesus Christ, Mrs. Robinson!"

Unfortunately, this is about the only scene which allows us to see that Ben is sexually attracted to Mrs. Robinson. Most of the time Nichols insists that Mrs. Robinson is repulsive because she is sexual and Benjamin lovable because he is not. Sheer boredom, Ben confesses, is the only thing which brings him to her time after time. And later he explains that bedding down with Mrs. Robinson meant nothing;

it was "just another thing that happened to me . . . just like shaking hands." Apparently we are to believe, as Stanley Kauffman has written, that Ben "sees the older woman's advances as a syndrome of a suspect society," and that he deserves congratulations for his indifference; what seems an astonishing blindness to Mrs. Robinson's very real sexiness is to be taken as a moral victory.

Ben's voice of morality, though, is rather unpleasantly self-righteous: "Do you think I'm proud that I spend my time with a broken-down alcoholic?" The scene in which he tries to liven up their evenings by getting Mrs. Robinson to [38–39] *talk* to him has been much praised, and it *is* an interesting scene, though not for the reasons given, but because it presents Mrs. Robinson with more complexity than usual. When, in the middle of their abortive conversation, she orders Ben not to take out her daughter, the only reason he can guess for the command is that she thinks he isn't good enough for Elaine, and he announces angrily that he considers this liaison "sick and perverted." Bancroft's face, marvelously expressive of deeply rooted social and personal discontents, makes clear to us that this is *not* Mrs. Robinson's reason, that her reasons are much more intense and tortured than Ben suspects —mostly, presumably, an envy of youth and a fear of being cast off for her daughter— and deserve his sympathy, not his moralistic outrage. Ben is too insensitive to see that when she seems to acknowledge that she thinks her daughter too good for him, it's only out of desperation and confusion; she has feelings more intricate and disturbed than she knows how to explain to him. His rejection of her at this moment may look moral, but given the depth and the anguish of her emotional experience, it's a pretty ugly, unfeeling response. Mrs. Robinson's answer to Ben's plea that she talk to him— "I don't think we have much to say to each other"—proves to be quite accurate, but it doesn't expose her shallowness, as Nichols seems to have intended, it exposes *Ben's*. She has so much more self-awareness than he, and so many more real problems, why *should* she talk to him? Anne Bancroft is really too interesting for Nichols's sentimentalities about the generational gap, so he treats her characterization with no respect; after this scene, he turns her into a hideous witch, an evil Furie maniacally insistent on keeping Ben and her daughter apart. This goes along with the current urge to see the generational conflict as a coloring-book morality play—the young in white, the old in black—but it's a cheap dramatic trick.

What really wins the young audience to Ben is his compulsive pursuit of Mrs. Robinson's daughter Elaine in the second half of the film. His single-minded dedication to securing the girl he pines after may be the oldest staple of movie romance, but it is also manna to today's Love Generation. Elaine, though, is a problem. She's gorgeous, all right, she's earnest, and she smiles nicely, but what Ben sees in her beyond her lovely face is kept a secret from us. She does seem to be as clean-cut and stupid as he is. But since she wears her hair long and uncombed and goes to Berkeley (another put-on, much like Hoffman's suffering face), we're to assume that she's an extraordinary catch. Doesn't the fact that she dates and almost marries a smooth, starched medical student confirm the opposite? Ben, incidentally, doesn't even admit her physical attractiveness; his excuse for wanting her so desperately is that at last he has found someone he can talk to. What two such uninteresting people could talk about is a real stumper; and Nichols must have thought so too, for he bars us from one of their few conversations, placing them behind the windshield of Ben's convertible. Perhaps if Nichols were a more experienced film director, he could have convinced us of the vitality of Ben's and Elaine's love with some pungent, seductive visuals; but he relies only on modish out-of-focus shots of flowers and foliage (shots that looked a lot prettier in *Two for the Road* anyway).

All that does express their love is an old-fashioned Hollywood Kiss. On their first date, after treating her quite wretchedly, Ben tries to get her to stop crying and kisses her. And that does it. She forgets her humiliation and smiles. It's love at first sight, just like in the [39–40] movies, but because the actors look casual and sensitive and alienated, audiences think their instant jello of a romance is "real." A little later Elaine learns of Ben's affair with her mother and flees back to Berkeley; he follows her there, and she comes to his room at night to ask why. But first she asks him to kiss her once more, and when he does, she's satisfied; her doubts are erased, and she's ready to marry him. It's all very reminiscent of Betty Grable cheerleader movies. And it's interesting that there seems to be no real sexual attraction between Ben and Elaine. Even their two or three kisses are awfully restrained. After receiving her second kiss, which looks about as exciting as a late-night cup of hot chocolate, Elaine darts quickly out of Ben's door. The movie is rather offensively prudish in splitting sex and love, implying that sexual relationships are sick and perverted, but that in a healthful Young Love relationship—why, sex is the furthest thing from the kids' minds. In this respect the film fits nicely with the flower talk about love, which for all of the bubbles and incense and the boast of promiscuity, is equally insipid, passionless, ultimately quite as sexless.

How bizarre it is that the vacuous Elaine, who has been so easily conned into marrying the fraternity's ace make-out king, can cause such a cataclysmic change in Ben. He throws off his lethargy, chases after her and breaks up her wedding at the last minute, bellowing an anguished "Elaine" as he beats against the glass that separates him from the congregation. A minute later, when Ben punches Elaine's father in the stomach, when he beats off the suburbanites with a giant cross and locks the door with it, the audience cheers vigorously—and to give Nichols his due, it's a pleasing, outrageous image. But it's much too glib to turn Ben suddenly into a rebel hero—this same Ben who's spent most of the film staring blankly into his acquarium and lounging by his pool, transformed by a kiss from a sweet little coed into a fighter for his generation. The motivation may be phony, but we can all laugh at how the old folks get theirs in the end.

The Graduate, like Nichols's film of *Virginia Woolf,* has been applauded for its boldness—never before in an American movie, it is said, could a hero have slept with a woman and married her daughter. The premise *is* arresting, but it's interesting how Nichols blunts it, makes it as easy as possible for his audiences to accept the outrageous. By minimizing Ben's participation in the affair with Mrs. Robinson, by suggesting that it's boring and unpleasant to him, and then by leaving sex out of the relationship with Elaine altogether, the film scampers away from a situation that would be truly challenging and compelling—a young man with strong sexual desire for mother and daughter. Ben doesn't have any sexual desires, apparently, and his unwilling involvement in the affair with Mrs. Robinson lets us off too comfortably. And at a time of much irrelevant nudity and bedroom talk in the movies, this is one film that's entirely too fastidious; the absence of sex in *The Grad-*

uate is a real failure (as it was in *The Family Way*) because the film is, to a large extent, *about* sexuality. But the urgency of Ben's triangular predicament is lost because we don't know much about what goes on in the bedroom, or even in Ben's fantasies. The incestuous longings that lie beneath the surface of the relationships are too uneasily sketched to carry much force. Any development of the oedipal rivalry between mother and daughter is also skimped. This hostility must be behind Mrs. Robinson's command that Ben not see Elaine, and if Elaine is human, she would have certain feelings of jealousy toward her mother. By making her outrage at Ben's affair *purely moral,* by ignoring its psychological content, the film misses an opportunity to explore its potentially explosive situation with depth and humanity—just as it cheated earlier by defining Ben's response to Mrs. Robinson in purely moral terms. Nichols titillates us with an intrigue that we haven't seen before in a movie, but he never gets close to feelings that would upset us. He knows how to startle, but he also knows how to please.

The movie as a whole is a Youth-grooving movie for old people. Nichols's young people have senile virtues—they're clean, innocent, upright, [40–41] and cute too. Tired rich audiences can relax and say, "So *that's* what this youthful rebellion is all about; the kids want just what you and I want, Daddy—a happy marriage, a nice home, and they're really so well-behaved." Nichols doesn't risk showing young people who are doing truly daring, irreverent things, or even young people intelligent enough to seriously challenge the way old people live. All that ennobles Ben, after four years of college, is his virginity. He and Elaine are very bland, and that suits the old folks just fine; bankers and dowagers know that it's "in" to celebrate the young, and in *The Graduate* they can join the celebration with a minimum of fret or identification. The film is actually an insult to the young who aren't so goody-goody—young people who have complicated conflicts of loyalty and affection and who aren't able to make such a decisive moral rejection before they marry the most beautiful sweetheart of Sigma Chi.

Yet young people are falling for the film along with the old people, because it satisfies their most infantile fantasies of alienation and purity in a hostile world, their most simplistic notions of the generation gap, and their mushiest daydreams about the saving power of love. The movie swings on their side, though from a safe, rather patronizing position, and bleats that even when the middle-aged degenerates are cruelest, all you need is a closed-mouth kiss.

As for Nichols's film sense, he does seem to be learning. He still holds shots much too long or dresses them up much too self-consciously—as in the scuba-diving episode, a good idea ruined by clumsy direction. His images are mostly clichéd—not just blurs of flowers and sun-rippled water and car headlights reflecting on his lens, but even monkeys in the San Francisco zoo. He's good when you feel he's enjoying an unpretentiously silly, charming comic touch for its own sake, and he shows a nice eye for good-natured satiric detail (he's hardly a caustic talent) —Mrs. Robinson watching *The Newlywed Game* on TV, a daffy, myopic lady organist at Elaine's wedding. And perhaps it's not fair to give the impression that the film fails because of expediency and calculated compromise; it may be that Nichols actually did not know what he was doing. He has stated recently, in an interview, that Ben and Elaine are not to be envied at film's conclusion, and that Ben will end up exactly like his parents—which suggests attempts at a more harshly sardonic point of view than the film manages to convey. Why do people cheer so exuberantly and walk out so happily if the film means to criticize Ben? Have they all missed the point? Whatever Nichols's intentions, *The Graduate* never really seems to be attacking the young people; all that can be said is that it celebrates them with a strange lack of conviction, which may once have been meant as savage irony, but comes across only as particularly hollow and ineffective film-making. Along with his handling of actors, Nichols's only real success in the movie is with the same sort of lighthearted, inconsequential farce routines he's provided for Neil Simon's comedies on Broadway; there's no point in encouraging him to believe that he's the serio-comic prophet of the plastic generation. Maybe Nichols does have the talent to do something more important—so far he has the energy and the ambition—but we're not going to find out as long as an evasive gimmicky hoax like *The Graduate* is trumpeted as a milestone in American film history.   [*41*]

1. Do you agree that Ben is not really very deep?

2. Compare the viewpoints of Stanley Kauffmann and the authors of this review on the subject of Ben's motives for falling in love with Elaine. Whose argument seems more convincing?

3. Mr. Farber and Miss Changas make two comments about the film's portrayal of sex and love: 1) that *The Graduate* prudishly separates the two, and 2) that this separation is appealing to the audience that likes the film. Do you agree with these assertions?

4. Which of the critics gives the most convincing analysis of the film's popularity? What would you say on this subject?

THE GRADUATE

Jacob Brackman

. . . The tensions of the first third of the movie—ending with Benjamin's phone call to Mrs. Robinson—arise from the question: What is Benjamin going to do with himself? Mike Nichols, the director, handles its exposition boldly, and we are given every reason to expect that what the movie will try to do is answer it. In more general terms, the first part of the film seems to be asking what it means to be a promising young man in America today. What does it add up to now, in this country, to be twenty-one, with a high-quality education behind you and a brilliant future ahead of you? Naturally gifted, with a family of wealth and position to back him up, an impressive degree, a fellowship award, the ability to excel in almost any career he might choose, Benjamin exists, as [36–37] the film opens, in that condition of voluptuous potentiality which is supposed to define young men. The condition fills him with anguish and confusion. And this is fine material for a story, because what was once a predicament confined to the sons of a tiny élite has become a mass predicament in middle-class America. The shared assumptions about what one will do with oneself no longer hold together. Not only is Benjamin interesting to us because of the predicament he is in; he could not be interesting, and perhaps not even recognizable as a youth, if he weren't in it. We could no longer be taken with a young man who stood smiling confidently upon the threshold of his future as a doctor or a businessman. Benjamin's parents and their friends struggled, we can assume, to achieve what hard times had denied *their* parents. For Benjamin to make their youthful hopes his own would be preposterous. A son can pursue ambitions that his parents cherished and failed to fulfill but not ambitions that they fulfilled and then found wanting. From Benjamin's vantage point, his parents and their friends exist in a world of murmuring emptiness. Upon his arrival home, he finds himself

Formerly with *The New Yorker*, JACOB BRACKMAN is now film critic for *Esquire* magazine.

From "The Graduate," *The New Yorker*, July 27, 1968, pp. 36–41, 50–58. Reprinted by permisson; © 1968 The New Yorker Magazine, Inc.

surrounded by fawning adults who have, in a way that escapes them, made a mess of their lives. He sees himself on the threshold only of making a mess of his own life. In the first segment of the film, Nichols himself occupies this limited vantage point so thoroughly as to make Benjamin's perceptions his own, and the audience's. He has managed to translate Benjamin's vision of adult grotesquerie into such striking cinematic terms that even the most conventional moviegoers are hard pressed to see through Benjamin's problem along such lines as "Spoiled brat, what's he belly-aching about? My kid should have it so good!" Nichols' conception, early in the film, is uncompromisingly anti-adult—perhaps the most anti-adult ever to come out of Hollywood. In the party scene, he uses huge, smothering closeups to impose Benjamin's claustrophobia on the audience when his parents seek to show him off as part of their panoply of success. Even though Benjamin is in a position to accomplish no more, really, than they have accomplished, the guests claw at him hungrily. A tippler promises Benjamin the single word that will unlock the riddle of his future, draws him out onto the patio, and whispers portentously, "Plastics." Benjamin seems momentarily stunned. Even, or precisely, through our laughter, something inside us cries out, with him, "No, that cannot be the word! That must be the *opposite* of the word!" But Benjamin can't escape the clutches of the people who seem to live by it—except by standing at the dark bottom of his parents' pool, breathing from a scuba tank.

A quick survey of parents who have seen "The Graduate" has turned up only a few who fancied Benjamin the villain of the piece. (For these, his mother and father were "bad" only insofar as they'd "spoiled" him.) Most, if they didn't exactly identify themselves with Benjamin, were at least on his *side*, in an avuncular way. They managed to feel this sympathy by seeing Benjamin's parents as terribly extreme. Parents who are in life as intellectually [37–38] vulgar as the Braddocks urged their children to go to the movie and see how lucky they were. ("We aren't *that* bad, are we, Andy?") Actually, Mr. Braddock is a more reasonable figure than the usual suburban stereotype, that Hollywood blending of Jewish and WASP garishness—say, the father from Darien in "Auntie Mame," who could be ridiculed because of his bigotry. There is some boldness to the disparagement of Braddock's fatherhood. Braddock stands for nothing readily impugnable; he simply fails to stand for anything worthy of respect. The film condemns him because he is not a fit model, and because his ambitions for his son are misguided. Indeed, *no one* gives Benjamin any sense of direction, much less inspiration. Had there been a single great teacher —or, for that matter, a great hanger-on—back at his nameless Eastern college, he would not be quite so mopily lost. His adulthood looks bleak largely because his environment offers no decent ideal of adulthood—not even a clue to what that ideal might be.

The question posed in the middle third of the film, which ends when Benjamin realizes he's in love with Elaine, is: How is he going to get out of his affair with Mrs. Robinson? We know that an entanglement with a married woman—especially one so awful—can come to no good end, and that the movie, in order to resolve itself, is going to have to get Benjamin out of it and into something else. More important, we understand that the whole Robinson episode is but a distraction from the problem of Benjamin's future—worse than a distraction, though, for it helps make up the very syndrome Benjamin wants no part of. Mechanical sex—a bitchy adultery—is as indispensable to the vacuous suburban scene as a few tall, cool ones hoisted over the hibachi. Mrs. Robinson might be his emblem for the plastic world. Benjamin knows he can devote no attention to mapping out his life as long as he has her to deal with. We feel that "The Graduate" will have to return to its initial theme, which the affair has futilely tried to evade.

The question we expect the final third to answer is something like: Will Benjamin find his way back to his initial dilemma, come to terms with it at last, and resolve it? Or, at least, we would expect such a question if we could halt the progress of the film until we were ready to proceed, the way we lay a book down on our lap to mull over what has happened and anticipate what is to come. Luckily for "The Graduate," film affords no opportunity for immediate reflection, except at the risk of missing out on the ongoing action. For this reason, we must replay movies (or their most interesting parts, anyway) in our minds, and judge them largely in retrospect. We do watch movies in our minds rather as we read books: slow the pace at will to get into a particular scene, or even stop the action to get into a single frame; pause to take stock of what the author is doing to us; turn backward to reexamine something that we didn't realize would become important. (Marshall McLuhan might dismiss all this as clinging to linear-text methodologies, but I think most people go over movies this way. A number of film critics, one gathers, try to perform the same mental operations while they are actually watching a film. Not only can they not do it; they keep missing more. They go back mentally to retrieve something, only to discover that they hadn't fully caught it the first time around.) Many films mellow in leisurely recollection; perhaps a fine film must. But "The Graduate," although it is terrific fun to watch, begins to fall apart under reflection. The final third, in which the best scenes occur, is able to preoccupy us only as long as light is still flickering on the screen. Just when we have greeted Elaine as the catalytic agent to extricate Benjamin from his distracting entanglement with her mother, just when we have braced ourselves for a renewed confrontation with his future, the film, hurtling relentlessly onward, places terrible obstacles between Benjamin and Elaine. Soon it loses sight of its initial problem entirely. The winning of Elaine, which we might properly have regarded as a preliminary step on Benjamin's road to deliverance, supplants the very question of deliverance. As we watch him driving up to Berkeley from Los Angeles, his Alfa Romeo gliding swiftly across the Bay Bridge, he is changing inside. Suddenly, we see him behaving like a man of absolute purpose—a man who knows what he wants and fights for it. Suddenly, he is overflowing with energy and sense of direction. After moping aimlessly through two-thirds of the picture, he is transformed, through his pursuit of Elaine, into the conventional man, resolved upon his chase. On these terms, his success is assured. Once you really know what you're after, in the movies, it's mostly a question of going out and getting it.

Despite its bizarre antecedents, the last few hundred feet of the film have a *healthy* American quality: Benjamin and his girl racing across a green lawn, he in his chinos and stained windbreaker, weary with work well done, and she in her lovely white wedding dress, looking so pure. And she *is* pure, as far as we know— the first pure flesh amid the plastic. However unnatural what led up to it may have been, they will have a proper wedding night! The clambering onto the bus filled with good common folk. Off on their honeymoon! "What crazy things happen in—well, America!" Somehow, the elation of the scene is almost untainted by any residue of Benjamin's confusion or by the "bad" implications of the relationship. The unseen bourgeois, looking [38–39] very much like the man who spoke the single word "Plastics," puts his arm fraternally around our shoulder: "See—the kid just needed a sweet little woman to straighten him out." And we, perhaps clinging to a last-ditch reservation, ask, "But what about his marrying the daughter on the basis of *nothing,* after he'd been sleeping with the mother, the wife of his father's partner, who looks so much like his own mother?" And the voice replies, "Are you talking about these two lovely American kids? Sitting in the bus there? Are you going to try and make something nasty out of that?" "For once," wrote Stanley Kauffmann, "a happy ending makes *us* feel happy."

"The Graduate" engages its audience almost exclusively at the level of events until the grandly satisfying conclusion, when its problems (Benjamin's problems) seem to arrive at a happy solution. The pace of the film is swift and smooth, but its emotional progress—its movement toward resolution—is deeply illogical. The ending does answer the question: How will Benjamin get to marry Elaine, whom he loves? But this union—indeed, the entire boy-meets-loses-gets-girl theme—shapes into a line of resolution only after "The Graduate" is two-thirds over. At one level, the film proceeds awkwardly, deceptively, through a series of less and less interesting problems, sidestepping difficulties of its own authorship, until it can solve only the least interesting of them. All that remains when the bus drives Benjamin and Elaine off into a presumably roseate adulthood is the bare convention of young love triumphant. The trials that Benjamin seemed to forget once he had fixed upon getting the girl, we, too, are encouraged to forget.

Benjamin's acquisition of Elaine is not an apt resolution of Charles Webb's novel "The Graduate," either—the book from which the movie was adapted—but then Webb doesn't try to pass it off as one. The book is peculiarly spare for a long piece of fiction, reading more like a scenario treatment than a novel. In the manner of a scenario, Webb's book tries to float its meanings on the surface of events—on easily visible changes in attitude and setting, and on what characters say rather than on what they think and feel.

In the book, Benjamin's sudden infatuation with Elaine seems purposely unmotivated. Nothing about her presents a good reason for his falling in love with her. The novel, in dialogue that is omitted from the film, makes this abundantly clear at a number of points. For example:

> He nodded. "So," he said, taking her hand. "We're getting married then."
> "But Benjamin?" she said.
> "What."
> "I can't see why I'm so attractive to you."
> "You just are."
> "But why?"
> "You just are, I said. You're reasonably intelligent. You're striking looking."
> "Striking?"
> "Sure."

"My ears are too prominent to be striking looking."
Benjamin frowned at her ears. "They're all right," he said.

What was, then, an artful point in the novel is wholly lost in the movie: the
fact that Benjamin's precipitate and (one wants to say "therefore") consuming love
for Elaine makes very little sense. We find ourselves sucked in by a cinematic convention: That's how people fall in love in the movies; it doesn't *have* to make sense.
Katharine Ross's scrumptiousness becomes a more than sufficient cause. Yet because
the romance has now grown crucial to the scheme of Benjamin's life, because we
are encouraged to imagine Elaine as the light at the end of his darkness, the film
seems suddenly top-heavy. The affair—the preliminary relationship—has been
pictured in endless detail; now the love that promises salvation is treated skimpily.

In the film, when Elaine tells Benjamin she doesn't want him to leave
Berkeley until he has "some definite plan," we appreciate only her coy desire for
him to stay—a certain bubble-headed righteousness that Miss Ross makes adorable.
In the book, we never overcome the anxiety created in us by Benjamin's planless-
ness. Elaine perpetually reminds him, and us, that she is a distraction: "'Well, I just
think you're wasting your time sitting around in this room,' she said. 'Or sitting
around in a room with me if we got married.'" Webb can permit such revealing
lines because although he lets his protagonist escape from the essential, he isn't
trying to pretend otherwise. Nichols could not have included Elaine's keen remark;
it is fundamental to his upbeat resolution of the movie that we do not stop to reconsider Elaine's relation to Benjamin's anguish about his life. Nichols cannot let us
leave the theatre feeling that nothing has changed, so he gives us what he thinks we
want by packing the last thirty minutes with passages of tremendous emotional
power. The passages begin when Benjamin finds Mr. Robinson waiting in his room
(Hoffman's terrified scream is perfect), and keep coming, all but torrentially, until
the final hundred feet of film. Their tension has to do with the horror of confronting
brute, implacable stupidity—*wrongheadedness*—in others. With the over-obvious
exception of Benjamin, people all appear to see the world so wackily that, like Benjamin, we have no idea what would be involved in getting them to see it straight.
The adults will sacrifice him, and sacrifice Elaine, too. There is no reasoning with
them. They cannot "win" (Elaine will obviously get an annulment; the couple can
no longer be kept apart), but they will still destroy Benjamin, pointlessly, if they
can. If he doesn't [39–40] escape with his girl, they'll crack his head against a pew
and have him thrown in jail.

Like Benjamin's graduation party, the wedding guests are all middle-aged
and elderly people. (Don't kids in California ever get to invite any of *their* friends?)
Benjamin's creators have thus provided him with an absolutely sound reason for a
thinly disguised orgy of parricide—or plain adulticide. If he lit into the congregation
without the perfect rationale of self-defense, the scene would appear vengeful, even
sadistic. But because the adults' mindless attack seems to leave him no alternative
his aggression seems fitting. The scene takes on overtones of Jesus driving the money-
lenders from the temple. An author must manipulate his plot skillfully to legitimize

so impermissible a release. Webb swung into his most dramatic prose:

> Mr. Robinson dove in toward him and grabbed him around the waist. Benjamin twisted away, but before he could reach Elaine he felt Mr. Robinson grabbing at his neck and then grabbing at the collar of his shirt and pulling him backward and ripping the shirt down his back. He spun around and slammed his fist into Mr. Robinson's face. Mr. Robinson reeled backward and crumpled into a corner.

Nichols has muted the smash to the face into an elbow to the solar plexus, but Mr. Robinson still lands senseless on the floor, and the scene begins to build to an Oedipal jubilee. If Benjamin could have handled the situation in any other way, or if he had really injured Mr. Robinson (or had killed him), Nichols might have led his young audiences to feel the guilt that lies just beyond, and sometimes mingles with, triumph. But "The Graduate's" solution aims at gratifying not our understanding of its problems but our insecurities about them. Snatching away the bride at the altar—a pleasing fantasy that has turned up in movies often, at least since "It Happened One Night" and "The Philadelphia Story"—is regenerated by an inspired directorial stroke. Benjamin arrives *after*—instead of, as in the novel and in previous films, before—the ceremony is over. Benjamin's crying out to Elaine *before* the vows would mean simply "Don't marry him! Marry me!" After the sacramental kiss, his cry means "It doesn't *matter* that you married him—or that I slept with your mother! *We* know what is real!" The chase to the altar puts us in a familiar frame of mind: We forget that the vows are only a ritual; the chase assumes a conventional urgency— *maybe he will be too late!* Then Nichols craftily steps outside the convention.

The wedding finale has been compared, largely because of its disruptiveness, with the wedding scene in "Morgan!" Yet there was no chance that Morgan would "get" Vanessa Redgrave; his busting up the post-wedding party meant simply that he'd gone over the brink, fallen victim to his unbalanced fantasies. Where Morgan hurts and humiliates no one but himself, Benjamin, like an Ivy League Douglas Fairbanks, outmaneuvers and routs the hostile wedding party. Anyone who has seen "The Graduate" when a fair number of young people were in the audience can have had no doubt about what was happening. Benjamin's contemporaries aren't apprehensive about his escaping safely; they stomp and hoot and cheer when he plows into the cluster of parents. And when he starts swinging the cross like a battle-axe they go wild. Hip Negro audiences respond the same way when Sidney Poitier returns the Southern patrician's genteel slap in "In the Heat of the Night," or when Jimmy Brown gets to slug a couple of white men—enemy soldiers—in "The Dirty Dozen." Kids at "The Graduate" can let go because Benjamin kicks hell out of a whole entourage of parents—and with an unassailable motive. As far as I know, no movie has ever shown a black man beating up a white man outside a war setting (though in life it's not uncommon)—not even in a situation that favors the white man. But one can imagine a screenplay with sufficient art to justify a Negro's physically humiliating a crowd of dreadful whites. Like Benjamin, he would have to have no choice but the ordinarily forbidden.

Benjamin's battle for Elaine is so sudden and ferocious that we involve ourselves in it completely. When they finally escape their tormentors, and the tension of the chase is relaxed, our relief is consummate. To Nichols' credit, he has not permitted "The Graduate" to fade from the screen on a shot of the couple in a clinch, or even on grins of idiotic triumph. They stare blankly ahead, because at last things have stopped happening at a preoccupying clip. Now they have a chance to consider the momentous consequences of what they have done, and the difficulties that lie ahead. This final moment of thoughtfulness—Nichols has painstakingly established the use of full-screen expressionless faces to indicate thought and emotion—lessens only slightly the exuberant tone of his finale. But after the lights go on in the theatre we, for our part, have a chance to realize that Benjamin's capture of Elaine was, at the outside, a secondary aim. What, after all, is Benjamin going to do with his life? Do we infer from the vigor of his pursuit, and from the conventionality of Elaine, that they will soon be discussing a mortgage on a split-level in Tarzana? That the whole "problem" upon which the film established itself was just a sort of "post-grad blues"—a phase that Benjamin simply had to be jolted out of? Or are these clues illusory? Will Benjamin now, with Elaine in tow, return to grapple with the confusions that unsettled him before the Robinson ladies turned up? These are crucial questions, and "The Graduate" has balked at them. Indeed, Nichols recently told a group of college-newspaper editors that as the movie ends, the real problems are just beginning (we must assume that Benjamin somehow *needed* Elaine before he could face them), and that the marriage would never work out. Nichols' remarks were surprising, for none of their pertinent, even crucial extensions come across in his dénouement. The last third of the film implies either that "The Graduate" is about a boy passing through a difficult stage on his way to Normality or that Elaine represents, at best, Benjamin's cowardly desire to simplify the complex issues of his life-to-be. (At worst, he has fixed upon her as a distraction, exactly as he fixed upon her mother.) The option is hardly satisfactory, so most of the critics have steadfastly ignored the evidence of the text and insisted that Benjamin's long search for himself arrives at its payoff. The Philadelphia *Evening Bulletin,* typically, informed us that "The Graduate" is "rooted in the affirmative premise that the young can escape the traps of a society created by their parents." And *Glamour* explained Benjamin's barely controlled hysteria at the wedding by saying, "He doesn't care what other people think because [now] he knows who he is. That's growing up."

The condition of being altogether lost may be unbearable; it is understandable that people usually take false roads out. The false roads don't lead toward being found, exactly, or toward any particular wisdom, but at least they allow one a comforting feeling of movement, an illusion of progress—at least they consume energy. For an artist to detour onto such roads is also understandable, [40–41] I suppose; in any event, it happens often enough. Resisting the lure of such detours and remaining still, in stark perplexity, to watch and listen is the nerviest course, in art as in life. The artist cannot afford to let himself get away with things; if he does, he cheats his characters and, consequently, his audience. If he cannot long maintain himself in the condition of being lost, he cannot long maintain his characters in that condition, either, because he has no sure sense of where it leads, or even of what its resolution might look like. He grows adept not at solving problems but at overcoming them—transmuting them, removing them, "settling" them, directing them toward false outcomes. The higher an artist's distractability is, the less tenaciously he clings to the essential, and the easier, and emptier, his aesthetic choices become.   [41]

*   *   *

Nichols (and Webb before him) clearly aimed at that comedy which arises naturally out of a scrupulous observation of life—that vision of human frustration and inadequacy which is devastatingly true yet devoutly compassionate. This is probably the highest form of comedy and, at its most successful, the funniest. It is the comedy of Chekhov, of some Mark Twain stories and some of Chaplin's movies, of Lenny Bruce, of Salinger—the wise laughter rising above apparent tragedy. Now, there can also be a certain condemnation in such laughter, but never so much as to overwhelm charity with contempt. The song that Simon and Garfunkel do on the sound track after Benjamin flees from Mrs. Robinson's cops suggests its temper: "And here's to you, Mrs. Robinson, Jesus loves you more than you will know." Great comedy is naturally subversive, by virtue of its accuracy, but it is never venomous. It may give exquisite pleasure over long periods without making us laugh out loud. Then, when the sidesplitters do come, they have a quality almost of spiritual purgation. Nichols would have liked, one imagines, to make "The Graduate" this sort of comedy, but he was trained in a theatre—cabaret and Broadway—where comedy's success is meter-measured: How many in the audience laugh? How often and how loud? Nichols seems to care about getting the laughs, even easy ones; he doesn't particularly care who it is he's laughing at, and he apparently believes that a laugh is as good a way out of an artistic problem as any other.

An odd change occurs in Nichols' point of view at the beginning of the middle section of the film (when Benjamin telephones Mrs. Robinson) and persists until the end of that section (when Benjamin realizes he loves Elaine): Benjamin himself becomes the butt of the jokes. In the first part of the film, adults seemed laughable, or pitiable, yet basically well intentioned. Here they seem wicked (Mrs. Robinson) or dangerously insensitive (Benjamin's parents). Having become sinister, the grownups no longer seem fit objects for comedy. Nonetheless, this middle section of "The Graduate" is the most comically intended of the three, and, to judge by the reactions of the audience, it is the most comically successful. Benjamin turns into a victim here—not only a victim of Mrs. Robinson's wiles but a victim of his own ineptitude. It is the second victim, in particular, that we are meant to laugh at. Nichols has filled the section with the sort of broad funny business he polished in staging Neil Simon's comedies on Broadway. Benjamin should be uncomfortable with Mrs. Robinson partly because of his naïveté but more because he understands that she can have no real place in the scheme of his life. Nichols, however, exaggerates the naïveté until it becomes farcical. About fifteen minutes of running time elapses, for example, between the time Benjamin telephones Mrs. Robinson and the time they hit the hotel bed together—fifteen minutes of sight and sound gags on the theme of nervousness. Benjamin fumbles through the arrangements for their rendezvous—nodding maniacally, scratching, wheezing from deep in his throat, like a frightened animal— as though he expected a vice squad to descend on him at any instant. In some business with the room clerk that centers on his having no luggage, Benjamin loses his cool completely. The single, frenetic joke—the ninny doesn't know what he's doing —continues after Mrs. Robinson gets up to the bedroom: Benjamin kisses her just after she has inhaled smoke from a cigarette, so she must hold the smoke in until the kiss is over; Benjamin tries to bring her a wooden hanger for her dress, but it's attached to the closet rod; and so forth. We quickly exhaust our ways of receiving the joke, and our laughter becomes similarly frenetic.

Critics have remarked that the excruciating exchanges between Benjamin and Mrs. Robinson are reminiscent of some of the bits that Nichols used to do with Elaine May. Their [50–51] work together often portrayed men and women coming on with each other, and Nichols and May were particularly sharp at skewering common dishonesties, egotistical little games, and ulterior desperation. Yet the one scene in "The Graduate" in which Benjamin lets his hair down to Elaine ("I feel like I'm playing this game somebody else made up the rules to . . .") is closer to a Nichols and May routine than any conversation with Mrs. Robinson—though heaven forbid we should laugh at it. Their comedy almost never took sides—one of them didn't become the other's butt. Nichols' character was just as derisible as May's, and neither used gag lines to make us laugh; instead, each tried to express himself with the utmost seriousness and wound up—partly to our embarrassment, because each said things that any of us might hear ourselves saying—fatuous. In "The Graduate," Nichols treats as revelation the kind of material he would once have used for his comedy, and makes comedy out of the kind of material that would once have been beneath him. When Benjamin first arrives at the hotel, he does a double take when the clerk asks him, "Are you here for an affair?" Soon we are asked to laugh at every hint of his anguish. Mrs. Robinson becomes more than a domineering female. The traditional sexual roles are reversed: she clearly wants nothing more than a good time in bed, and Benjamin, like a Vassar girl, keeps working the conversation around to his misgivings about not having a "meaningful relationship." Her frank, predatory sexuality begins to look like derision of Benjamin. His compliance begins to suggest that he must despise himself. Had Nichols made a more substantial case against Benjamin's surroundings—had that issue survived the first third of the film—his self-degradation would have made sense, at least dramatically: he might have felt so sullied by his inability to break connections with society that he could not foresee ever feeling pride in himself.

After the surprising credibility of the first third, the tight structure of plot and character begin falling to pieces. We are assaulted by a series of unbelievable details. Presumably vital questions of plot become irrelevant, because of incredible elements within the plot. Is Benjamin a virgin or isn't he? After the first hotel-room scene with Mrs. Robinson, we could equally well decide either way. Since Benjamin's entire motivation in the scene hinges upon the "true" answer, we may assume that [51–52] Nichols at least whispered it in Dustin Hoffman's ear, and, without very much extra effort, could have tipped off the audience. If Benjamin *is* a virgin, we may chalk up most of his terrible distress to first-time jitters. (Many of the critics made exactly this assumption, and consequently took Benjamin's sexual initiation, or "coming of age," to be the major theme of the film.) If he is not, we must look for more interesting and disturbing causes. Having read the book, as John Lennon says,

I can report that although the Benjamin of the film usually acts as though he'd never even seen *Playboy,* the Benjamin of the novel is not a virgin. Ten pages are devoted to his departure for and return from three weeks on the road, undertaken, after graduation, to relieve his metaphysical distress, and he informs his father afterward, "There were a few whores included in the tour." Nor is there any indication that they were Benjamin's first. Just as Nichols has declined to let us know about Benjamin's previous sexual experience, he has left out the trip altogether, even though many of its incidents might have had tremendous cinematic potential. Benjamin tells his father of fighting a forest fire in Shasta country, of hitching rides from common folk, of sex in "a cow pasture, Dad," going on to say of this, "It was about three in the morning and there was ice in the grass and cows walking around us." And he asks, rhetorically, "Have you ever had a queer Indian approach you while you're trying to keep your clothes from burning up?" The stuff a Dylan song is made of! Yet Nichols omits the whole diminished *Bildungsroman,* possibly because it so forcefully underscores the proper problem of "The Graduate;" it shows beyond doubt that Benjamin is desperately in earnest about trying to determine what sort of life he wants to construct for himself. By concealing Benjamin's sexual experience from us, Nichols is able to get mileage out of the boy's naïveté and ineptitude. We could not laugh in quite the same way if we knew that Benjamin had just returned from sleeping with prostitutes on the road; we would have to treat him more seriously. We would have to interpret his reluctance to embark upon an affair with Mrs. Robinson as more sensible and telling.

The virginity question is just one example of what happens as "The Graduate" veers from its early course. As soon as Nichols starts fudging on his material, he gets caught up in a web of implausibilities. First, we have the B.M.O.C. Benjamin —evidently head of the debating club, campus editor, captain of the cross-country team, social chairman of his house—transformed into a somnambulistic, clowny schlepp, and, again, into an aggressive tiger. It's natural for a guy to manifest different aspects of his personality with different girls, but the "cool" Benjamin, in shades, who knows his way around tough Sunset Strip burlesque joints simply cannot be the shook-up fellow with the big-eyed stare who assures Mrs. Robinson as he prepares to grant her fondest wish, "I want you to know how much I appreciate this." Next, Mrs. Robinson—a handsome, worldly, unhappily married woman—is transformed first into a businesslike mistress and then into a hellhound. Nichols seems on the verge of making her human in the fight after Benjamin pleads, of their affair, "Couldn't we liven this up with a little conversation?" For a moment, he allows us to realize that the young man has the position of strength in a liaison of this kind, and that the older woman—worn out, fearful about wrinkles and flab and her waning capacity for arousing desire or affection—is the one who is truly vulnerable. Just as we begin to feel some sympathy for this wretched woman, Nichols snaps the witch mask back on her. The remarkable thing is that there is not the slightest necessity for either of these sequences of transformation. Nothing essential to the story requires that Benjamin ever be less than bright and competent. Nor does anything demand Mrs. Robinson's consummate villainy; the wooing of a girl after an affair with her mother would by itself present a hero with plenty of obstacles —especially once the father-husband found out. So Nichols has introduced these two distortions of personality as though to help captivate us away from our initial focus, and from them spring a litter of false bits. Benjamin would not continue to call Mrs. Robinson by her surname after they have been sleeping together for weeks. He would not make such an idiot of himself over retrieving his toothbrush from his car. He would not drive his car literally off the road at [52] Elaine's casual mention of the hotel where he and Mrs. Robinson have been trysting. Mrs. Robinson would not be so insanely touchy on the subject of her daughter. She would not perpetually address Benjamin in that excessively clear tone one reserves for small children. She would not lean over indifferently to rub out a smudge on her slip when Benjamin puts a hand on her brassiered breast—her hungers could not be so cold. She would not be so ready to tell Elaine of the affair, nor would Benjamin—they would not race each other home to break the news. She would not then invent a preposterous story about Benjamin's getting her drunk and raping her—stab him in the back and then try to hang him on a concealed-weapons rap—and if she did, neither her daughter nor her husband would believe her, because they could not live twenty years with such a woman and know nothing of her treachery. Indeed, Mrs. Robinson becomes so impossible that her machinations have to take place offscreen for almost the last hour of the movie, except for a two-minute confrontation with Benjamin when he appears searching for Elaine, and a one-line appearance in the wedding finale. With Mrs. Robinson out of the way, Elaine must share the burden of uncertain characterization. She falls for the rape story completely and dismisses Benjamin for good, then immediately believes his denial and falls in love with him. We might make allowances for that much, but suddenly she becomes inexplicably flighty; her feelings seem to be serving some unfathomable higher demands—the director's, we cannot help suspecting. Precisely when the course of the film hinges upon her response to Benjamin, she grows so wildly fickle that even the conventions of "femininity" will not excuse her. For no apparent reason, she shatters our picture of the obstacles arising from a misguided adult world.

Much of the excitement surrounding "The Graduate" has stemmed from the proposition that, in Glamour's words, it "gets to the very heart of what youth is about," and is also a superbly "adult" movie. (Very few children's movies come out of Hollywood anymore, but producers still reserve the term "adult" for films they regard as uncommonly truthful.) Critics who previously had only scorn for film renderings of Youth hail "The Graduate" as the first American motion picture to deal authentically with today's much discussed generation gap. Yet in representing the gap between [54–55] contemporary adults and youth the film unwittingly calls urgent attention to the gap between the America of today and the America of ten years ago, from which its generational vision might more credibly have emerged.

"The Graduate" hinges upon Benjamin's interestingness, and it is an interestingness not so much portrayed as established by a tautological convention: People who don't say much and who look pained in frequent closeups are deep and interesting because why else would they be pictured that way? Carl Smith is introduced and limned to underscore our impression of Benjamin. Carl is the Lane Coutell figure—tweedy, suave, "giving the impression of having at least three lighted cigarettes in each hand." His fraternity brothers, naturally, refer to him as "the make-out king." But what, after all, does the contrast between Carl and Benjamin amount to? I asked a number of people who saw the movie. Most of them, in fascinating departures from the text, immediately replied that the two were as different as Jacob and Esau, and went on to paint subjective portraits of Carl as an unfeeling square and Benjamin as a sort of radical-hippie—a logical extension of his "interesting-ness." But an interesting young man of the late fifties transplanted into the America of 1968 would be barely conscious. Ten years ago, a primitive rejection of adult emptiness and hypocrisy was a sufficient condition for interestingness. Today, by itself, it isn't nearly enough. It may not even be necessary.

On the basis of all we can learn directly from the film, the differences between Carl and Benjamin are these: Benjamin is the sloppier dresser, the more awkward, the more sour, the more confused, and—almost logically—the more interesting. But isn't he, really, awfully straight arrow? Poor Carl, like the President, is condemned for his idiom. (He proposes to Elaine by saying, "I think we'd make a pretty good team.") He sees the course of his life stretching clearly ahead of him and prepares to traverse it without ambivalence, confident in the relevance of his past (primarily, we assume, his studies) to his business in the world. He carries himself in a way that suggests he envisions not so much a future as a beneficent destiny. Benjamin, on the contrary, lacks the pleasant conviction of progress. By common definitions, he has already proved he can succeed, but he is unable to gain any satisfaction from that excellence. He finds himself unexpectedly disenchanted with award-winning [55–56] and aunt-kissing, and he regards his education as useless, but nothing that looks like an option has presented itself to him. Webb's novel continually emphasizes these points:

> ". . . I'm finished with schools, Dad." A section of grapefruit fell off his spoon and onto the table. "I never want to see another school again. I never want to see another educated person again in my life."
> "Come on, Ben."
> "Come on!" Benjamin said, standing up. "Now I have wasted twenty-one years of my life. As of yesterday. And that is a hell of a lot to waste."
> "Sit down."
> "Dad," Benjamin said, "for twenty-one years I have been shuffling back and forth between classrooms and libraries. Now you tell me what the hell it's got me."
> "A damn fine education."
> "Are you kidding me?"
> "No."
> "You call me educated?"
> "I do."
> "Well, I don't," Benjamin said, sitting down again. "Because if that's what it means to be educated then the hell with it."
> "Ben?" his mother said. "What are you talking about."
> "I am trying to tell you," Benjamin said, "I'm trying to tell you that I am through with all this."
> "All what?"
> "All this!" he said, holding his arms out beside him. "I don't know what it is but I'm sick of it. I want something else."
> "What do you want?"
> "I don't know."

Now, for a man to be twenty-one years old in America today, for a man to have grown up around Los Angeles and have been through four years at the nerve center of an Eastern college, and for him suddenly to wrestle with dissatisfactions so unfamiliar to him that their articulation is as primitive as this—and it is *more* primitive in the movie—can only be a sign of some serious retardation. Such a man is "interesting" only insofar as we might marvel at how soundly he has slept through the life that was going on around him, at how thoroughly he has managed to avoid exposure to a dozen explanations for his malaise. Yet the movie's importance rests upon our assumption that Benjamin represents the best, the vanguard, of his generation. Nichols cannot be permitted the line of defense divined by those polls that are forever showing comfortable majorities of students supporting the war, abhorring drugs, and so forth—polls that never point out that at Harvard, for example, six per cent of the students support the war, a quarter have indicated they will go into exile or prison rather than submit to the draft, and fewer than half have never turned on. Benjamin is not supposed to be a "typical" collegian. (He doesn't wear a *"State"* sweater.) He is supposed to be pointing toward the future—showing us which way the wind is blowing. Even in the late fifties, any harbinger would have had much clearer ideas about what he was rejecting. (There were beatniks then, after all, issuing position papers on American society.) The true Benjamin of Eisenhower America would have spoken to his father more in this vein: "Dad, you're worried about my 'negative attitude.' But I can't see keeping on with the scramble anymore. Don't take this personally, but you and your friends look dead to me. The system is a trap, huh? It whooshes you along in frantic, meaningless patterns—college, mixers, grad school. And then the whole Good Life in America syndrome—career, tony wife, kids in good schools, Martinis, intelligent friends, two-week vacations, *Newsweek* . . . No adventure, no honesty, no *break*-through. Well, I see how impoverished my ambitions have been so far." Vanguard youth went on like that in the fifties; they accepted the seriousness of their parents' beliefs and life styles, and could therefore address themselves to adult society in the manner of prosecuting attorneys. In the sixties, a paradigmatic father-and-son conversation would begin just where Webb's conversation ends:

"What do you want?"
"I don't know."

And that would probably be the whole of the conversation, because one or both of them would then get up and leave the room, weary of preaching to the wind, racked (or delighted) by the impossibility of saving the other, no longer caring. When the Benjamin of the fifties finally said "I don't know," he had run out of ways to explain himself but he still believed in the possibility of explanation, if he were but a little more articulate, his parents a little more sensitive. The Benjamin of today would say "I don't know" right at the start because he wouldn't consider explanation pertinent, or even feasible. The very language given him by the adult world, he would feel, leads perniciously, inexorably back into that world. "So you've got no *respect!*" a father accuses, and as soon as the son tries to redefine the word his case is lost. Instead of the old heated philosophical debates, almost grown children now simply attempt to humor or manipulate their parents—ideally, creating the impression that they are allowing [56] themselves to be manipulated. Indeed, many young people have made this faculty a criterion of being grown: When you finally understand where it's at, you abandon fruitless argument.

Twenty-year-olds today can dismiss their parents' vision without a lot of agonizing partly because they have the sense of being into much that their parents can't even know about. Some adults continue to maintain that Blind Youth always suffers from this delusion: "You'll look back in ten years and realize how right I was." But those who have paid closer attention to their children perhaps have felt more deeply put down than any generation of parents in history. For the first time, parents have taken to heart the feedback they got from their kids, have come to suspect they may be leading pointless lives and have thereby been rendered unable to take pride in what they have achieved. Properly, the Braddocks display no such defensive doubts in relation to their son: Benjamin cannot even begin to formulate precisely what it is that's wrong. More critically, his "rebellion" seems to arise, unprompted, from a *tabula rasa* of experience; he sees into *less,* not more, than his parents, and he has little appreciation of their needs and binds. He is unable to lie to them, let alone manipulate them. He gives the impression of having investigated little and "been through" even less. Has Benjamin already checked out psychedelics, heavy sex, solitude, S.D.S., mysticism, and so on? Unaccountably, a number of people I spoke with guessed that he had, even though there is no evidence for it in the film, nor does anything in his personality, as it comes across on the screen, give the "feel" of such experience. Eisenhower America: In the late fifties, a young man could leap directly from a normal middle-class scene into this paralyzing condition of being altogether lost. The culture had not prepared him for the violence of his disillusionment, nor had it offered him a series of seductive alternate routes. "The Graduate" is largely the work of people who experienced some version of this dilemma a decade ago. They've now apparently decided that America is ready to be told—told not that her very best youth despairs for her but that some eccentric few are having unspecified "misgivings."   [58]

1. Much of Mr. Brackman's criticism is based on his assumptions about what the audience's reactions were. Does he formulate these assumptions convincingly? Is this a sound critical technique? How many of the volume's other critics use presumed audience response to make their points?

2. Do you agree with Mr. Brackman's summary (on page 162) of the technique of film criticism?

3. Outline the arguments which Mr. Brackman makes against the film's comedy. What is his general point?

4. Do you agree with Mr. Brackman's final sketch of the contemporary twenty-year-old's state of mind?

BONNIE AND CLYDE

TWO VIEWS

JOSEPH MORGENSTERN

I

In "Bonnie and Clyde," the heroes of which are a pair of 1930s bank robbers, some of the most gruesome carnage since Verdun is accompanied by some of the most gleeful off-screen fiddling since Grand Ole Opry. The effect is ear-catching, to say the least. For those who find killing less than hilarious, the effect is also stomach-turning.

That is the fatal flaw of this otherwise interesting film, directed by Arthur Penn and produced by Warren Beatty, who also plays Clyde. It does not know what to make of its own violence. Were the people in charge of its production actually amused by scores of cops being gunned down or blown up by hand grenades hitting armored cars? Did they feel there was simply no use crying over spilt blood? Or did they use the music as a last-ditch effort to take the curse off their film's essential ugliness?

Whatever the case, the people in charge were not really in charge, and what begins as an engagingly perverse Depression saga, fully equipped with Burma Shave signs, Roosevelt posters, tin Lizzies, rumble seats and a few vignettes derived from "Let Us Now Praise Famous Men," transforms itself, willy-nilly, into a squalid shoot-'em for the moron trade. Try to imagine "In Cold Blood" being played as a William Inge comedy, including an attempt at lyricism consisting of a slow-motion sequence in which the inert bodies of Bonnie and Clyde, being perforated by the law's lead, rise and fall and pitch and turn with something of the same grace that Vittorio Mussolini must have seen in Ethiopia when he compared bomb bursts to rose petals.

JOSEPH MORGENSTERN writes film criticism for *Newsweek,* which allowed him to break with reviewing practice by retracting his original piece on *Bonnie and Clyde.*

Within the ugliness lies some beauty, suggestions of humanity and even some legitimate humor. Bonnie, a West Dallas waitress played well and attractively by Faye Dunaway, strikes up a strange, sexless and yet spirited alliance with Clyde, a back-country bumpkin fresh out of prison. Clyde does what he does in banks because he cannot do what he wants to do in bed. Bonnie, who must have a beautiful soul because she writes clandestine doggerel, keeps telling Clyde not to worry and to let nature take its course, which it finally does in a field with flowers. It is "The Family Way" all over again, except that if the hero had found his potency sooner a hundred lives or more could have been saved.   [65]

II

Last week this magazine said that "Bonnie and Clyde," a tale of two young bank robbers in the 1930s, turns into a "squalid shoot-'em for the moron trade" because it does not know what to make of its own violence. I am sorry to say I consider that review grossly unfair and regrettably inaccurate. I am sorrier to say I wrote it.

Seeing the film a second time and surrounded by an audience no more or less moronic than I, but enjoying itself almost to the point of rapture, I realized that "Bonnie and Clyde" knows perfectly well what to make of its violence, and makes a cogent statement with it—that violence is not necessarily perpetrated by shambling cavemen or quivering psychopaths but may also be the casual, easy expression of only slightly aberrated citizens, of jes' folks.

I had become so surfeited and preoccupied by violence in daily life that my reaction was as excessive as the stimulus. There are indeed a few moments in which the gore goes too far, becomes stock shockery that invites standard revulsion. And yet, precisely because "Bonnie and Clyde" combines these gratuitous crudities with scene after scene of dazzling artistry, precisely because it has the power both to enthrall and appall, it is an ideal laboratory for the study of violence, a subject in which we are all matriculating these days.

Violent movies are an inevitable consequence of violent life. They may also transmit the violence virus, but they do not breed it any more than the Los Angeles television stations caused Watts to riot. Distinctions can and must be made between violent films that pander and violent films that enlighten, between camp, comment and utter cynicism. And there is nothing like the movies for giving us historical perspective on violence we have known, and in many cases loved.

No one but Charlie Chaplin's competitors ever deplored his early comedies, though they served up staggeringly large helpings of mayhem. Cruelty to animals, children and adults was the crucial ingredient in W. C. Fields's social satire. No one ever accused Cagney of excess gentility in "Public Enemy," but people consoled themselves in those days with the notion that violence was the particular province of a particular minority, namely the violent. They called the group The Underworld, at least until 1939.

World War II brought back primitivism, which had been on the skids ever since 1918, and its popularity today has not discernibly declined. A fair amount of contemporary movie violence is still conventionally primitive, unadorned by anything but gangrenous nostalgia—"Battle of the Bulge," for instance. Some movie violence is stylishly primitive—"St. Valentine's Day Massacre" pumps slugs into lugs by the thousands, but a few good performances lift the sleazy legend from the sewer to the gutter. Some is pretentiously primitive—"The Chase" was all awash with racial and social symbols, yet seemed most pleased with itself when Marlon Brando's battered face was awash with ketchup. And some is ingeniously primitive —"The Dirty Dozen" spends more than two hours on an outlandishly detailed setup for a half-hour payoff in which the GI demolition squad really demolishes, the charges explode, the Kraut machine guns chatter and the victims (including lots of screaming females) cry themselves a river of blood.

Such stuff as this is trash, and at least has the bad grace to give itself away. More serious complications arise when the overlay of comedy or comment is done more artfully. "A Fistful of Dollars" and its sequel, "For a Few Dollars More," were synthetic Westerns made on the cheap in Italy and unmistakably brutal. But their director, Sergio Leone, had done his homework and studied the [82–83] models he wanted to copy and/or parody. His primary motive clearly was profit, and therefore imitation, but that did not prevent him from adding a pinch of put-on, and a dollop of dubious satire.

Yet violence can serve thoroughly satiric or artistic ends, and not only in Shakespeare, Marlowe, Buñuel, "Marat/Sade" or the coming film version of "In Cold Blood." Violence was downright charming in "The Quiet Man," delightful in "The Crimson Pirate," enthralling in "Psycho" and "The Hill," relevant in "Dutchman." "West Side Story" might well have done with more of it to stiffen its spine, and so might "Up the Down Staircase," which only tiptoed timorously around the crazy chaos of America's slum schools.

There is nothing timorous about "Bonnie and Clyde," in which violence is at once a virtue and a vice. Director Arthur Penn and his colleagues perform poignant and intricate wonders with a *Loony Tunes* gang of outlaws who bumble along from one bank job to another, from one blood bath to another, in an inchoate, uncomprehending and foredoomed attempt to fulfill their stunted selves. Both "Bonnie and Clyde" and "St. Valentine's Day Massacre" deal with the same slice of life, yet the characters in the latter are gun racks and the characters in "Bonnie" have a rushing of blood in their veins and a torrent of thought in their minds.

From time to time, however, all artistry falls by the wayside: when a cop trying to stop the getaway car is shot in the face, when a grocer is bludgeoned in a close-up, when a grenade demolishes a police tank, when one outlaw has his skull blown open and another has her eye shot out. These scenes are reprehensible not because they are ugly, or shocking, but because they are familiar, gross and demeaning. When artists are able to bring characters to life and keep them alive, they should not leave death to the special-effects department.

There is, in the depiction of violence, a thin red line between the precisely appropriate and the imprecisely offensive. Sometimes a few too many frames of film may mean the difference between a shot that makes its point concisely and one that lingers slobberingly. These few frames or scenes in "Bonnie and Clyde" will hardly change the course of human events. When we talk about movies, even artistic movies, we are not talking about urban-renewal programs, nuclear nonproliferation treaties or rat-control bills. Art cannot dictate to life and movies cannot transform life, unless we want to retool the entire industry for the production of propaganda. But art can certainly reflect life, clarify and improve life; and since most of humanity teeters on the edge of violence every day, there is no earthly reason why art should not turn violence to its own good ends, showing us what we do and why. The clear danger, of course, is that violence begets violence in life and engenders confusion in art. It is a potent weapon, but it tends to aim the marksman.   [83]

1.   Summarize the development of Mr. Morgenstern's argument that *Bonnie and Clyde* has a serious purpose for its depiction of violence. Is the argument well-made?

2.   Do you agree that the characters in *Bonnie and Clyde* have "a torrent of thoughts in their minds"?

3.   What is the function of Mr. Morgenstern's final paragraph? Is it consistent with the rest of his review?

BONNIE AND CLYDE

Pauline Kael

How do you make a good movie in this country without being jumped on?
Bonnie and Clyde is the most excitingly American American movie since *The Manchurian Candidate*. The audience is alive to it. Our experience as we watch it has
some connection with the way we reacted to movies in childhood: with how we
came to love them and to feel they were ours—not an art that we learned over the
years to appreciate but simply and immediately ours. When an American movie is
contemporary in feeling, like this one, it makes a different kind of contact with an
American audience from the kind that is made by European films, however contemporary. Yet any movie that is contemporary in feeling is likely to go further than
other movies—go too far for some tastes—and *Bonnie and Clyde* divides audiences,
as *The Manchurian Candidate* did, and it is being jumped on almost as hard. Though
we may dismiss the attacks with "What good movie doesn't give some offense?"
the fact that it is generally *only* good movies that provoke attacks by many people
suggests that the innocuousness of most of our movies is accepted with such com-
placence that when an American movie reaches people, when it makes them react,
some of them think there must be something the matter with it—perhaps a law
should be passed against it. *Bonnie and Clyde* brings into the almost frighteningly
public world of movies things that people have been feeling and saying and writing
about. And once something is said or done on the screens of the world, once it has
entered mass art, it can never again belong to a minority, never again be the private
possession of an educated, or "knowing," group. But even for that group there is an
excitement in hearing its own private thoughts expressed out loud and in seeing
something of its own sensibility become part of our common culture.

One of America's most widely-published film critics, PAULINE KAEL has been a film distributor and theater manager. Most recently film critic for *The New Republic*, she now reviews regularly for *The New
Yorker*. Two collections of her work have appeared: *I Lost It at the Movies* and *Kiss Kiss Bang Bang*.

Our best movies have always made entertainment out of the anti-heroism of American life; they bring to the surface what, in its newest forms and fashions, is always just below the surface. The romanticism in American [47–48] movies lies in the cynical tough guy's independence; the sentimentality lies, traditionally, in the falsified finish when the anti-hero turns hero. In 1967, this kind of sentimentality wouldn't work with the audience, and *Bonnie and Clyde* substitutes sexual fulfillment for a change of heart. (This doesn't quite work, either; audiences sophisticated enough to enjoy a movie like this one are too sophisticated for the dramatic uplift of the triumph over impotence.)

Structurally, *Bonnie and Clyde* is a story of love on the run, like the old Clark Gable–Claudette Colbert *It Happened One Night* but turned inside out; the walls of Jericho are psychological this time, but they fall anyway. If the story of Bonnie Parker and Clyde Barrow seemed almost from the start, and even to them while they were living it, to be the material of legend, it's because robbers who are loyal to each other—like the James brothers—are a grade up from garden-variety robbers, and if they're male and female partners in crime and young and attractive they're a rare breed. The Barrow gang had both family loyalty and sex appeal working for their legend. David Newman and Robert Benton, who wrote the script for *Bonnie and Clyde,* were able to use the knowledge that, like many of our other famous outlaws and gangsters, the real Bonnie and Clyde seemed to others to be acting out forbidden roles and to relish their roles. In contrast with secret criminals—the furtive embezzlers and other crooks who lead seemingly honest lives—the known outlaws capture the public imagination, because they take chances, and because, often, they enjoy dramatizing their lives. They know that newspaper readers want all the details they can get about the criminals who do the terrible things they themselves don't dare to do, and also want the satisfaction of reading about the punishment after feasting on the crimes. Outlaws play to this public; they show off their big guns and fancy clothes and their defiance of the law. Bonnie and Clyde established the images for their own legend in the photographs they posed for: the gunman and the gun moll. The naïve, touching doggerel ballad that Bonnie Parker wrote and had published in newspapers is about the roles they play for other people contrasted with the coming end for them. It concludes:

> Someday they'll go down together;
> They'll bury them side by side;
> To few it'll be grief—
> To the law a relief—
> But it's death for Bonnie and Clyde.

That they did capture the public imagination is evidenced by the many movies based on their lives. In the late forties, there were *They Live by Night,* with Farley Granger and Cathy O'Donnell, and *Gun Crazy,* with John Dall and Peggy Cummins. (Alfred Hitchcock, in the same period, cast these two Clyde Barrows, Dall and Granger, as Loeb and Leopold, in *Rope.*) And there was a cheap—in every sense—1958 exploitation film, [48–49] *The Bonnie Parker Story,* starring Dorothy Provine. But the most important earlier version was Fritz Lang's *You Only Live Once,* starring Sylvia Sidney as "Joan" and Henry Fonda as "Eddie," which was made in

1937; this version, which was one of the best American films of the thirties, as *Bonnie and Clyde* is of the sixties, expressed certain feelings of its time, as this film expresses certain feelings of ours. (*They Live by Night,* produced by John Houseman under the aegis of Dore Schary, and directed by Nicholas Ray, was a very serious and socially significant tragic melodrama, but its attitudes were already dated thirties attitudes: the lovers were very young and pure and frightened and underprivileged; the hardened criminals were sordid; the settings were committedly grim. It made no impact on the postwar audience, though it was a great success in England, where our moldy socially significant movies could pass for courageous.)

Just how contemporary in feeling *Bonnie and Clyde* is may be indicated by contrasting it with *You Only Live Once,* which, though almost totally false to the historical facts, was *told* straight. It is a peculiarity of our times—perhaps it's one of the few specifically modern characteristics—that we don't take our stories straight any more. This isn't necessarily bad. *Bonnie and Clyde* is the first film demonstration that the put-on can be used for the purposes of art. *The Manchurian Candidate almost* succeeded in that, but what was implicitly wild and far-out in the material was nevertheless presented on screen as a straight thriller. *Bonnie and Clyde* keeps the audience in a kind of eager, nervous imbalance—holds our attention by throwing our disbelief back in our faces. To be put on is to be put on the spot, put on the stage, made the stooge in a comedy act. People in the audience at *Bonnie and Clyde* are laughing, demonstrating that they're not stooges—that they appreciate the joke —when they catch the first bullet right in the face. The movie keeps them off balance to the end. During the first part of the picture, a woman in my row was gleefully assuring her companions, "It's a comedy. It's a comedy." After a while, she didn't say anything. Instead of the movie spoof, which tells the audience that it doesn't need to feel or care, that it's all just in fun, that "we were only kidding," *Bonnie and Clyde* disrupts us with "And you thought we were only kidding."

This is the way the story was told in 1937. Eddie (Clyde) is a three-time loser who wants to work for a living, but nobody will give him a chance. Once you get on the wrong side of the law, "they" won't let you get back. Eddie knows it's hopeless—once a loser, always a loser. But his girl, Joan (Bonnie) —the only person who believes in him—thinks that an innocent man has nothing to fear. She marries him, and learns better. Arrested again and sentenced to death for a crime he didn't commit, Eddie asks her to smuggle a gun to him in prison, and she protests, "If I get you a gun, you'll kill somebody." He stares at her sullenly and asks, "What do you think they're going to do to me?" He becomes a murderer while escaping from [49–50] prison; "society" has made him what it thought he was all along. *You Only Live Once* was an indictment of "society," of the forces of order that will not give Eddie the outcast a chance. "We have a right to live," Joan says as they set out across the country. During the time they are on the run, they become notorious outlaws; they are blamed for a series of crimes they didn't commit. (They do commit holdups, but only to get gas or groceries or medicine.) While the press pictures them as desperadoes robbing and killing and living high on the proceeds of crime, she is having a baby in a shack in a hobo jungle, and Eddie brings her a bouquet of wild flowers. Caught in a police trap, they die in each other's arms; they have been denied the right to live.

Because *You Only Live Once* was so well done, and because the audience in the thirties shared this view of the indifference and cruelty of "society," there were no protests against the sympathetic way the outlaws were pictured—and, indeed, there was no reason for any. In 1958, in *I Want to Live!* (a very popular, though not very good, movie), Barbara Graham, a drug-addict prostitute who had been executed for her share in the bludgeoning to death of an elderly woman, was presented as gallant, wronged, morally superior to everybody else in the movie, in order to strengthen the argument against capital punishment, and the director, Robert Wise, and his associates weren't accused of glorifying criminals, because the "criminals," as in *You Only Live Once,* weren't criminals but innocent victims. Why the protests, why are so many people upset (and not just the people who enjoy indignation), about *Bonnie and Clyde,* in which the criminals *are* criminals—Clyde an ignorant, sly near psychopath who thinks his crimes are accomplishments, and Bonnie a bored, restless waitress-slut who robs for excitement? And why so many accusations of historical inaccuracy, particularly against a work that is far more accurate historically than most and in which historical accuracy hardly matters anyway? There is always an issue of historical accuracy involved in any dramatic or literary work set in the past; indeed, it's fun to read about Richard III vs. Shakespeare's Richard III. The issue is always with us, and will always be with us as long as artists find stimulus in historical figures and want to present their versions of them. But why didn't movie critics attack, for example, *A Man for All Seasons*—which involves material of much more historical importance—for being historically inaccurate? Why attack *Bonnie and Clyde* more than the other movies based on the same pair, or more than the movie treatments of Jesse James or Billy the Kid or Dillinger or Capone or any of our other fictionalized outlaws? I would suggest that when a movie so clearly conceived as a new version of a legend is attacked as historically inaccurate, it's because it shakes people a little. I know this is based on some pretty sneaky psychological suppositions, but I don't see how else to account for the use only against a *good* movie of arguments that could be used against almost all [50–51] movies. When I asked a nineteen-year-old boy who was raging against the movie as "a cliché-ridden fraud" if he got so worked up about other movies, he informed me that that was an argument *ad hominem.* And it is indeed. To ask why people react so angrily to the best movies and have so little negative reaction to poor ones is to imply that they are so unused to the experience of art in movies that they fight it.

Audiences at *Bonnie and Clyde* are not given a simple, secure basis for identification; they are made to feel but are not told *how* to feel. *Bonnie and Clyde* is not a serious melodrama involving us in the plight of the innocent but a movie that assumes—as William Wellman did in 1931 when he made *The Public Enemy,* with James Cagney as a smart, cocky, mean little crook—that we don't need to pretend we're interested only in the falsely accused, as if real criminals had no connection with us. There wouldn't be the popular excitement there is about outlaws if we didn't all suspect that—in some cases, at least—gangsters must take pleasure in the profits and glory of a life of crime. Outlaws wouldn't become legendary figures if we didn't suspect that there's more to crime than the social workers' case studies may show. And though what we've always been told will happen to them—that they'll come to a bad end—does seem to happen, some part of us wants to believe in the tiny possibility that they can get away with it. Is that really so terrible? Yet when it comes to movies people get nervous about acknowledging that there must be some fun in crime (though the gleam in Cagney's eye told its own story). *Bonnie and Clyde* shows the fun but uses it, too, making comedy out of the banality and conventionality of that fun. What looks ludicrous in this movie isn't *merely* ludicrous, and after we have laughed at ignorance and helplessness and emptiness and stupidity and idiotic deviltry, the laughs keep sticking in our throats, because what's funny isn't only funny.

In 1937, the movie-makers knew that the audience wanted to believe in the innocence of Joan and Eddie, because these two were lovers, and innocent lovers hunted down like animals made a tragic love story. In 1967, the movie-makers know that the audience wants to believe—maybe even prefers to believe—that Bonnie and Clyde were guilty of crimes, all right, but that they were innocent in general; that is, naïve and ignorant *compared with us.* The distancing of the sixties version shows the gangsters in an already legendary period, and part of what makes a legend for Americans is viewing anything that happened in the past as much simpler than what we are involved in now. We tend to find the past funny and the recent past campy-funny. The getaway cars of the early thirties are made to seem hilarious. (Imagine anyone getting away from a bank holdup in a tin lizzie like that!) In *You Only Live Once,* the outlaws existed in the same present as the audience, and there was (and still is, I'm sure) nothing funny about them; in *Bonnie and Clyde* that audience is in the movie, transformed into [51–52] the poor people, the Depression people, of legend—with faces and poses out of Dorothea Lange and Walker Evans and *Let Us Now Praise Famous Men.* In 1937, the audience felt sympathy for the fugitives because they weren't allowed to lead normal lives; in 1967, the "normality" of the Barrow gang and their individual aspirations toward respectability are the craziest things about them—not just because they're killers but because thirties "normality" is in itself funny to us. The writers and the director of *Bonnie and Clyde* play upon our attitudes toward the American past by making the hats and guns and holdups look as dated as two-reel comedy; emphasizing the absurdity with banjo music, they make the period seem even farther away than it is. The Depression reminiscences are not used for purposes of social consciousness; hard times are not the reason for the Barrows' crimes, just the excuse. "We" didn't make Clyde a killer; the movie deliberately avoids easy sympathy by picking up Clyde when he is already a cheap crook. But Clyde is not the urban sharpster of *The Public Enemy;* he is the hick as bank robber—a countrified gangster, a hillbilly killer who doesn't mean any harm. People so simple that they are alienated from the results of their actions—like the primitives who don't connect babies with copulation—provide a kind of archetypal comedy for us. It may seem like a minor point that Bonnie and Clyde are presented as not mean and sadistic, as having killed only when cornered; but in terms of legend, and particularly movie legend, it's a major one. The "classic" gangster films showed gang members betraying each other and viciously murdering the renegade who left to join another gang; the gang-leader hero no sooner got to the top than he was betrayed by someone he had trusted or someone he had double-crossed. In contrast, the Barrow gang represents family-style crime. And Newman and Benton have been acute in emphasizing this—not making them victims of society (they are never that, despite Penn's cloudy efforts along these lines) but making them absurdly "just-folks" ordinary. When Bonnie tells Clyde to pull off the road—"I want to talk to you"—they are in a getaway car, leaving the scene of a robbery, with the police right behind them, but they are absorbed in family bickering: the traditional all-American use of the family automobile. In a sense, it is the absence of sadism—it is the violence without sadism—that throws the audience off balance at *Bonnie and Clyde*. The brutality that comes out of this innocence is far more shocking than the calculated brutalities of mean killers.

Playfully posing with their guns, the real Bonnie and Clyde mocked the "Bloody Barrows" of the Hearst press. One photograph shows slim, pretty Bonnie, smiling and impeccably dressed, pointing a huge gun at Clyde's chest as he, a dimpled dude with a cigar, smiles back. The famous picture of Bonnie in the same clothes but looking ugly squinting into the sun, with a foot on the car, a gun on her hip, and a cigar in her mouth, is obviously a joke—her caricature of herself as a gun moll. Probably, since they never [52–53] meant to kill, they thought the "Bloody Barrows" were a joke—a creation of the lying newspapers.

There's something new working for the Bonnie-and-Clyde legend now: our nostalgia for the thirties—the unpredictable, contrary affection of the prosperous for poverty, or at least for the artifacts, the tokens, of poverty, for Pop culture seen in the dreariest rural settings, where it truly seems to belong. Did people in the cities listen to the Eddie Cantor show? No doubt they did, but the sound of his voice, like the sound of Ed Sullivan now, evokes a primordial, pre-urban existence—the child-hood of the race. Our comic-melancholic affection for thirties Pop has become sixties Pop, and those who made *Bonnie and Clyde* are smart enough to use it that way. Being knowing is not an artist's highest gift, but it can make a hell of a lot of difference in a movie. In the American experience, the miseries of the Depression are funny in the way that the Army is funny to draftees—a shared catastrophe, a leveling, forming part of our common background. Those too young to remember the Depression have heard about it from their parents. (When I was at college, we used to top each other's stories about how our families had survived: the fathers who had committed suicide so that their wives and children could live off the in-surance; the mothers trying to make a game out of the meals of potatoes cooked on an open fire.) Though the American derision of the past has many offensive aspects, it has some good ones, too, because it's a way of making fun not only of our fore-bears but of ourselves and our pretentions. The toughness about what we've come out of and what we've been through—the honesty to see ourselves as the Yahoo children of yokels—is a good part of American popular art. There is a kind of American poetry in a stickup gang seen chasing across the bedraggled backdrop of the Depression (as true in its way as Nabokov's vision of Humbert Humbert and Lolita in the cross-country world of motels)—as if crime were the only activity in a country stupefied by poverty. But Arthur Penn doesn't quite have the toughness of mind to know it; it's not what he means by poetry. His squatters' jungle scene is too "eloquent," like a poster making an appeal, and the Parker family reunion se-quence is poetic in the gauzy mode. He makes the sequence a fancy lyric inter-lude, like a number in a musical (*Funny Face*, to be exact); it's too "imaginative"— a literal dust bowl, as thoroughly becalmed as Sleeping Beauty's garden. The movie becomes dreamy-soft where it should be hard (and hard-edged).

If there is such a thing as an American tragedy, it must be funny. O'Neill undoubtedly felt this when he had James Tyrone get up to turn off the lights in *Long Day's Journey Into Night*. We are bumpkins, haunted by the bottle of ketchup on the dining table at San Simeon. We garble our foreign words and phrases and hope that at least we've used them right. Our heroes pick up the wrong fork, and the basic figure of fun in the American theatre and American movies is the man who puts on airs. Children of peddlers and hod [53–54] carriers don't feel at home in tragedy; we are used to failure. But, because of the quality of American life at the present time, perhaps there can be no real comedy—nothing more than stupidity and "spoof"— without true horror in it. Bonnie and Clyde and their partners in crime are comically bad bank robbers, and the backdrop of poverty makes their holdups seem pathetically tacky, yet they rob banks and kill people; Clyde and his good natured brother are so shallow they never think much about anything, yet they suffer and die.

If this way of holding more than one attitude toward life is already familiar to us—if we recognize the make-believe robbers whose toy guns produce real blood, and the Keystone cops who shoot them dead, from Truffaut's *Shoot the Piano Player* and Godard's gangster pictures, *Breathless* and *Band of Outsiders*—it's because the young French directors discovered the poetry of crime in American life (from our movies) and showed the Americans how to put it on the screen in a new, "existential" way. Melodramas and gangster movies and comedies were always more our speed than "prestigious," "distinguished" pictures; the French directors who grew up on American pictures found poetry in our fast action, laconic speech, plain gestures. And because they understood that you don't express your love of life by denying the comedy or the horror of it, they brought out the poetry in our tawdry subjects. Now Arthur Penn, working with a script heavily influenced—one might almost say inspired—by Truffaut's *Shoot the Piano Player*, unfortunately imitates Truffaut's artistry instead of going back to its tough American sources. The French may tenderize their American material, but we shouldn't. That turns into another way of making "prestigious," "distinguished" pictures.

Probably part of the discomfort that people feel about *Bonnie and Clyde* grows out of its compromises and its failures. I wish the script hadn't provided the upbeat of the hero's sexual success as a kind of sop to the audience. I think what makes us not believe in it is that it isn't consistent with the intelligence of the rest of the writing—that it isn't on the same level because it's too manipulatively clever, too much of a gimmick. (The scene that shows the gnomish gang member called C. W. sleeping in the same room with Bonnie and Clyde suggests other possibilities, perhaps discarded, as does C. W.'s reference to Bonnie's liking his tattoo.) Compromises are not new to the Bonnie-and-Clyde story; *You Only Live Once* had a tacked-on coda featuring a Heavenly choir and William Gargan as a dead priest, patronizing Eddie even in the afterlife, welcoming him to Heaven with "You're free, Eddie!" The kind of people who make a movie like *You Only Live Once* are not the kind who write endings like that, and, by the same sort of internal evidence, I'd guess that Newman and Benton, whose Bonnie seems to owe so much to Catherine in *Jules and Jim*, had more interesting ideas originally about Bonnie's and Clyde's (and maybe C.W.'s) sex lives.   [54–55]

But people also feel uncomfortable about the violence, and here I think they're wrong. That is to say, they *should* feel uncomfortable, but this isn't an argument *against* the movie. Only a few years ago, a good director would have suggested the violence obliquely, with reaction shots (like the famous one in *The Golden Coach*, when we see a whole bullfight reflected in Anna Magnani's face), and death might have been symbolized by a light going out, or stylized, with blood and wounds kept to a minimum. In many ways, this method is more effective; we feel the violence more because so much is left to our imaginations. But the whole point of *Bonnie and Clyde* is to rub our noses in it, to make us pay our dues for laughing. The dirty reality of death—not suggestions but blood and holes—is necessary. Though I generally respect a director's skill and intelligence in inverse ratio to the violence he shows on the screen, and though I questioned even the Annie Sullivan–Helen Keller fight scenes in Arthur Penn's *The Miracle Worker*, I think that this time Penn is right. (I think he was also right when he showed violence in his first film, *The Left Handed Gun*, in 1958.) Suddenly, in the last few years, our view of the world has gone beyond "good taste." Tasteful suggestions of violence would at this point be a more grotesque form of comedy than *Bonny and Clyde* attempts. *Bonnie and Clyde* needs violence; violence is its meaning. When, during a comically botched-up getaway, a man is shot in the face, the image is obviously based on one of the most famous sequences in Eisenstein's *Potemkin*, and the startled face is used the same way it was in *Potemkin*—to convey in an instant how someone who just happens to be in the wrong place at the wrong time, the irrelevant "innocent" bystander, can get it full in the face. And at that instant the meaning of Clyde Barrow's character changes; he's still a clown, but *we've* become the butt of the joke.

It is a kind of violence that says something to us; it is something that movies must be free to use. And it is just because artists must be free to use violence—a legal right that is beginning to come under attack—that we must also defend the legal rights of those film-makers who use violence to sell tickets, for it is not the province of the law to decide that one man is an artist and another man a no-talent. The no-talent has as much right to produce works as the artist has, and not only because he has a surprising way of shifting from one category to the other but also because men have an inalienable right to be untalented, and the law should not discriminate against lousy "artists." I am not saying that the violence in *Bonnie and Clyde* is legally acceptable because the film is a work of art; I think that *Bonnie and Clyde*, though flawed, is a work of art, but I think that the violence in *The Dirty Dozen*, which isn't a work of art, and whose violence offends me *personally*, should also be legally defensible, however morally questionable. Too many people—including some movie reviewers—want the law to take over the job of movie criticism; perhaps what they really [55–56] want is for their own criticisms to have the force of law. Such people see *Bonnie and Clyde* as a danger to public morality; they think an audience goes to a play or a movie and takes the actions in it as examples for imitation. They look at the world and blame the movies. But if women who are angry with their husbands take it out on the kids, I don't think we can blame *Medea* for it; if, as has been said, we are a nation of mother-lovers, I don't think we can place the blame on *Oedipus Rex*. Part of the power of art lies in showing us what we are *not* capable of. We see that killers are not a different breed but are *us* without the insight or understanding or self-control that works of art strengthen. The tragedy of *Macbeth* is in the fall from nobility to horror; the comic tragedy of *Bonnie and Clyde* is that although you can't fall from the bottom you can reach the same horror. The movies may set styles in dress- or love-making, they may advertise cars or beverages, but art is not examples for imitation—that is not what a work of art does for us—though that is what guardians of morality *think* art is and what they want it to be and why they think a good movie is one that sets "healthy," "cheerful" examples of behavior, like a giant all-purpose commercial for the American way of life. But people don't "buy" what they see in a movie quite so simply; Louis B. Mayer did not turn us into a nation of Andy Hardys, and if, in a film, we see a frightened man wantonly take the life of another, it does not encourage us to do the same any more than seeing an ivory hunter shoot an elephant makes us want to shoot one. It may, on the contrary, so sensitize us that we get a pang in the gut if we accidentally step on a moth.

Will we, as some people have suggested, be lured into imitating the violent crimes of Clyde and Bonnie because Warren Beatty and Faye Dunaway are "glamorous"? Do they, as some people have charged, confer glamour on violence? It's difficult to see how, since the characters they play are horrified by it and ultimately destroyed by it. Nobody in the movie gets pleasure from violence. Is the charge based on the notion that simply by their presence in the movie Warren Beatty and Faye Dunaway make crime attractive? If movie stars can't play criminals without our all wanting to be criminals then maybe the only safe roles for them to play are movie stars—which, in this assumption, everybody wants to be anyway. After all, if they played factory workers, the economy might be dislocated by everybody's trying to become a factory worker. (Would having criminals played by dwarfs or fatties discourage crime? It seems rather doubtful.) The accusation that the beauty of movie stars makes the anti-social acts of their characters dangerously attractive is the kind of contrived argument we get from people who are bothered by something and are clutching at straws. Actors and actresses are *usually* more beautiful than ordinary people. And why not? Garbo's beauty notwithstanding, her Anna Christie did not turn us into whores, her Mata Hari did not turn us into spies, her Anna Karenina did not make us suicides. [56–57] We did not want her to be ordinary looking. Why should we be deprived of the pleasure of beauty? Garbo could be all women in love because, being more beautiful than life, she could more beautifully express emotions. It is a supreme asset for actors and actresses to be beautiful; it gives them greater range and greater possibilities for expressiveness. The handsomer thay are, the more roles they can play; Olivier can be anything, but who would want to see Ralph Richardson, great as he is, play Antony? Actors and actresses who are beautiful start with an enormous advantage, because we love to look at them. The joke in the glamour charge is that Faye Dunaway has the magazine-illustration look of countless uninterestingly pretty girls, and Warren Beatty has the kind of high-school good looks that are generally lost fast. It's the roles that make *them* seem glamorous. Good roles do that for actors.

There is a story told against Beatty in a recent *Esquire*—how during the shooting of *Lilith* he "delayed a scene for three days demanding the line 'I've read *Crime and Punishment* and *The Brothers Karamazov*' be changed to 'I've read *Crime and Punishment* and *half* of *The Brothers Karamazov.'"* Considerations of professional conduct aside, what is odd is why his adversaries waited three days to give in, because, of course, he was right. That's what the character he played *should* say; the other way, the line has no point at all. But this kind of intuition isn't enough to make an actor, and in a number of roles Beatty, probably because he doesn't have the technique to make the most of his lines in the least possible time, has depended too much on intuitive non-acting—holding the screen far too long as he acted out self-preoccupied characters in a lifelike, boringly self-conscious way. He has a gift for slyness, though, as he showed in *The Roman Spring of Mrs. Stone,* and in most of his films he could hold the screen—maybe because there seemed to be something going on in his mind, some kind of calculation. There was something smart about him —something shrewdly private in those squeezed-up little non-actor's eyes—that didn't fit the clean-cut juvenile roles. Beatty was the producer of *Bonnie and Clyde,* responsible for keeping the company on schedule, and he has been quoted as saying, "There's not a scene that we have done that we couldn't do better by taking another day." This is the hell of the expensive way of making movies, but it probably helps to explain why Beatty is more intense than he has been before and why he has picked up his pace. His business sense may have improved his timing. The role of Clyde Barrow seems to have released something in him. As Clyde, Beatty is good with his eyes and mouth and his hat, but his body is still inexpressive; he doesn't have a trained actor's use of his body, and, watching him move, one is never for a minute convinced he's impotent. It is, however, a tribute to his performance that one singles this failure out. His slow timing works perfectly in the sequence in which he offers the dispossessed farmer his gun; there may not be another actor who [57–58] would have dared to prolong the scene that way, and the prolongation until the final "We rob banks" gives the sequence its comic force. I have suggested elsewhere that one of the reasons that rules are impossible in the arts is that in movies (and in the other arts, too) the new "genius"—the genuine as well as the fraudulent or the dubious —is often the man who has enough audacity, or is simpleminded enough, to do what others had the good taste not to do. Actors before Brando did not mumble and scratch and show their sweat; dramatists before Tennessee Williams did not make explicit a particular substratum of American erotic fantasy; movie directors before Orson Welles did not dramatize the techniques of film-making; directors before Richard Lester did not lay out the whole movie as cleverly as the opening credits; actresses before Marilyn Monroe did not make an asset of their ineptitude by turning faltering misreadings into an appealing style. Each, in a large way, did something that people had always enjoyed and were often embarrassed or ashamed about enjoying. Their "bad taste" shaped a new accepted taste. Beatty's non-actor's "bad" timing may be this kind of "genius"; we seem to be watching him *think out* his next move.

It's difficult to know how Bonnie should have been played, because the character isn't worked out. Here the script seems weak. She is made too warmly sympathetic—and sympathetic in a style that antedates the style of the movie. Being frustrated and moody, she's not funny enough—neither ordinary, which, in the circumstances, would be comic, nor perverse, which might be rather funny, too. Her attitude toward her mother is too loving. There could be something funny about her

wanting to run home to her mama, but as it has been done, her heading home, running off through the fields, is unconvincing—incompletely motivated. And because
the element of the ridiculous that makes the others so individual has been left out
of her character she doesn't seem to belong to the period as the others do. Faye
Dunaway has a sixties look anyway—not just because her eyes are made up in a
sixties way and her hair is wrong but because her personal style and her acting are
sixties. (This may help to make her popular; she can seem prettier to those who don't
recognize prettiness except in the latest styles.) Furthermore, in some difficult-to-
define way, Faye Dunaway as Bonnie doesn't keep her distance—that is to say, an
actor's distance—either from the role or from the audience. She doesn't hold a characterization; she's in and out of emotions all the time, and though she often hits
effective ones, the emotions seem *hers,* not the character's. She has some talent,
but she comes on too strong; she makes one conscious that she's a willing worker,
but she doesn't seem to know what she's doing—rather like Bonnie in her attempts to
overcome Clyde's sexual difficulties.

Although many daily movie reviewers judge a movie in isolation, as if
the people who made it had no previous history, more serious critics now commonly attempt to judge a movie as an expressive vehicle of the director, and
[58–59] a working out of his personal themes. Auden has written, "Our judgment
of an established author is never simply an aesthetic judgment. In addition to any
literary merit it may have, a new book by him has a historic interest for us as the act
of a person in whom we have long been interested. He is not only a poet . . . he is
also a character in our biography." For a while, people went to the newest Bergman
and the newest Fellini that way; these movies were greeted like the latest novels of a
favorite author. But Arthur Penn is not a writer-director like Bergman or Fellini, both
of whom began as writers, and who (even though Fellini employs several collaborators) compose their spiritual autobiographies step by step on film. Penn is far more
dependent on the talents of others, and his primary material—what he starts with—
does not come out of his own experience. If the popular audience is generally uninterested in the director (unless he is heavily publicized, like DeMille or Hitchcock), the audience that is interested in the art of movies has begun, with many of
the critics, to think of movies as a directors' medium to the point where they tend
to ignore the contribution of the writers—and the directors may be almost obscenely
content to omit mention of the writers. The history of the movies is being rewritten
to disregard facts in favor of celebrating the director as the sole "creative" force.
One can read Josef von Sternberg's autobiography and the text of the latest books
on his movies without ever finding the name of Jules Furthman, the writer who
worked on nine of his most famous movies (including *Morocco* and *Shanghai Express*). Yet the appearance of Furthman's name in the credits of such Howard Hawks
films as *Only Angels Have Wings, To Have and Have Not, The Big Sleep,* and *Rio
Bravo* suggests the reason for the similar qualities of good-bad-girl glamour in the
roles played by Dietrich and Bacall and in other von Sternberg and Hawks heroines,
and also in the Jean Harlow and Constance Bennett roles in the movies he wrote for
them. Furthman, who has written about half of the most entertaining movies to
come out of Hollywood (Ben Hecht wrote most of the other half), isn't even listed

in new encyclopedias of the film. David Newman and Robert Benton may be good enough to join this category of unmentionable men who do what the directors are glorified for. The Hollywood writer is becoming a ghostwriter. The writers who succeed in the struggle to protect their identity and their material by becoming writer-directors or writer-producers soon become too rich and powerful to bother doing their own writing. And they rarely have the visual sense or the training to make good movie directors.

Anyone who goes to big American movies like *Grand Prix* and *The Sand Pebbles* recognizes that movies with scripts like those don't have a chance to be anything more than exercises in technology, and that this is what is meant by the decadence of American movies. In the past, directors used to say that they were no better than their material. (Sometimes they said it when they weren't even up to their material.) A good director can attempt to [59–60] camouflage poor writing with craftsmanship and style, but ultimately no amount of director's skill can conceal a writer's failure; a poor script, even well directed, results in a stupid movie—as, unfortunately, does a good script poorly directed. Despite the new notion that the direction is everything, Penn can't redeem bad material, nor, as one may surmise from his *Mickey One,* does he necessarily know when it's bad. It is not fair to judge Penn by a film like *The Chase,* because he evidently did not have artistic control over the production, but what happens when he does have control and is working with a poor, pretentious mess of a script is painfully apparent in *Mickey One*—an art film in the worst sense of that term. Though one cannot say of *Bonnie and Clyde* to what degree it shows the work of Newman and Benton and to what degree they merely enabled Penn to "express himself," there are ways of making guesses. As we hear the lines, we can detect the intentions even when the intentions are not quite carried out. Penn is a little clumsy and rather too fancy; he's too much interested in being cinematically creative and artistic to know when to trust the script. *Bonnie and Clyde* could be better if it were simpler. Nevertheless, Penn is a remarkable director when he has something to work with. His most interesting previous work was in his first film, *The Left Handed Gun* (and a few bits of *The Miracle Worker,* a good movie version of the William Gibson play, which he had also directed on the stage and on television). *The Left Handed Gun,* with Paul Newman as an ignorant Billy the Kid in the sex-starved, male-dominated Old West, has the same kind of violent, legendary, nostalgic material as *Bonnie and Clyde;* its script, a rather startling one, was adapted by Leslie Stevens from a Gore Vidal television play. In interviews, Penn makes high, dull sounds—more like a politician than a movie director. But he has a gift for violence, and, despite all the violence in movies, a gift for it is rare. (Eisenstein had it, and Dovzhenko, and Buñuel, but not many others.) There are few memorable violent moments in American movies, but there is one in Penn's first film: Billy's shotgun blasts a man right out of one of his boots; the man falls in the street, but his boot remains upright; a little girl's giggle at the boot is interrupted by her mother's slapping her. The mother's slap—the seal of the awareness of horror—says that even children must learn that some things that look funny are not only funny. That slap, saying that only idiots would laugh at pain and death, that a child must develop sensibility, is the same slap that *Bonnie and Clyde* delivers to the woman saying "It's a comedy." In *The Left Handed Gun,* the slap is itself funny, and yet we suck in our breath; we do not dare to laugh.

Some of the best American movies show the seams of cuts and the confusions of compromises and still hold together, because there is enough energy
and spirit to carry the audience over each of the weak episodes to the next good one.
The solid intelligence of the writing and Penn's aura of sensitivity help *Bonnie and
Clyde* triumph over many poorly directed scenes: [60–61] Bonnie posing for the
photograph with the Texas Ranger, or—the worst sequence—the Ranger getting
information out of Blanche Barrow in the hospital. The attempt to make the Texas
Ranger an old-time villain doesn't work. He's in the tradition of the mustachioed
heavy who foreclosed mortgages and pursued heroines in turn-of-the-century plays,
and this one-dimensional villainy belongs, glaringly, to spoof. In some cases, I
think, the writing and the conception of the scenes are better (potentially, that is)
than the way the scenes have been directed and acted. If Gene Hackman's Buck
Barrow is a beautifully controlled performance, the best in the film, several of the
other players—though they are very good—needed a tighter rein. They act too much.
But it is in other ways that Penn's limitations show—in his excessive reliance on
meaning-laden closeups, for one. And it's no wonder he wasn't able to bring out the
character of Bonnie in scenes like the one showing her appreciation of the fingernails
on the figurine, for in other scenes his own sense of beauty appears to be only a few
rungs farther up that same cultural ladder.

The showpiece sequence, Bonnie's visit to her mother (which is a bit
reminiscent of Humphrey Bogart's confrontation with his mother, Marjorie Main, in
the movie version of *Dead End*), aims for an effect of alienation, but that effect is
confused by all the other things attempted in the sequence: the poetic echoes of
childhood (which also echo the child sliding down the hill in *Jules and Jim*) and a
general attempt to create a frieze from our national past—a poetry of poverty. Penn
isn't quite up to it, though he is at least good enough to communicate what he is
trying to do, and it is an attempt that one can respect. In 1939, John Ford attempted
a similar poetic evocation of the legendary American past in *Young Mr. Lincoln*;
this kind of evocation, by getting at how we *feel* about the past, moves us far more
than attempts at historical re-creation. When Ford's Western evocations fail, they
become languorous; when they succeed, they are the West of our dreams, and his
Lincoln, the man so humane and so smart that he can outwit the unjust and save the
innocent, is the Lincoln of our dreams, as the Depression of *Bonnie and Clyde* is
the Depression of our dreams—the nation in a kind of trance, as in a dim memory.
In this sense, the effect of blur is justified, is "right." Our memories *have* become
hazy; this is what the Depression has faded into. But we are too conscious of the
technical means used to achieve this blur, of the *attempt* at poetry. We are aware that
the filtered effects already include our responses, and it's too easy; the lines are
good enough so that the stylization wouldn't have been necessary if the scene had
been played right. A simple frozen frame might have been more appropriate.

The editing of this movie is, however, the best editing in an American
movie in a long time, and one may assume that Penn deserves credit for it along with
the editor, Dede Allen. It's particularly inventive in the robberies [61–62] and in
the comedy sequence of Blanche running through the police barricades with her
kitchen spatula in her hand. (There is, however, one bad bit of editing: the end of the
hospital scene, when Blanche's voice makes an emotional shift without a corresponding change in her facial position.) The quick panic of Bonnie and Clyde

looking at each other's face for the last time is a stunning example of the art of editing.

The end of the picture, the rag-doll dance of death as the gun blasts keep the bodies of Bonnie and Clyde in motion, is brilliant. It is a horror that seems to go on for eternity, and yet it doesn't last a second beyond what it should. The audience leaving the theatre is the quietest audience imaginable.

Still, that woman near me was saying "It's a comedy" for a little too long, and although this could have been, and probably was, a demonstration of plain old-fashioned insensitivity, it suggests that those who have attuned themselves to the "total" comedy of the last few years may not know when to stop laughing. Movie audiences have been getting a steady diet of "black" comedy since 1964 and *Dr. Strangelove, Or: How I Learned to Stop Worrying and Love the Bomb.* Spoof and satire have been entertaining audiences since the two-reelers; because it is so easy to do on film things that are difficult or impossible in nature, movies are ideally suited to exaggerations of heroic prowess and to the kind of lighthearted nonsense we used to get when even the newsreels couldn't resist the kidding finish of the speeded-up athletic competition or the diver flying up from the water. The targets have usually been social and political fads and abuses, together with the heroes and the clichés of the just preceding period of film-making. *Dr. Strangelove* opened a new movie era. It ridiculed *everything* and *everybody* it showed, but concealed its own liberal pieties, thus protecting itself from ridicule. A professor who had told me that *The Manchurian Candidate* was "irresponsible," adding, "I didn't like it—I can suspend disbelief only so far," was overwhelmed by *Dr. Strangelove*: "I've never been so involved. I had to keep reminding myself it was only a movie." *Dr. Strangelove* was clearly intended as a cautionary movie; it meant to jolt us awake to the dangers of the bomb by showing us the insanity of the course we were pursuing. But artists' warnings about war and the dangers of total annihilation never tell us how we are supposed to regain control, and *Dr. Strangelove,* chortling over madness, did not indicate any possibilities for sanity. It was experienced not as satire but as a confirmation of fears. Total laughter carried the day. A new generation enjoyed seeing the world as insane; they *literally* learned to stop worrying and love the bomb. Conceptually, we had already been living with the bomb; now the mass audience of the movies—which is the youth of America—grasped the idea that the threat of extinction can be used to devaluate everything, to turn it all into a joke. And the members of this audience do love the bomb; they love feeling that the worst has happened and [62–63] the irrational are the sane, because there is the bomb as the proof that the rational are insane. They love the bomb because it intensifies their feelings of hopelessness and powerlessness and innocence. It's only three years since Lewis Mumford was widely acclaimed for saying about *Dr. Strangelove* that "unless the spectator was purged by laughter he would be paralyzed by the unendurable anxiety this policy, once it were honestly appraised, would produce." Far from being purged, the spectators are paralyzed, but they're still laughing. And how odd it is now to read, "*Dr. Strangelove* would be a silly, ineffective picture if its purpose were to ridicule the characters of our military and political leaders by showing them as clownish monsters—stupid, psychotic, obsessed." From *Dr. Strangelove* it's a quick leap to *MacBird* and to a belief in exactly what it was said we weren't meant to find in *Dr. Strangelove*. It is not war that has been laughed to scorn but the possibility of sane action.

    Once something enters mass culture, it travels fast. In the spoofs of the last few years, everything is gross, ridiculous, insane; to make sense would be to risk being square. A brutal new melodrama is called *Point Blank* and it is. So are most of the new movies. This is the context in which *Bonnie and Clyde,* an entertaining movie that has some feeling in it, upsets people—people who didn't get upset even by *Mondo Cane.* Maybe it's because *Bonnie and Clyde,* by making us care about the robber lovers, has put the sting back into death.   [63]

1.   How does Miss Kael treat counterarguments? Is her method convincing?

2.   Do you agree with her defense of the film's comic treatment of crime?

3.   Why does Miss Kael deride the director's presentation of Depression America? Do you agree with her?

4.   How convincing is her defense of the film's violence? Compare her article with that by Joseph Morgenstern. What are your own conclusions about the place of violence in films?

5.   Why does Miss Kael raise the issue of censorship? Is this relevant to her argument? See the piece by Charles Thomas Samuels on this point. Do you agree with his explanation of Miss Kael's concern with censorship?

6.   Outline this essay. What observations can you make about Miss Kael's method of organization? Its relationship to her arguments?

7.   What is Pauline Kael's explanation for the anger produced by *Bonnie and Clyde?* How is this related to her previous points?

BONNIE AND CLYDE

CHARLES THOMAS SAMUELS

A bunch of decayed cabbage leaves smeared with catsup, *Bonnie and Clyde* has been judged an artistic bouquet; not by middlebrow critics like Bosley Crowther but by reviewers whose very names stand for the setting and guiding of taste. Admittedly, the film is well-acted, slickly paced, and brilliantly edited. Yet after granting its technical polish, one is left with its meaning, which is heavily obvious when not confused; its tone and characterization, which are both implausible and inconsistent; and its violence, which is stomach-turning. One who measures its cynical falsity will realize how worrisome is its success.

To begin with, *Bonnie and Clyde* is presumed to be making serious comments about crime. So far as I can see, the comments are these: crime is joyless, it is sick, it is less concerned with money than fame. As an example of the first point, we have the scene at a motel in which Clyde's brother hoots and hollers, "Whooee, we'll have ourselves a time."—Long pause—"What we gonna do?"—followed by Clyde's account of how he avoided prison work by cutting off two toes, concluded with a broad smile and an "Ain't life grand!" To establish the bankrobber's sickness, we have at least four instances of Clyde's impotence that presumably explain his reliance on more lethal weapons. By way of asserting that the criminals seek publicity rather than gain, we have the Barrows stealing a newspaper from a rural mailbox before they count the proceeds from their latest bank. It is difficult to understand how insights so dramatized can be taken seriously; but Joseph Morgenstern, who on first viewing thought *Bonnie and Clyde* "a squalid shoot-'em-up for the moron trade," acknowledged great purposiveness and subtlety when *Newsweek* permitted him a public reversal the following week.

CHARLES THOMAS SAMUELS, of the Williams College English department, has published a pamphlet on John Updike (1969) and film and literary criticism in *The Atlantic Monthly, The Kenyon Review, The New Republic* and other magazines.

This article originally appeared in *The Hudson Review*, Vol. XXI, No. 1, pp. 10–22.

Viewers might well find themselves confused, for the film shuttles back and forth between radically different tones. Through most of the gang's activities, fast pacing and banjo music contrive to turn mayhem into zaniness and the bloody Barrows into charming hicks; but, in addition to being primitive, these scenes violate characterization and plausibility. Take, for example, Clyde's first bank robbery. As Bonnie drives him to the site of the crime, he seems as nervous as a raw recruit, yet we know that he has already served time for what he here contemplates with dread. (One might argue that this shows Clyde to be a frightened punk, but usually, as in the woods or the café before this job, he is made to seem authoritative, even sensitive.) When Bonnie finally shames him into action, he discovers that the bank is out of business. Considerately, the management has left a teller [10] behind to inform him of the fact; but, of course, without the teller, there would be no comedy. Even more absurd is their second job, during which the get-away man, C. W. Moss, nearly ruins everything by backing into a parking place—guided less by his own stupidity than by the scriptwriters' desire for laughs. Eventually Moss pulls out, but his delay permits the bank's employees to chase him. Here the film turns suddenly gory, a fact that has occasioned its admirers' most sophistical argument.

Pauline Kael asserts that the comedy purposefully turns into violence in order to implicate the viewer, who will be harrowed when he realizes that crime isn't, after all, fun: "the whole point of *Bonnie and Clyde* is to rub our noses in it, to make us pay our dues for laughing." What Miss Kael neglects to admit is that we laugh only because the director and writers have forced us—by wrenching their materials to fit a comic mold. Penelope Gilliatt recognizes that "the movie is full of scenes of giggling and show-off, but the mood belongs to the characters, not the film." One would be interested to see how she might go about arguing this distinction.

When sexually motivating the protagonists' crimes—that is to say, when introducing psychology to tone matters up—the film becomes not only implausible but dishonest. Scenarists David Newman and Robert Benton have recently confessed that Clyde was originally to have been homosexual rather than impotent, "but we [made the change] because homosexuality took over the whole movie and colored all responses." Translated less ingenuously, this comes out: whereas homosexuality repels the average spectator, impotence is likely to make him sympathetic. After all, Clyde is a hero.

Similarly motivated are the many hints that Bonnie and Clyde were heroes because America was undergoing a Depression. This note is first struck when Clyde invites a dispossessed farmer to shoot the sign placed before his house by the bank. Throughout the film, its director and set designer take great trouble duplicating the thirties in order to surround the Barrows with an ambience of social decay so palpable that mere presence might suggest causality. Thus we are disposed to believe Clyde when he promises Bonnie's mother that they will stop stealing as soon as times improve, and we can sympathize when the couple is forced to steal food because the bank they had previously attempted had already failed. But apart from the offensive facility with which it yokes public circumstance and private crime, occasionally the film argues against its own implication. Before they are killed, for example, when Bonnie asks Clyde what he would do with his life to live over, after an intense moment of concentration, he replies that he would pull his jobs in other states.

   Bonnie and Clyde runs off in many directions at once (even Pauline Kael, who runs off in quite a few herself, calls it at one point, "the first film demonstration that the put-on can be used for the purposes [12] of art"). Yet though all of its admirers are aware that the film might be called wayward, they either de-emphasize or ignore its banal confusion. But since *Bonnie and Clyde* is so confused, its violence shows all the more lurid against the vague thematic background. The interesting questions to raise about the film therefore are why so many reputable critics condone violence lacking expressive purpose and why customers are willing to pay for a movie both repulsive in its bloodshed and disorienting in its tonal shifts. What holds the film together for these groups who themselves form so unexpected a combination?

   We can approach an answer by way of the movie's most discussed episode. When Bonnie returns to her mother, the director shoots the scene in soft focus, emphasizing not only the dusty atmosphere in which it transpires but the haze of nostalgia and family feeling through which its participants perceive themselves. Bonnie's family is delighted to welcome the returning prodigals; they have kept a scrapbook of the gang's exploits. Bonnie romps with the children; Clyde, the good son-in-law, enjoys the vittles. We might be witnessing the family picnic of all our dreams—until Bonnie's mother tells her daughter and Clyde to keep on running from the cops. This ironic reversal, however, is too pat and unsurprising to dissipate the foregoing effect of lyricism, especially since the picnic is preceded by another scene of lyricism so fruity that we are now thoroughly confused. In the earlier scene, Clyde pursues Bonnie as she flees the gang to make her way home. Catching up with her in a golden wheatfield, he wails plaintively, "Please don't never leave me without sayin' nuttin.'" Accompanied by soulful music, the loving couple embraces, while the camera draws back, leaving them a poor tangled speck in a giant sea of grain over which portentous clouds glide, casting shadows. Under the circumstances, this might seem a sick joke: casting the crooks—previously clowns or desperadoes—in the roles of Mr. Newlywed and the young wife who wants to run home to mother. But like several other scenes, it creates unmistakable identification between the Barrows and the audience; and it is this identification which holds the spectator. Then, having persuaded the audience to identify with the Barrows, the film goes on to suggest that the crooks are superior to society. Here the serious critics seem to have found their delight.

   It may seem tedious to recall the many ways in which the film slanders society, but I don't think one can understand its current popularity until this motif has been explored. Its presentation is relentless, beginning when the hungry but penniless Clyde attempts to steal groceries. While he inquires after peach pie, a piggish clerk flies down at him with a meat cleaver, thus nearly validating his subsequent chagrin: "He tried to kill me. I didn' wanna hurt him. You try to get somep'n to eat round here, they come at you with a meat cleaver." Throughout the film, the forces of property and law respond with [14] excessive, even sadistic zeal. Not only do they require 1000 rounds of ammunition to finish the lovers off but when the gang tries to settle down in tidy domesticity, the cops intrude without even the chivalrous warning one has come to expect from earlier gangster movies ("All right, come out now; the house is surrounded!"). Ambushing the Barrows at a motel, the police unfairly arrive in an armored car at just the moment when Bonnie is showing Clyde how she has taken in an old dress; and when they kill Clyde's brother by surrounding him as he's down, the deputies shout like Comanche savages, in whose classic formation they have been staged. Yet though the besieged gang kills its share, the lawmen, unlike the criminals, never bleed.

If we turn our attention to the Barrows' only differentiated antagonists, the film's bias becomes unmistakable. The sheriff who finally kills the lovers sports a devilish mustache and, in the death scene, wears a black shirt, though everything about Bonnie and Clyde, including their car, is white. Critics have admired the film's insight into the crooks' pathetic desire for publicity. Sheriff Hamer is similarly motivated, but in his case the impulse is bad: he goes after Bonnie and Clyde out of vengeance, because they humiliated him by circulating the photo in which they forced him to pose as their captive.

Because the gang's antagonists are pigs and devils who wear black shirts and don't bleed, and because they have formed a society actually inferior to that of the criminals,[1] in which brotherhood and love predominate, we can sympathize with the Barrows, even though they are hard to keep in rational focus. But because the criminals are sick, dumb, and ludicrous, we can bear to watch them die. Citing this latter characteristic, Pauline Kael argues that *Bonnie and Clyde* is less sentimental than standard Hollywood gangster films because they used to make the criminals innocent. But in drama, if not in life, innocence is relative. The movie clearly authorizes Bonnie's doggerel characterization of herself and Clyde as scapegoats whom society will not leave in peace.

Thereby forced into partisanship, a spectator can actually approve the blood as the red badge of Bonnie and Clyde's undeserved suffering. Critics, of course, have found something deeper in it. More or less overt in every favorable review is the notion that *Bonnie and Clyde* makes a valid comment not so much on their lives as on ours. We know better than the thirties that violence may substitute for love, [16] that it is often perpetrated by moral morons, that America today incites violence by its disrespect for law and people. "All this should strike the viewer with icy familiarity," asserts Robert Hatch (an editor of *The Nation*) "in our day of motorcycle gangs and flower children, Nazi insignia, cheap beads, incense, drugs, apathy and motiveless violence." Whereas the audience probably identifies with Bonnie and Clyde as surrogate social victims, serious reviewers identify them as surrogate social problems. No wonder, despite the bloodshed, that everyone is happy.

But the movie's inventors give a less edifying account of their product's appeal: violence in the arts, they say, is "fun," "and if that idea causes you to blanch

---

[1] At no time is the film's comedy more heavily thematic than when the gang kidnaps the couple, Eugene and Velma. By turns, we are treated to exposures of the couple's prurience, cowardice, and secret regard for crime. Though blatant, all this has some relevance. Why though, do we get the revelation that Velma has lied to Eugene about her age? For the same reason that the respectable Mr. Moss, who will betray Bonne and Clyde, shouts at his son, "I'm glad that your ma ain't alive to see this thing," meaning not C. W.'s crime but his tattoo. And for the same reason that the one member of the gang who is disloyal, dishonest, and greedy is Blanche—the preacher's daughter.

or cluck the tongue reprovingly . . . then you are not only soft . . . you are something worse: out of step." As Pauline Kael reports with equanimity, "in the spoofs of the last few years, everything is gross, ridiculous, insane; to make sense would be to risk being square."

Ironically, whereas Newman and Benton (creators of Esquire's "What's In and What's Out" and Dubious Achievement Awards) think violence fun and significance a drag, reviewers and moviegoers have, through their earnest pursuit of the movie's purpose, turned Bonnie and Clyde into the year's most successful and —the ads bray—"most talked-about film." This irony is the true key to the film's meaning, for as Newsweek reports, Newman and Benton "always seem to know what's going to pop up next in American culture."

Lurid example of a vulgar, wornout genre, Bonnie and Clyde nevertheless seems up-to-date. Not because of its technique, out of Godard and the vaudeville blackout; not because of its ideas, out of Sanctuary (the impotent gunman) or Erik Erikson (the identity crisis), but because of an attitude which persuades the viewer to swallow its violence: the attitude—it is precisely nothing more—that society and normality are frauds. Since this is close to having become a contemporary article of faith, it is no wonder that violence has become as entertaining in art as it seems to have become excusable in politics. Oppose the latter, and you are a soft-hearted liberal; oppose the former, and you are "something worse: out of step."

That Bosley Crowther is "out of step" should come as no surprise. When for once, however, he marched slowly in a good cause, he brought down upon his head anger so fierce that we can now see how precious a possession the film's attitude has become. Thus Penelope Gilliat, obviously thinking of Crowther, said that one would need "a head full of wooden shavings" to think that the movie glamorized crime, though if the word "glamorize" is correctly understood it is entirely to the point. Thus Pauline Kael, obviously thinking of Crowther, begins her piece in a manner uniquely wistful: "How do you make a good movie in this country without being jumped on?" (Miss Kael, it should be explained, thinks "Bonnie and Clyde . . . the most excitingly [18] American American movie since The Manchurian Candidate!"). Thus Andrew Sarris felt called upon to begin his review in The Village Voice by informing readers that "Bonnie and Clyde has become the subject of a Crowther crusade that makes the 100-Years-War look like a border incident" (a remark whose inaptness would inspire hyperbole had Sarris not already pre-empted the heights). In fact, so enraged is Sarris that he charges poor Crowther with a crime of which Crowther was manifestly innocent: calling for censorship, "at a time when too many bigots see a golden opportunity to lash the Negro with fake rhetoric of law and order."

Sarris' absurd political analogy suggests the covertly political basis of most of the film's support, a phenomenon even more strikingly displayed by the irate letter-writers who bombarded the Times after Crowther's review appeared. But at the same time that the film's attitude suggests affinities with some current political notions, its supporters don't want it taken too seriously. One almost hears them tremble: if the establishment really sees what is going on in Bonnie and Clyde they may spoil the fun by taking it away from us! Thus, after coming to realize that its use of violence was relevant, Joseph Morgenstern spins about to assert that "when we talk about movies, even artistic movies, we are not talking about urban-renewal programs, nuclear non-proliferation treaties or rat-control bills." Yet Morgenstern then goes on to argue that the film's violence takes its significance from the fact that "most of humanity teeters on the edge of violence every day."

Does Bonnie and Clyde have political or social significance far beyond its significance as a work of art? To answer "yes" is not to contend that the film incites acts directly, for against such a contention Morgenstern would be right and Sarris would have reason to fear thought control. But art initiates action in more subtle ways: by reflecting contemporary attitudes and thus, through the power of reflection, confirming them. How much more potent is this process when performed by a piece of mass entertainment.

It would be foolish to equate the growing approval of violence, even among humane and liberal persons, with the specific advocacy of a bloodthirsty, cheap film. Those who riot against conditions in the Negro ghetto or the war in Vietnam can claim precisely the moral validation for their acts which the Barrow Gang so conspicuously lacks. But each form of behavior embodies a similar lapse of commitment to organized society, and in accepting one we may find ourselves accepting the other. Each expresses the underlying belief that society represents not law and order but only convention and force. When society is no longer felt to represent legitimacy, protest itself becomes the only legitimate response. But with standards of legitimacy confounded, the criminal may seem to resemble the rebel, the hippie to merge with the reformer. Surely Bonnie and Clyde did not produce [20] society's current disrepute or our desperate reaching out for any alternative. Just as surely, by playing with the disrepute it exploits the desperation, helping us to celebrate what we once condemned.

If seeing the film as a reflection of larger social issues seems far-fetched, I commend the reader's attention to an important study of the German expressionist film after World War I: Siegfried Kracauer's From Caligari to Hitler (Princeton, 1947; reissued, 1966). Assuming that movies are an index to national mentality because they are collectively produced and massively consumed, Kracauer traces through the period's chief films the rise of Nazism. In short, he implies that popular entertainment acts as a national fever chart. In the thirties in Germany, the disease was authoritarianism; in the sixties in America, it is anarchy. Through the stream of anarchic art which flows high and low in our culture today, Bonnie and Clyde thrashes prominently, its protagonists folk heroes in a national epic struggle.

The day after I saw the film, at the school where I teach—a very good school with intelligent students from comfortable homes—I saw scrawled on a bathroom wall, "C.W. in '68." If this example of collegiate graffiti is portentous to even a small degree, then investigating the importance of Bonnie and Clyde can't be left to reviewers.   [22]

1. Mr. Samuels claims that the film Bonnie and Clyde slanders society. Do you agree? If not, how would you counter his argument?

2. Do you agree that the assertion of society's fraudulence has become "a contemporary article of faith?" Where would one look for evidence?

3. Does *Bonnie and Clyde* bear out Robert Warshow's theories concerning the gangster film?

FOGGY BOTTOM

JERRY RICHARD

Bonnie and Clyde is a great film, as long as you don't think about it. After their first successful bank robbery, when Bonnie and Clyde and their loony driver C.W. are chased across open country by two police cars, crisscrossing and bouncing off rocks to the frolicking musical background of Flatt and Scrugg's *Foggy Mountain Breakdown,* the scene brilliantly reincarnates the Keystone Kops comedies to show us how lighthearted, how a little bit daft the whole adventure is. Or at the end the way Bonnie and Clyde are betrayed and ambushed and the camera dwells on their already dead bodies still being shot, still being brutalized by a straight-faced Texas ranger who never did see the humor of it all, and the motion is slowed a bit, making something important of their end, something tragic of their lives. Cinematically, they are both great scenes, and it is not until later, thinking about it, that you realize they could hardly have both been in the same film, or that if they were, it could hardly have been a great film.

It isn't that Arthur Penn, the director, saw the tragic underpinnings of Bonnie and Clyde's mad career, or that he saw the comic overtones to their essentially tragic lives; the impression finally left by the film is that he saw both the comedy and the tragedy but he saw them alternately. One attitude doesn't seem to relieve the other, it only follows it. When you mix blue and yellow you expect to get green; in *Bonnie and Clyde,* somehow, you get blue and yellow.

It is not as if what started out to be a lark (either the film or their lives) ended up a tragedy, or at least a case of hard luck. We do not even get a sense of their increasing isolation or disillusionment. In fact, it is not even Bonnie and Clyde who are revealed to us in the final scene but the Texas Ranger, that otherwise minor

JERRY RICHARD teaches literature at Godard College and has published short stories and reviews in *The Nation, The Progressive,* and other magazines.

This review originally appeared in the *Antioch Review,* Vol. XXVIII, No. 3, pp. 388–392. Reprinted by permission.

character. Earlier in the film we [388–389] see him brave as he attempts to round up the gang all by himself and defiant when, even handcuffed, he spits in Bonnie's eye. He is the image of the stereotypical Ranger. At the end he is revealed as sneaky and sadistic. Nothing, except perhaps our suspicions of Texas Rangers, accounts for this apparent change. All we learn about Bonnie and Clyde is that they are dead.

Of course, if you are against interpretation, these things don't bother you. One can look at the weird rhythms of those slowly bouncing bodies in the superbly photographed last scene and not think about the character of the Texas Ranger at all. I suppose one could even not think about the fact that Bonnie and Clyde are being killed.

The popularity of *Bonnie and Clyde* is symptomatic. In the *Village Voice* of December 27, 1967, Charles Marowitz, writing from London, reports that *"Bonnie and Clyde* is the apotheosis of the New Style." The young people there (presumably in heart as well as in age) are apparently imitating the costumes worn by Warren Beatty and Faye Dunaway in the film. "If you are a bonnie-and-clyder, you are pro-camp and anti-Ugly." And the style in art as well as in personal dress and demeanor hearkens back to the twenties and thirties for its inspiration. We see that here too of course. It is difficult to guess who has a more unrealistic picture of the thirties, those who were there or those who weren't.

One can understand the reluctance to think about the film: it spoils the fun. If you cannot, alternatively, derive pleasure from the process of thinking then all the fun is gone. Anyway, thinking, these days, is in bad repute. For the hippie it is the exercise of a faculty that has got the world in the mess it's in. For the activist it too seldom leads to practical, much less immediate results. Spontaneity, happenings, experience, these are the words of the day. If you think at all you must think about not thinking. If you are of a religious or philosophical frame of mind, you turn to mysticism; if political you eschew ideology. If esthetic you will find that drugs will expand an artistic experience, while thinking risks diminishing it.

This is not an argument against experiencing things, much less a suggestion that there is too much pleasure in the world. There is room in the same body for the guts and the mind. Certainly, where interpretation is vengeful, where it is "the compliment that mediocrity pays to genius," then it deserves the bad reputation that Susan Sontag has hung on it. But I think that is seldom the critic's motive (amateur or professional). Perhaps people are reluctant to criticize a work because they don't want to find out how few first-rate things there are in the world. That is something to be afraid of. I suspect, however, that it stems more from a kind [389–390] of laziness. ("That's a great book," says the freshman, "but don't ask me why.")

A kind of laziness because it does not result from want of energy. Rather it stems from the shifting balance of values from work towards pleasure. We have been getting away from the Puritan code, a process considerably accelerated by the announcement of that fact so that by now everyone knows not only that we are ridding ourselves of Puritan restraints, but that we should do so. Films, for instance, are only slowly being introduced in our schools. They were previously banned on suspicion of being inherently entertaining. In truth it is easier to watch a film than to read a book. But while we are freeing ourselves from the idea of work for the sake of working, we have not yet seen the pleasure of working for the sake of the work. I suppose that automation and the scarcity of jobs that it threatens has contributed to this process. Surely, it is one of the things that has shaken up the Puritan ethic. However, it would be useful here to keep in mind the distinction that Hannah Arendt makes (or resurrects, really) between *work* and *labor*. In *The Human Condition* she reminds us that work is the term properly applied to a creative and individually productive (in the sense that the activity culminates in a product and not just part of a product) job; labor is the term for repetitive, assembly-line type jobs. Most work, during the industrial revolution, has turned to labor, but this is precisely the sort of activity threatened by automation. No one really wants to labor; the rewards are all extrinsic, and it is the pay that we work for. The rewards of work, however, are partly, sometimes largely, intrinsic. There is a need to work and this explains the rise of do-it-yourselfism. Even if the result looks like—in the words of the title of a book of some years ago—How To Make An Orange Crate Out of Old Pieces of Furniture—there is still a good deal of intrinsic satisfaction. The maker of the orange crate will feel proud of having made something, but we needn't admire it as if we couldn't tell it from a beautiful table. I have built a bookcase and I am secretly proud of having accomplished it, but I have to warn people not to pass too closely to it and I know that it is neither structurally sound nor beautiful.

Perhaps criticism had gone too far in one direction. Certainly it had if the idea got around that anything amusing could not be profound and that a truly significant work of art was incompatible with entertainment. I think that idea did get around to many occasional readers and some artists. If that is the case, then a little retrenching was in order, and the real significance of *Against Interpretation* may have been that it called a truce between critic and artist. A truce between critic and artist, however, [390–391] quickly becomes a truce between audience and artist, since the reader or viewer too is inevitably a critic. We want to use this truce to get back to a simpler time, a time of innocence; a time when things just happened, and there was beauty in the label of a soup can and pleasure in those corny musicals of the thirties. (A time, I suppose, when one could go around the country stealing and killing, and it was all right until it happened to you.) Innocence becomes amateurishness (or is it the other way around?), and we are more tolerant of lack of technique. Then we come to admire it, not only sympathetic to a film that is overexposed and out of focus but regarding such crudities as virtues. (Ronald Reagan has already capitalized on these sympathies.)

To talk about amateurishness, however, is to get far away from *Bonnie and Clyde*, a fully conscious, deliberate, and very professionally made film. I am talking about technique. The form is skillfully executed; the content is naive. The style of the film conveys a sense, accurately or more probably inaccurately, of the carefree, no-tomorrow, sensation-filled life of the thirties. Mr. Marowitz in his *Village Voice* article writes: ". . . the film has captured the rollicking dream-life-cum-reality of thousands of young Britons who hanker after the romanticized joys that gambols Bonnie and Clyde across bullet-riddled American highways." If this was what Arthur Penn, the director, intended, the film would have been a splendid artistic achievement, but in the *New York Times* of Sunday, September 17, 1967, he is quoted as saying: "I think it shows the squalor, the isolation, the terrible boredom of these people." Obviously, that is not what a lot of people who saw the film, some of them several times, thought it showed.

What all this shows is not an obtuse audience but a naive director. Even a careful, critical viewing of the film does not give us the feeling Penn intends. The "bonnie-and-clyders" are right in their interpretation. Even the background music clearly tells us Bonnie and Clyde are having fun. (In an attempt to lend Bonnie and Clyde an air of social consciousness there are two scenes, isolated from anything else the film tells us about them, in which Bonnie and Clyde, or at least Clyde, chew the grapes of wrath. In one Clyde sympathizes with an evicted farmer, loaning the man his gun so he can shoot out the windows of his former house; in the other, Clyde allows a poor man at a bank to withhold his money from the loot. In the *New York Times* article Penn says these two scenes were added to the original screenplay. They look it.)

While the medium in this case was certainly the message to most of the viewers, it does not prove that McLuhan is right. In *Bonnie and Clyde* the content is not so much at odds with the style as it is at odds [391–392] with itself. No wonder most viewers ignored it. I think it is true though that many people do pay more attention to style these days than they do to content, but it may be because they are influenced by the fashionable ideas of Marshall McLuhan. In other words, McLuhan may turn out to be right not because his analysis is correct but because it was published. Anyway, what critics should worry about is not McLuhan's law but Gresham's.

A great work of art should not only be immediately titillating, it should expand in retrospect. It's fun to relax with a good mystery novel, but we are in danger of relaxation becoming our only occupation, and that would be all right too if there weren't still a need in this world, if not in ourselves, for an alert critical faculty. Already the writer with something to say feels he has to be strident just to get through (Mailer's *Why Are We In Vietnam?*, for example). And in the end, this critical truce will have dulled our receptivity even to pleasure. When we uncritically expand the range of experience we submit ourselves to, it only seems to expand in one direction.

Experimenting with new forms and new styles in old forms used to be for the sake of finding new ways to say something; now these experiments are increasingly for the sake of finding new forms or new styles. I suppose some people expect that after the new forms are mastered, artists will use them to say something, but that attitude is for people able to keep their eye firmly on the doughnut, even after it has been eaten. Art should be seductive; with much of today's art we are seduced and abandoned.

So young men put on wide-brim straw hats and Big Max ties and a manic smile and court their ankle-length dressed Bonnies without apparently knowing that Clyde is impotent. Or is bank robbing as potent as sex? Perhaps it is now since it is vicarious, as so much sex used to be. In the film, of course, Clyde finally does have an orgasm, either as a substitute for robbing banks or else, as some critics have suggested, made healthy again by Bonnie's poetry. Like much else, it isn't clear in the film. But I haven't noticed many "bonnie-and-clyders" either robbing banks or writing poetry. (Both occupations do seem to be on the upswing, but I don't think this is attributable to the movie.) Meanwhile, enjoying *Bonnie and Clyde* is another exercise in dry intercourse.   [392]

1. Compare Miss Kael and Messrs. Richard and Samuels on the mixture of comedy and violence in *Bonnie and Clyde*. Which argument is most convincing? Why?

2. Do you agree with Mr. Richard that people today don't want to think about the films they see? What would be relevant evidence?

3. Can you find other evidence for Mr. Richard's general position? How relevant is it to *Bonnie and Clyde*?

BLOW-UP

A BIT OVERBLOWN

JOHN SIMON

Michelangelo Antonioni's *Blow-Up,* ignoring the precept of Archibald MacLeish, means more than it is. A film, I feel, should *be* before it means, should have a reality of its own before making metaphysical pronouncements. The metaphysics of *Blow-Up* are in limbo, which may not be a bad place for metaphysics, but is no place for people. Even if people are lost souls, as those in the film certainly are, their relationships to one another, to their surroundings, to the work of art in which they figure, should be firmly apprehended and made convincing.

A synopsis of the wispy plot is unfortunately unavoidable. Dawn in London: A noisy rag-party of students with their faces painted white rides in a jeep into a building complex; a bunch of ragged men emerge from a flophouse. One of the latter gets into a Rolls-Royce; he is a highly successful photographer who has spent the night taking pictures for his forthcoming book of photographs. The mimes start collecting money for some cause or other and touch him for a bill. He drives back to his large studio *cum* apartment in a charming mews. A battery of models and personnel awaits him. In his filthy bum's attire, he rushes to his work, photographing first a sexy model (played by Verouchka, a sexy model) in a series of extremely erotic, scantily clad poses. He washes and changes, and proceeds to shoot a group of fashion models in suggestive mod clothes and weird groupings. He saunters over to a neighboring studio where an artist friend refuses to sell him one of his abstractions. He casts some yearning glances at the artist's wife, and returns to his own studio where two silly, pushy teenyboppers intrude on him in the hope he will photograph them. He gets rid of them and drives off to an out-of-the-way antique shop he wants to buy.

The shop owner is out, and the photographer wanders into a neighborhood park, taking pictures of pigeons and such, until he comes upon a couple, a young

girl and a middle-aged man, in a rather quaint love-ballet and starts avidly photographing them. The girl has a curious way of both leading the man on and dancing
away from him. As the photographer is about to leave, the girl, who has just caught
on, runs after him and tries to beg, buy, or wrest the film from him. He refuses, takes
some shots of her running away, and returns to the antique shop. He haggles with
the owner, a young girl who is tired of the business and wants to travel (everyone
wants what he hasn't got), and buys from her an old-fashioned airplane propeller.
Then he drives to a lunch appointment with a literary friend who is writing the
text for his picture book. He tells the writer that the idyllic shots of the lovers in the
park will be a perfect conclusion for an otherwise violent book. Through the plate-
glass window someone has been spying on them, but disappears when followed.
As our hero drives home, a peace demonstrator sticks a sign [265–266] into his car,
but the sign is presently blown out of the convertible.

Back at the studio, the photographer is met by the girl from the park. She
must have those negatives; she has been tailing him, and will tail him into bed to
get them. A dalliance begins that might lead to a little more than a quick sex bout,
when they are interrupted by the delivery of the propeller. The staging and editing
do not make clear whether intercourse occurs, but the girl leaves, having received a
roll of film. The film is a phoney, as is the phone number the girl gives the aroused
photographer. He now proceeds to develop the real film, and, in studying the blowups carefully, notices something fishy. After a series of hectic magnifications, detec-
tions, further magnifications, it emerges that a man with a gun was hiding in the
bushes. Apparently he killed the man in the tryst, for something like a body appears
in the shrubbery in the pictures of the girl running away.

Our hero calls his writer friend with the startling revelation, but his story
is not believed. He is interrupted by the return of the mini-skirted would-be models,
drifts into a mini-orgy with them, packs them off, and goes back to the by now nocturnal park. The man's body is indeed there. A noise, as of a camera clicking, fright-
ens the photographer and he drives away. He wanders into the apartment of his
painter friend and finds the couple copulating. The wife looks at him longingly even
as she is being made love to by her husband. Our hero returns to his studio and finds it
ransacked, his photographic evidence of a crime stolen or destroyed. He is visited by
the painter's wife who tells him she can't leave her husband for him. She wants to
talk to him about her problem, while he can go on only about the body in the park.
Neither can help the other.

The photographer is driving to a party where his writer friend is, but, en
route, he glimpses the mystery girl. He thinks she has ducked into a rock'n'roll club,
and looks for her there in vain. All that happens is that one of the performers, an-
gered, stomps his electric guitar to bits, a melee ensues as the kids fight over the
pieces, and our hero somehow ends up with the biggest chunk, runs out with it, and
promptly discards it.   [266–267]

He finds the writer at what proves to be a marijuana party, and urges him
to come inspect and photograph the body with him. The friend, high on the stuff,
refuses; the exhausted photographer falls asleep. He gets back to the park at dawn,
but the body is gone. Now the mimes from the previous morning arrive in the park,
and two of them proceed to mime a tennis game, while the rest mime engrossed

spectators. Our hero finds himself caught up in the imaginary game. When the imaginary ball is hit out into the park, he actually mimes picking it up and tossing it back onto the court. Suddenly he begins to hear the nonexisting ball: its puck-puck grows louder as the camera comes in for an overhead shot of the bemused photographer, forlornly heading for home.

The essential point of the film is Pirandellian: the real and the imaginary encroach upon each other and become, finally, inseparable. Most obviously so at film's end: the corpse has vanished as has all evidence of the murder—the very real killing has been rendered nonexistent; conversely the illusory tennis game has been willed, believed into existence. Related to this notion is that of the interpenetration of opposites, whereby the grave and the trivial, the earnest pursuit and the game, become interchangeable. We see this at the very beginning: The idle, roisterous mimes turn out to be collecting for some "worthy" cause, while the grim, shabby young man emerging from the flophouse with nothing but a small, grimy parcel unwraps an expensive camera from it and gets into his luxury car.

Or take the session when the young man photographs his luscious model. The foolish business of taking suggestive pictures is converted into, indeed usurps the place of, sexual fulfillment. He gets closer and closer to her as he photographs away, and disarranges and disarrays her more and more. Occasionally there is even a piddling, nibbling proto-kiss. The girl finally sinks back supine and the man straddles her as he and his camera swoop down for a clicking climax. All along, he rattles off clucking, hectoring, spasmodic verbiage, which, in its accelerandos and crescendos as well as in its ambiguity, is the very deverbalized language of intercourse: "Lurch, lurch more . . . That's great! . . . Now give it to me! More of that, as fast as you can . . . Very good, [267–268] marvelous, great! Much more, much more! . . . Now really give it! . . . Go, go, and again! Lovely, make it come, luv, for me, for me! Yeah, yeah, yes!" The girl now falls back on the floor and feebly stirs her limbs to relax them; she is deliciously, narcissistically satisfied. Our hero, all pseudo-passion spent, collapses on a near-by sofa.

Amid all this a twinge of real jealousy occurs: "Whom the hell were you with last night?" the photographer at one point asks the girl whom he has himself just kept waiting an hour; she merely smiles, mysteriously, bitchily. She tells him she's off to Paris. Later, he meets her at the pot party and exclaims, "I thought you were in Paris!" She drawls, "I am in Paris." Shades of des Esseintes, who sets out for England but, on a rainy night in Calais, as he dines on mutton chops at an English-looking inn, concludes that he has had the English experience. But Huysmans' dilettante still had to dislodge himself a bit; today's trips, in a cigarette or sugar cube, come to us. And for those to whom Paris is a drug-orgy, why shouldn't a drug-orgy be Paris?

As one's husband makes love to one, one's face clutches that of a lover; illusion and reality, seriousness and play have become identical; all things end by floating into one another. So when our hero looks at his blow-ups of the park scene, the soundtrack rustles with wind-stirred leaves; when he is out inspecting the cadaver, he is frightened by what sounds like the click of a shutter—he may have been transferred to someone else's incriminating film. In the studio, strange photo-

graphs have their strident aliveness; while people, grotesquely costumed and en-
vironed, seen in reflections or through semitransparencies, become dehumanized
and reified before our eyes.

Fusing—or confusing—similitudes suffuse the whole work. When the
girl from the peace march sticks her "GO AWAY" placard into a Rolls convertible,
she thinks she has planted her banner on the enemy's stronghold; but our callous
hero, whose car it is, is just as indifferent then as a bit later, when the placard is
swept out of his fast-moving car. Similarly, when the neck of a guitar over which
teenagers fought like ravening beasts ends up in the hero's possession, he can only
throw it away; even the typical mod [268–269] passers-by, who next pick it up,
discard it with utmost indifference. Those who march for peace and those who disturb it are, ultimately, equally disoriented, their sacred symbols equally inefficacious.

Even more striking is the echo of colors. When the hero is photographing
his model, he is dressed in pale colors (blue, beige), she in a black quasi-nightgown,
and the flat backdrops are of a dark, brooding blue-green (this device of surrounding characters with a large, flat, monochrome expanse was well used by Antonioni before: the white hospital walls for the demented girl in *La Notte*; the red
interior of the shack for the "siesta" in *Red Desert*.) Against this lowering virides-
cence, the pseudosexuality of the photography session takes on an even more stylized, artificial look. But when the hero is in the park, shooting the temptress and her
victim, his own attire echoes all the colors from the studio session (black jacket,
blueish shirt, white trousers), while the surrounding vegetation repeats the same,
somewhat lurid, blue-green coloration of the backdrop. Antonioni, we learn, actually
had the grass dyed for this sequence. The cold colors thus juxtaposed create the
same kind of elegant detachment in the studio as in the park, and help suggest that
both photography as lovemaking, and lovemaking as a subject for shooting (with
camera or gun!) are rather alike: unnatural and unwholesome.

So, too, when the hero visits the painter, he admires an abstraction of his
which, to quote Francis Wyndham, has "colored dots arranged to give an effect of
explosion." When the hero discovers the painter and his wife during intercourse,
the camera pans to those explosive dots again—rather like the colored lights Tennessee Williams' Stella says she sees when her husband makes love to her. And
when the painter's wife comes to see the photographer and looks at the one remaining blow-up that the ransackers neglected to destroy—possibly because the corpse,
in desperate magnification, shows only as a vague blur of dots—she exclaims,
"Looks like one of those paintings!" There you have it: sex, murder, artistic creation
—nothing but the same swirling shapes and colors slightly rearranged. It is almost
Baudelaire's forests of symbols[269–270] where *"les parfums, les couleurs et les
sons se répondent,"* except that here nature is not a temple; or, if so, the temple of
a god who is malign, oblivious, or dead.

Characteristically, in a world where sensations, colors, sounds, and the
perfume of available (which is to say all) flesh take on the functions of ratiocination
and discourse, the word becomes debased and obsolete as a caudal appendage.
Dialogue becomes a perfunctory caress or a sudden blow. When a group of absurd
models in bizarre get-ups, posing among square transparent screens inside a ghostly

white parallelepiped—the whole thing looking like a cubist-surrealist hallucination —fail to achieve the desired expression of breathless hebetude, the photographer barks at them, "Start agaìn! Rethink it!" These fruging gum-chewers rethink? Or even think? But the angry tone tells all. Quite consistently, the film depends to an unprecedented degree on noises, and may be the first in which the climactic revelation is a sound: the dull but loud and persistent whacking of a nonexistent tennis ball. So, too, the lines spoken by the actors—the ably devious Vanessa Redgrave, the suitably subliminal Sarah Miles, and the (regrettably) charmless David Hemmings —are mostly balls of caprice batted about by backhanded drives.

The two basic statements of the film seem to be the painter's comment on his works, "They don't mean anything when I do them, just a mess. Afterward I find something to hang onto, like that leg. Then it all sorts itself out; it's like finding a clue in a detective story"; and the photographer's praise of his undeveloped park pictures, "very peaceful, very still," with which he wants to end his violent book to make it "ring truer." Life, like art, Antonioni appears to say, can be figured out only a *posteriori*; but we are in for some nasty surprises: the final truth does not ring true, or, rather, what rings true isn't the truth. (The film, by the way, is based on a story by Julio Cortázar, of whose novel, *Hopscotch*, it has been said that it must be read twice to be read at all; and the English adaptation is by Edward Bond, whose play, *Saved*, is a notable contribution to the theatre of cruelty.)

An essentially ironic relation between illusion and reality, why not? I believed Pirandello, and I am prepared to believe Antonioni, particularly since his photography, design, and direction [270–271] are all spectacular. But there is a hitch. The grand philosophic stance is not, as in Pirandello, attached to characters and plots that have a life of their own.

It is the real that has to become illusory, after all, and the illusory real. When everything is evanescent, wraith-like, superficial—even the genuinely fleshly orgy with the mini-skirters is finally unreal because locomotion is substituted for emotion—only nebulae whirl into other nebulae, atoms into other configurations of atoms. There is nothing for me to make human contact with and become genuinely drawn to. It may all sort itself out in the end, but just what is that initial "it"? Unlike in a detective story, I haven't a clue.   [271]

1. Does John Simon's analysis of the film support the assertions he makes in his first paragraph?

2. How accurate is Mr. Simon's synopsis? To what extent is his reading helped by his plot summary?

3. Do you agree that David Hemmings is charmless? How does one define this quality in an actor or performance?

4. Compare this review with Mr. Simon's critical credo. How is his practice related to his theory of film criticism?

WATCHING ANTONIONI

Robert Garis

. . . And now I am about to praise *Blow-Up* with an enthusiasm that may also seem unreasonable, since I am going to dismiss as a minor flaw something that I can imagine taking very hard in another movie. The fact is that, thanks to one of those irritating illusion-and-reality puzzles, and a clumsily managed one at that, interpretation of *Blow-Up* can't be quite secure.

The mechanism of this puzzle is the first thing you see in the movie: a glaringly symbolic carload of heavily made-up pantomimers, or whatever they are —why, they don't even look British. They disappear quickly, and the movie begins to follow a day in the life of a young London photographer who, about a third of the way through, takes some atmosphere shots of a man and a woman dallying with each other romantically in a park. When the woman goes to extreme lengths to try, unsuccessfully, to get the roll of film, he develops it and studies the pictures closely to find out what she's so upset about. As he blows up detail after detail he gradually discovers that he has apparently photographed a murder in which the woman must have been implicated. He returns to the park at night to look for the corpse and he finds it; in the meantime somebody breaks into his studio and steals all the evidence. When he returns to the park again at dawn he finds the body gone without a trace and then Antonioni wheels in the symbol again: the pantomimers drive up, run to some tennis courts, and begin (very beautifully, I'll agree) to mime

---

ROBERT GARIS is Professor of English at Wellesley College and a frequent contributor to *Partisan Review*, *Commentary* and other magazines. He is author of *The Dickens Theatre*.

a tennis match with an imaginary tennis ball. One of the players hits it out of the court onto the grass where the photographer is standing, and he is mutely asked to throw it back. He does so, and the camera focuses on his face while the sound track registers for the first time the sound of a tennis ball in play: by consenting to enter their illusion, he seems to have turned it into reality for himself, which is to say that there may have been no murder.

The crux of the puzzle is, of course, the dead body: as the photographer looks down at it there is a click on the sound track which sounds more like the click of a gun being cocked than the click of his camera but may be supposed to be either or both in his imagination. Is the body also imaginary? Or is Antonioni counting on the native realism of the movies to tell us that what the camera sees must really exist?   [87–88]

Now if these questions were rooted in the rest of the movie one would have to take them seriously, but then one would want to, because an Antonioni movie deeply concerned with illusion and reality would be worth seeing. *Blow-Up* is not that movie, and the right response to the arch and superficial questions raised by the symbol is exactly the response of the photographer—mild curiosity. It suits his character perfectly that he should entertain the possibility that he imagined the murder, but it doesn't suit it at all that he should actually have imagined it. Though Antonioni has pasted in a few little reminders of the puzzle throughout the movie, everything about the main character shows that he is a contriver, not an experiencer of illusions. He dresses up as a bum in order to take pictures in a doss-house and he verbally jazzes up a model to get the right expression of sexual ecstasy on her face. But this is all conscious expertise, not vicarious experience, and nothing in the movie suggests that the photographer's fantasy life centers around things like revolvers and murders. Antonioni's symbol won't bear serious consideration.

But the shot of David Hemming's face as he takes in the puzzle *is* important, because it is the last stroke in a characterization that represents Antonioni at nearly his best. Characterization is the right word. It is Antonioni's specialty to use the film medium idiomatically to represent human beings and human relations with a depth and subtlety that we are more used to finding in novels than in movies. In *Blow-Up* he does it again, though you will miss it if you are tired in advance of movies about cool, uncommitted modern youth and if you aren't willing to watch and wait while Antonioni's beautifully managed structure reveals his meaning.

The characterization begins by delivering a sequence of vivid images in a non-committal tone and at a brilliantly fast but sensitive pace. Certain information is given, but positive judgments about the information are frustrated by the tone and speed. The photographer first seems to be a bum leaving a doss-house; when he is sure none of the other bums is looking, he races around the corner and gets into a snazzy Rolls-Royce convertible and puts an expensive-looking camera into the glove-compartment; as he drives off, he talks to somebody on a two-way radio, using standard Roger-Over vocabulary. All this is attention-getting but quite neutral information, its implications yet unfocused, and the same thing is true of the even more striking imagery that follows. Back at his studio, we learn that the young man is a successful professional photographer working in three fields: art (he took some "fabulous" pictures in the doss-house), arty semi-pornography, and far-out fashion photography. The information is still neutral but since it's now getting into areas where negative judgments would be natural, neutrality begins to create tension. It is clear that he takes all three kinds of work in stride and doesn't in the least mind producing junk: he is not a committed type, then, though he seems good at his job. But what we are to make of him in any broader terms is a question Antonioni holds in abeyance by giving us plenty to look at and by some coolly witty incongruities. Meanwhile, the flexible fast editing, which is geared to the photographer's actions and his day, generates an interest in him that is of course augmented by the indefinability of David Hemming's appearance and performance—peculiar and ordinary, sensitive and coarse, beautiful and ugly, restless and assured.

When the photographer enters the park, Antonioni changes the tempo radically to prepare for an unequivocally sympathetic stroke of characterization: the photographer responds to the atmosphere by making an instinctive leap of agile, youthfully awkward-graceful, self-delighting high spirits. And Antonioni underlines his meaning by using all his resources to make that atmosphere as fully concrete a sensuous experience as any I have ever had at the movies. The thick palpability of the wind in the trees, the totality of sunlight, the slow, full, even pace of the sequence, the illusion that the park is a life toward which the photographer is drawn and to which his leap is a tribute—all this is so central and simple in mood, so non-eccentric, so familiar a view of nature, that when Antonioni expresses it with the boldest possible inflection the effect is overwhelming in itself and dramatically decisive. For the photographer's response is also very boldly inflected and very central, so that a current of sympathy is set up between him and the audience strong enough to bring the whole characterization into focus and to control the meaning of the whole movie.

This control keeps the ambiguity of almost everything that follows perfectly secure and clear. It establishes the fact that the photographer is genuinely alive and free in an indisputably valuable way, and that he is consequently a figure of some dignity, interest, and concern. With this assured, we are in a good position to notice that there are many much less attractive aspects to his freedom. Though his body can express energy and enthusiasm, his face rarely does. His inner life, if it exists at all, remains hidden because he won't reveal it to anyone, but we can feel no assurance in holding that against him. Sometimes his isolation seems almost poignantly independent, sometimes less than human; and though his friendship with the artist and his mistress is easy and familiar, it is extremely casual. He knows swinging London inside out, and yet it doesn't really seem to be his "world." Incidentally, Pauline Kael notwithstanding, Antonioni's lurid images of marijuana parties and the like seldom amount to a heavy indictment of aimless modern living because they are always parts of the characterization of the photographer, who moves through them with such unsurprised and even uninterested acceptance that, instead of feeling how corrupt and sterile it all is, we are led rather to wonder whether this cool type can in fact respond to anything. But then he does momentarily get caught up in the struggle for the ruined guitar in the rock-and-roll sequence. And when he meets that incredibly hostile old man in the antique shop, it seems attractive that he should call his bluff with [88–89] such good humor, without irritation or surprise. By these qualifications and questionings, Antonioni gradually shapes his essentially sympathetic interest in this "cool" and "uncommitted" young man into a complex view that seems to me extremely interesting and original, and also quite decent and humane. It is not moralistic, nor in the least pretentiously meaningful and important, but it is in touch with moral concerns about human and social responsibility, as it should be.

The murder in the park keeps us in touch with these concerns in a particularly interesting way because of its oblique relation with the photographer's way of life. It is, of course, nonsense to say that this mysterious melodrama is the real life of significant human relations into which the photographer cannot enter responsibly. On the contrary, this event conveys almost no depth of feeling, nor does the character played by Vanessa Redgrave—though here it seems to me that Antonioni has failed to make his meaning entirely clear, and there's a chance that she is supposed to suggest more than the synthetic overbred tension that I saw. In any case, this event is convincingly hard for the photographer to deal with. It is hard to take seriously because it's so plotty, yet it does seem actually to have happened to real people. It is, then, just a special and single event, obviously exciting and puzzling, but just as obviously unrepresentative and perhaps even inauthentic.

Because of this, we watch with friendly sympathy while the photographer tries to figure out how to handle it. And because of Antonioni's mastery, the superb sequence in which the photographer examines his pictures is something we watch with total absorption. To make this process so exciting to watch without inflating its meaning—that is something only a great artist can accomplish.   [89]

1.   Mr. Garis's main point is that Antonioni gives us so much so fast about the photographer that we can't form any clear, unequivocal judgments and that, as a result, the film asks us to watch rather than judge the protagonist. Is this argument convincing? Does it fit your experience of the film?

2.   What is Mr. Garis's method of dispensing with counterarguments. Is it effective?

3.   What definition of art underlies Mr. Garis's final evaluation of *Blow-Up*?

BLOW-UP: ANTONIONI AND THE MOD WORLD

James F. Scott

On first viewing, *The Blow-Up* seems too clever, just too clever. How can anyone be so coy with a camera without losing himself in visual display? From the film's opening moment, when splinters of dramatic action burst through the titles until David Hemmings is erased from the last scene by a trick of the optical printer, Michaelangelo Antonioni never relaxes his insistence upon striking effects. Shots through layers of glass, props to complicate composition, splashes of expressionistic red, deep-focus and wide-angle fixes that draw the eye to incidental detail: the photography never ceases to dazzle. And yet I am now convinced this picture is much more than the cinematic equivalent of a Mary Quant dress. The mad mod world of London has found its poet, but has not found him in exactly a celebratory mood. Antonioni's highly complex reaction to contemporary English culture creates the thematic core of what must surely rank among the finest films of the sixties.

However brief his residence in London, the Italian director already knows this world well, its pace, its idiom, its style. He is not just the enthralled tourist, gawking at mini skirts and pink tights, even though such gear provides much of the surface phenomena of the film. As always, his bent is analytical and documentary, his attention devoted to the psychology underlying gesture and speech. His unnamed protagonist (played with supreme cool by Hemmings) might have been lifted from one

JAMES F. SCOTT is Associate Professor of English at St. Louis University.

of the Beatle records, for, like the musical hero fashioned by John Lennon, he's "a real Nowhere Man . . ." who "doesn't have a point of view/Knows not where he's going to." But in Antonioni the lyricism of the Beatles gives way to more ambiguous tonalities which, in spite of occasional dissonance, are arranged with great care, almost cunning. Down to the last stroke of the imaginary tennis game at its close, *The Blow-Up* is the work of a virtuoso. At the same time, though, it is a telling commentary upon the psychic defenses of man, particularly the man of artistic temper. Antonioni's seriousness about these matters reclaims the film, even when it comes close to triteness and sensationalism.

Paradoxically, this is perhaps Antonioni's most personal film. Like Bergman's *The Magician* and Fellini's *8½*, it is another version of "a portrait of the artist," here a commercial photographer. Of course, Antonioni avoids the confessional. The young man with the camera is no more the director himself than Herr Vogler, the traveling magician who does tricks with a magic lantern, is really Ingmar Bergman. But Antonioni surely feels the force of professional cousinship to his hero. Like the director who created him, the protagonist of *The Blow-Up* is intelligent, aloof, objective, technically expert, sometimes exploitative, and even a little worried about his obligations toward those who get into the view finder of his camera. He knows the strain of urban isolation but sees no relief from it; "I'm off London this week," he confides to a buddy, but these efforts at escape are no more significant than the chatter [227–228] of the girl in the secondhand shop about emigrating to Nepal. He also senses, at least vaguely, the ambiguous position of an artist working with mass media: Critical of the public taste that furnishes his livelihood, he must devote himself to representing the life of a community whose values mean almost nothing to him. Does aesthetic detachment require a purely spectatorial attitude? Does art do nothing more than freeze a moment of experience with a snap of the shutter or a stroke of the brush? These questions, arising naturally from the plight of the protagonist, are really Antonioni's own. Though the director never gets as close as to be unable to judge his hero, the verdict is delivered against a kindred spirit.

In characterizing the artist-hero, the film summons up polarities we have all grown familiar with—art and life, illusion and reality, style and impulse. Those who wish Keats had turned his back on the Grecian urn and Yeats had stayed clear of Byzantium will immediately be put off by this. Yet Antonioni is rarely cliché, though he crosses few philosophical thresholds. His fable is carefully built, and his characters, even when they resemble zombies, seem fully real. If the meaning expands into allegory, its generalized significance emerges from an ensemble of concrete sights, sounds, and gestures. The task he sets for himself as a film-maker is to "defend the principle of intelligence within the heart of the real" (*Bianco e Nero*, 1958). This scrupulous fidelity to the sensate world enables him in *The Blow-Up* both to assert the autonomy of art and measure the artist himself in moral terms.

To Antonioni, autonomy suggests distance, not escape, from life. But distance is crucial, because art imposes its claims indirectly; it does not have "meaning" in the ordinary journalistic sense. Bill the painter, Hemmings' closest associate, says of his own canvases: "They don't mean anything when I do them. Just a mess. Afterwards it sorts itself out—like a clue in a detective story." This echoes a remark

Antonioni once made about his own work: "It can happen that films acquire meanings, that is to say, the meanings appear afterwards . . ." (*Positif*, 1959). Whether or
not this parallel is significant, Bill's way of looking at his paintings provides a verbal
paradigm for the plot of *The Blow-Up*. Only by letting the meaning "sort itself out"
does Hemmings discover the real subject of his photography. This, however, complicates the prospect of action based on artistic insight.

The revelatory possibilities of art, Antonioni implies, spring from the
openness and curiosity of the artist. Hemmings plays the part of a good-natured
vagabond, exceptionally sensitive to light and shape, with fingers that move over
F-stops as smoothly as if he were performing on harp or violin. In the critical scene
in the park, he comes upon the lovers just accidentally, while collecting some landscape shots to balance the somber tone of a volume of photographs. The unexpected-
ness of the lovers' presence is emphasized in the way Antonioni shoots the scene, the
film camera first catching them as a colorful off-center blur in a few frames of a fast
pan. As Hemmings first begins to pursue them, he has (beyond some voyeuristic
interest) only an expectation that they will ornament the landscape more attractively
than the pigeons whom they replace as his subjects. Even after his altercation with
Vanessa Redgrave, (like Hemmings, nameless in the film), the photographer still
has no idea he has taken a picture of a murder. The [228–229] point is simple, but
well made. The real subject of art is distinct from the conscious designs of the artist,
to which it often does violence. A qualifying note is added upon Hemmings' return
to his studio: though art, like science, makes gains from serendipity, chance favors
only the properly disposed.

Hemmings is thus favored because he is, whatever else, a fine photographer. Sensitive to composition, he notices the eccentricity of his subject's sight-line.
Attentive to light, he sees a shadow he can't account for. He misarranges, then cor-
rects, the sequence of shots, entertaining and later rejecting the hypothesis that
Miss Redgrave is looking at him. From these notes a syndrome of details falls into
place, for association and implication are the substance of artistic insight. During
these moments as the prints are hung on the studio wall, the sound track effectively
reinforces an imaginative reconstruction of reality, Hemmings' absorption in the
world he has caught with his camera. While his concentration intensifies, the
sound of wind stirs through the trees, and the clouds of that fatal twilight seem to
regather. Now, too, we understand why Antonioni has made his protagonist specialize in black and white photography. Returning to the scene in the park, we go back
to a world drained of color, an unrealistic, self-evidently artificial world, yet one
whose tones are more real than reality. Only when the park episode is printed out
in black and white does the atmosphere seem sinister enough for murder. The film
stock itself serves to unmask the picturesque. Moreover, in this special world of
art, a meaningless, unfocused shadow gradually becomes a form, a man, a killer.
The parable is now complete. When Bill's mistress later remarks that one of the blowups looks "just like one of Bill's paintings," she just underscores verbally what the
action has already shown.

Art fixates, transforms, enlarges, and in so doing shows us aspects of reality
we could never see with an unguided eye. I discern in this a special message from
Antonioni to his critics, those who have looked askance at the seemingly arbitrary

imagery in some of his earlier films. Watch closely, gentlemen; trifles are not always a trifling matter. Beyond this, however, there is the more obvious public meaning, central to *The Blow-Up*. Art confers upon man a special kind of insight, yet not through magic or mystification, but through patience, craftsmanship, and mental alertness within an organized discipline.

Though if art is distinct from magic, this doesn't prevent its seeming magical to the uninitiate, or keep the artist himself from donning the robes of a mage. After all, the artist is a maker, and appears to create *ex nihilo*. There is something terribly beguiling about his office, which makes it a source of power. And that is why, I think, Antonioni's hero finds his profession so attractive. He is a weak man, rootless and confused, who uses his camera for ego support.

Camera in hand or in reach, the hero is sturdy and stylish. He can control his environment, choosing the roles he will play (worker, lover) and the terms on which he will play them (the escape clause of professional distance). This is not necessarily bad, of course, for every artist counterfeits those roles which extend an opportunity to create. The problem with Antonioni's protagonist is that behind the mask there seems to be no face. Personalities fall off him as readily as the roving picket's "Ban the Bomb" sign tumbles from the rear seat of his automobile. He needs the camera to [229–230] maintain his identity, for without it he is quickly caught up and lost in every crowd that gathers. At the mercy of his surroundings, his private self is too weak to withstand the world. Antonioni's interest in the camera as a power surrogate thus governs the argument of the film, offering the chief clue to the judgment he passes upon the central character.

The talismanic authority of the camera is nowhere more evident than when it is used as a sexual instrument, as in the sequence where Hemmings is first shown photographing a model. Much more than an isolated extravagance, this episode establishes a pattern running through all the scenes in which he exhibits strength. His camera, its threats and its promises, confers upon him a mastery over his associates. On this occasion, he feigns the role of lover, and with absolute success. His relationship with the model is purely professional, yet Antonioni composes the scene so as to make their encounter simulate sexual climax, complete with verbal enticements, erotic movement, gradual convergence, and eventual exhaustion. The clicking shutter of the camera marks the rhythm of this engagement, underscoring the importance Antonioni attaches to the visible badge of his hero's profession.

Having established this motif in a single scene, Antonioni now extends and complicates it, as Hemmings uses his camera to control the reactions of a wide range of persons—the sophisticated manikins of his studio, a desperate Vanessa Redgrave, and the absurd teen-agers who stumble into his path. For the painted creatures of the studio, the photographer's authority is absolute, whatever mockery and contempt is implicit in the way it is exercised. As for the girls who come calling after hours, they epitomize the same subservience at a comic level—the fantasy of male power associated with the camera. The mere promise of an eventual chance to model brings them stumbling out of their clothes in order to be sexually available to their benefactor. Flopping about like bewildered seals in an ocean of purple paper, these outrageously inept coquettes bring to grotesque summation the theme of ego-support derived from professional status.

As might be expected, the relationship between Hemmings and Miss Redgrave is more complex, exhibiting both the strength and weakness of the protagonist. While he plays the role of artist, his personal power is again reinforced by his camera. In the park, when Miss Redgrave protests his invasion of her privacy, he brushes her objections aside with brash clinical detachment: "It's not my fault if there's no privacy in the world." Apparently he has declared perpetual open season upon those who get in front of his camera. And he is still fully in command when she comes to the studio to plead for the incriminating film. So long as he holds it, he can have her as mistress or model, even restyle her personality according to his specifications and make a game of her incompetent efforts to steal the camera. The relationship changes, however, the moment he becomes personally implicated in her affairs. Suspecting nothing in her private life beyond a conventional liaison with an older man, he is shocked to find her connected with a murder plot. The discovery in the photo lab jars him completely out of the studied, easy composure he has turned into a rule of life. He loses his cool. Ironically, the honesty of his art explodes the artifice of his personal style, by forcing his attention upon a disturbing existential fact.   [230–231]

Significantly, in the scenes that follow his leaving the studio, he is without his camera. He can no longer control his environment. Alone, he is nervous and frightened. In crowds, he is immediately stamped with the collective image. Fumbling about the darkened streets of London, he is quite another person than the man who orders around the mascara-bedecked minions of his studio.

Look at the difference, for example, between the two scenes in the park, first when he is protected by his camera, then when he goes back to search for the corpse. Trailing the lovers, he was poised, self-assured, moving so bouncily as almost to dance. Returning to the scene, he is jittery, faltering, upset by incidental noises of the night, obsessed by a confused plan to "get help." His white garb against the deep green backdrop gives him something close to a spectral appearance. Should the police be telephoned? Apparently not before this impulse receives positive support from his friends.

Like nearly all Antonioni's heroes, Hemmings evades his spiritual crises with a benumbing emotional binge. First it's the Yardbirds' concert, which he blunders into but can't seem to leave. The audience, fixed in hypnotic stupor, traps him with its inertia, forcing him to listen to the adolescent vocalist who thumps out, ironically, a song about "goin' on." So close is Hemmings' inadvertent identification with this quivering glob that when he finally escapes during a moment of riot, he comes away with a sizeable hunk of a dismembered guitar. If this is the fruit of accident, his deliberate devices are still more disastrous. While the teen-agers go on jazz jags, their elders get high on pot. In the temple of narcotic euphoria he now visits, conscious life has collapsed altogether. "I thought you were going to Paris," he tells one of the guests. "This is Paris," she rejoins. The keynote of the scene is struck as the camera briefly lingers upon a volume of Van Gogh's paintings; madness and self-destructive brutality rule this world, though it lacks the redeeming assertiveness of Van Gogh. In the hell of Sartre's *No Exit*, the damned eternally confront one another with lidless eyes. But the marijuana enthusiasts are fully protected against this mark of existential awareness: their eyelids are permanently rolled down into a visionless squint. Quickly ennervated by this atmosphere, the protagonist himself settles down into unconsciousness.

"After such knowledge, what forgiveness?" Antonioni might well repeat T. S. Eliot's question. Confronted by the nasty reality of violent death, Hemmings is totally incapacitated. It's not that he should have played the hard-boiled private-eye, hunting down the guilty woman like some latter-day Bogart. What she's guilty of remains less than clear, perhaps active involvement, perhaps only accidental complicity. All we really know of the heroine comes from her own lips ("my private life is very confused"), hardly sufficient evidence for conviction. In any event, Antonioni isn't interested in pressing an accessory-after-the-fact charge against his hero. The focus of concern is this man's complete inability to cope with a violation of the world he has worked so patiently to make secure. His remedy for disturbance is distraction—sex, song, drink, drugs. In the morning he will have second thoughts, but by morning the chance to act will have vanished forever. This is why Antonioni's films so often end in the morning, not just *The Red Desert,* but *The Adventure* and *The Night* as well. Missed opportunities seem most poignant as one [231–232] carries an emotional hangover into a new, but unpromising, day.

In *The Blow-Up,* however, the conclusion is protracted to considerable length, allowing time for the now famous (or notorious) tennis match which white-faced revellers play with an imaginary ball. Giving up his sleuthing, Hemmings is ready to play too, as is evident from his willingness to chase a stray shot and return the ball to the court. But who are the players and what's the score? It's tempting to take this scene as summarizing the motifs of escape and evasion that permeate the entire dramatic texture. Their grease-paint associates these bizarre performers with the strangely tinted models of the studio; their collective hallucination brings to mind both the jazz concert and the marijuana party; their enthusiasm for racing around in an automobile resembles the nervous exuberance of Hemmings himself behind the wheel. Opening and closing the film, their antics seem to frame and evaluate everything in between. In accepting their game, the protagonist might be said to embrace a regressive fantasy-life which permanently corrupts his being. But maybe not. While perfectly plausible, this reading strikes me as overly simple.

Whether by intention or accident, Antonioni has left the last scene of *The Blow-Up* somewhat cryptic. I don't think he has quite made up his mind about the mods, or at least isn't ready to damn them *en masse.* One thing these youths have in their favor is their dissociation from the values of the past, which Antonioni so passionately rejected in a statement apropos of *The Adventure:*

> We make use of an aging morality, of outworn myths, of ancient conventions. And we do this in full consciousness of what we are doing. Why do we respect such a morality?

He resents fiercely that man "is impelled by moral forces and myths which were already old in the time of Homer" and that "in the realm of the emotions, a total conformity reigns." However irresponsible, the mods have escaped the burden of these inhibitions. Antonioni was of two minds when he talked about them in the *Life* interview last January:

> The young people among whom my film is situated are all aimless, without any other drive but to reach that aimless freedom. Freedom that for them means marijuana, sexual perversion, anything. . . .

Yet, on the other hand:

> To live as a "swinger" . . . I think it means to take a leave from certain norms, certain traditions at any cost. . . . But maybe it's also a legitimate way to get near a happier condition of life. Who can tell?

This mixture of feelings enters into the last scene of the *Blow-Up*.

The revellers, after all, are a little different from the marijuana crowd. We first see them collecting for charity, which may help no one, but seems well intentioned. They also appear to be really in touch with each other, not just rubbing shoulders while each pursues his private dream. Their eyes focus, too, if only on imaginary tennis balls. Though deliberately feigning, they apparently understand the difference between illusion and reality. Perhaps their posturing is an evasion of life, but it seems more like strategic retreat than unconditional surrender. We might make the same case for the artist-hero. He does not grow, but neither does he shrivel. In fact, the [232–233] tennis match—repeating a game he watched before photographing the murder—seems to return him to an earlier stage of his life. He has recovered his style, his manner, and perhaps acquired some insight into his inclination to indulge in posturing. At least this is a matter for further critical debate.

The *Blow-Up* is such an ocular *tour de force,* it is hard to avoid being either aggravated or overwhelmed by it. Balanced appraisal, however, must take account of both fault and achievement. To me, the defects seem minor, but they are there. I am still not sure, for example, why Miss Redgrave doesn't simply expose the film during the moment she has the camera in her possession. And why is the nude scene with the would-be models drawn out so lengthily, particularly since Antonioni has to bundle the characters in paper wrappers to get them past the vice squad? Yet the total effect of the picture is one of expert finesse. Appropriate nuances are everywhere, and little snips of footage speak with quiet eloquence. Take, for instance, some of the paraphernalia associated with the protagonist. An ornamental propeller —ready to twirl endlessly without moving anything anywhere. Or the drawing of an Arabian caravan—stylishly parading across an empty wall of the studio. Or a bust of Louis XV—remembered by history for a single phrase, "*apres moi, le deluge.*" Antonioni refuses to caress these objects with the affection of a symbol-monger. But how right they are, how fully relevant. The acting, too, is smooth, natural, while the composition and coloration will likely be studied by film technicians for the next decade.

The intellectual import of *The Blow-Up* is more difficult to assess. Like his protagonist, Antonioni seems to resent any encroachment upon his moral neutrality. Critics who insist upon social consciousness as a *sine qua non* will probably regret that the director gives so little attention to his hero's connection with the world of the doss house. An orthodox Marxist might easily have built this moment of hesitant contact with the proletariat into an elaborate statement upon the parasitism of bourgeois art. On the other hand, those who seek from this picture some "spirituality" of a kind usually associated with pulpits will come away frustrated. Antonioni debunks Hugh Haffner, but not from the perspective of either Talcott Parsons or Cardinal Ottaviani. Perhaps there is no controlling perspective in the film, which gives some force to the charge of evasion. It might be argued, surely, that the neat paradox of the tennis match offers theatrical finality in place of human judgment.

My personal sympathies, however, lie with Antonioni. I don't like *The Blow-Up* quite so much as *The Eclipse* or *The Red Desert,* but nothing in this film effaces my respect for the director's integrity, intelligence, and severe moral astringency. Rightly, he suspects both private mystiques and public orthodoxies. Of course, he merely sees *through,* never sees *to.* His visual rhetoric always shatters, never saves. At the end of *The Red Desert,* Giuliana tells her young son that the bird protects himself from sulfuric factory-smoke by learning to fly around it. At the human level, unfortunately, the problem is more complicated. I doubt that we will avoid the threats to our own survival by playing tennis in a London park, and gather that Antonioni doubts it too. But if anyone knows what we should be doing instead I wish he'd drop me a line.   [233]

1. Mr. Scott says that the hero uses his camera to control reality. Is he controlling reality in the park scene? Why not? How might Mr. Scott explain this?

2. Is Mr. Scott correct in saying that the Vanessa Redgrave character is not definitely guilty? Does Antonioni make the matter clear in the park scene?

3. Compare the readings of the last scene given by all four critics. Which man seems right? Why?

4. Do you agree that Antonioni doesn't have to judge his hero or the mod world in order to make a good film? In any case, how can one be sure that a director is judging what he photographs?

THE BLOW-UP: SORTING THINGS OUT

CHARLES THOMAS SAMUELS

. . . Some critics, notably Stanley Kauffmann and Ian Cameron, have accurately described Antonioni's effort to disentangle cinema from theater, but they have not perceived the radical lengths to which he has gone. Every important director, from popular artists like Hitchcock to serious *auteurs* like Kurosawa and Bergman, has exploited cinema's unique ability both to imprison the spectator in the lens's grip and to free him through speed and scope of movement; but Antonioni stands alone in making the visual image his fundamental mode of expression. He does not tell a story; he presents gestures and tableaux. He does not explore characters; he moves figures through a landscape. Yet, although his films are filled with things to look at, he does not shoot scenery.

To begin with: plot. Antonioni's plots are really antiplots, since his characters are chronically unable to engage in productive action. Thus, in *L'Avventura*, Claudia and Sandro cannot truly search for his lost fiancée because they cannot truly care whether she is found. In *La Notte*, the unhappily married protagonists accomplish nothing in their long, eventful day, while the lovers' appointment in *Eclipse* is never, so far as we can tell, kept. Giuliana, of *Red Desert*, performs the one significant act in Antonioni, but that is only a spiritual adjustment to the modern world. Plot suspense is utterly avoided; our desire for knowledge focuses on character.

But not on character as unique personage, with determinant past and significant future. Antonioni's people are simply what we see, which is why they are always defined by dead-end jobs. Sandro, once an architect, is now an appraiser;

This essay appeared originally in *The American Scholar*, Winter 1967–68, pp. 120–131. The present version omits the first page.

while Giovanni, in *La Notte,* is a writer who doubts the possibility of another book. The sensitive heroine of *Eclipse* is doomed to the soulless and the secondhand: her lover works for the stock exchange, while she translates for a living. Even Giuliana has a depleting job, that of full-time neurotic. Unlike characters in other works that are similarly focused, Antonioni's do not develop. Their stories show them assuming a role—Claudia becoming Sandro's lover—or understanding the roles they have always played—Sandro facing his emptiness.

Since Antonioni's characters do not really engage in action and do not radically change, their inward fixity calls for a new kind of film movement. Whereas most directors move your eye across the surface of the action, Antonioni tries to move your eye into its depths. For most directors, a close-up represents, as it were, the locus of event and dialogue. In Antonioni, events occur behind faces, which express themselves not in dialogue but in gesture: a flick of the eye, a grimace. Antonioni's close-ups must be "read." Furthermore, whereas most directors bombard the spectator with images or hurl him through space, Antonioni holds his eye in front of carefully composed scenes.

This last characteristic is the heart of [*121–122*] Antonioni's method. A director who emphasizes action will photograph the background as an agent; as, for example, Hitchcock photographs the windshield wipers of Janet Leigh's car in *Psycho:* normal servants turned by the plot into menacing blades. A director who explores character will arrange the background into an "objective correlative"; as, for example, Fellini does in *8½.* Antonioni handles decor in neither way. In his films, the background does not enhance or reflect the foreground but rather interacts with and interprets it.

In his first important film, *L'Avventura,* the two main female characters are established by the simplest visual means: Anna, who has dark hair and scowls a great deal, represents withdrawal from society to which blond, always smiling Claudia is innocently attracted. In the film's second scene, Anna leaves Claudia inspecting a Roman square while she deliberately stages a test of her love for Sandro. As we watch Anna's face disgustedly receiving Sandro's caress, we see the nullity of their relationship and, since we shall later see the faces of Sandro and Claudia turning in the same erotic dance, we preview the essential anonymity of relationships in this world.

That Claudia is destined to replace her, Anna realizes when, with a smirk, she forces Claudia to wear her blouse in the subsequent yachting scene. This image must come back to our minds when, at Taormina, Claudia playfully dons a black wig, accepting a life in which identities may so easily be changed. In the film's last scene, when Claudia is herself replaced by a common whore, she has no moral force left from which to condemn the fickle Sandro. Now totally sophisticated, she can only join him in a gesture of resignation at their common incapacity for commitment.

The plot, or aborted action, of *L'Avventura* advances by means of visual analogies and small appearances; Antonioni can spend seconds shooting Claudia as she sits exhaustedly in the train station where she hopes to escape Sandro's tempting importunities. Above her head, in this actionless scene, are some pictures of madonnas. The moment's meaning is a contrast between the despair registered on

Claudia's face and the serenity in the pictures. This is how Antonioni's decor interacts with and interprets the characters.

It also helps to establish the significance of their behavior through visual
symbols and allusions, like the modernist devices of *The Waste Land* or *The Magic
Mountain,* that realize Antonioni's modernist themes: lovelessness, paralysis of
will, loss of faith. Fundamentally, *L'Avventura* contains an implied parallel with the
Odyssey, which mostly took place in the same Sicilian locale, and which provides
the Western mind with its definitive image of adventure and search. The point of the
comparison, of course, is that the modern quest, indifferent to its object, must turn
inward. Thus Antonioni fills the background with symbols of former validity to point
up their debasement in the modern world. I will cite only a few examples. Patrizia,
the yacht's owner, works a jigsaw puzzle of a classic scene while the playboy Rai-
mondo fondles her breast in a gesture that is "unreproved, if undesired." On the island, while searching for Anna, the modern Romans find an ancient amphora, and
after some humorously uncomprehending guesses about its possible function, Rai-
mondo carelessly lets it fall. The *carabinieri* to whom Sandro goes at Messina are
housed in a baroque palace before whose splendid marble walls they have set up
ugly wooden slabs to form an office.

Throughout the island sequence, Antonioni is careful to train his cameras
on the rocks so that the humans are always seen entering large barren areas, as if
they come too late and too punily to dominate the alien landscape. For their humanity has been wrecked by a cultural debacle in which, as in much modern literature, a debilitated pursuit of pleasure competes with activities that had traditionally
nurtured the soul. This theme, which gives the meager events their large significance,
permeates the film. On the church tower at Noto, for example, when Sandro asks
Claudia to marry him, she refuses a proposal so lightly made by ringing the bells
which actualize attunement. The Sicilian men [122–123] milling about Claudia with
sidewise lust are visually counterpointed by the choir-boys marching in orderly
sexlessness from the cathedral. The Sicilian journey progresses through a culture in
ruins (symbolized by the succession of church towers progressively abandoned and
incomplete—one without a bell), coming to rest at Taormina, haunt of the rich, before a shattered building of which all that remains is a ruined tower and a fragment
of facade.

Because *L'Avventura* shows an unformed girl realizing her latent sophistication, it comes closer than any of Antonioni's films to presenting a character in
transition. Although we know little about Claudia (except that she was born poor),
we can sympathize with her decline. Thus *L'Avventura,* Antonioniesque though it be,
is moving in a conventional way. The later films are more representational in their
enactment of cultural malaise, their characters are more fully symbolic, and their
effect is more sensory and intellectual.

In *L'Avventura,* although hints exist only to demonstrate the deterioration
that is modern worldliness, we learn something not only of Claudia's but of Sandro's
past. Once a creator of buildings, Sandro now merely measures their cost. When he
vindictively spills ink on the young boy's sketch of the cathedral at Noto, the personal and public meanings of Sandro's behavior merge; he is both a success reacting
against lost innocence and modern man reacting against lost faith. In *La Notte,* we
do not know why Giovanni can no longer write; the personal drama now merely

illustrates the public meaning of a day that begins with the death of an intellectual and ends at an industrialist's party. Similarly, we do not know why Giovanni and Lydia have fallen out of love. Their unhappiness is not explained; it is merely displayed.

To establish Lydia's feelings, for example, Antonioni shoots the famous walking scene in which Lydia's state of mind is revealed through her reactions to a postman eating a sandwich, some fighting youths, a man firing off rockets, *et cetera*. Stopped clocks and flaking walls suggest the era's sickness; later, at the party, Antonioni achieves one of his best visual symbols of deterioration by showing the industrialist's cat staring fixedly at a Roman portrait bust. "Maybe he's waiting for him to wake up," the millionaire's wife announces. "Try and figure cats out." When Giovanni takes Lydia to a night club, they witness the erotic dance of two splendid Negroes; but the act turns out to be acrobatic, concluding when the female manages to get her legs around a glass of water. Milan's sterility is highlighted at the party which becomes vital only when a rainstorm strikes.

With few exceptions (the explicit last scene or some excessive business at the party), *La Notte* dramatizes its insights subtly. But the film is impure. As if frightened by its increased abstractness, Antonioni relies too heavily on dialogue to clarify his points; and, as we might expect from an artist who thinks with his eyes, the dialogue is banal.

Eclipse is more abstract than *La Notte,* heightening its emphasis on meaningful gesture and replacing dialogue, as often as possible, with expressive natural sound. Vittoria, the heroine, is even less explained than Giovanni and Lydia. We never learn why she has broken off her first affair or why she takes up with Piero. Although she has a job, it is minimally emblematic, whereas the jobs of Sandro and Giovanni represent obvious spiritual problems. Vittoria is created almost exclusively through what she does. She constantly fusses with flowers or disports herself with the primitive and the natural. These meanings come together when Vittoria is fascinated by one of the men who is wiped out by the stock market slide. Whereas the other investors sweat and fan themselves furiously, rush around, or, like Vittoria's mother, blasphemously turn religion to the service of Mammon, this man exits calmly. Vittoria follows him to a café, where he orders a drink and writes intently on a piece of paper. When he leaves, dropping the paper behind him, she retrieves it. It is covered with flowers. She is delighted. This is the moment before she begins her affair with Piero.   [*123–124*]

Living in a sterile modern world, Vittoria seeks escape on an airplane ride above the clouds, as well as through love. When down to earth in Piero's arms, however, she learns that people nowadays care only for things. The liveliest, noisiest scenes in *Eclipse* take place at the stock exchange (significantly, built in the ruins of a Roman temple), where men sweatingly pursue goods that truly excite them. But, try as they may to stir it, the air cannot cool their agitated bodies. Only above the clouds, or in one small moment when the Exchange halts out of respect for a deceased broker, does the air quicken; during that unique respite from noise in the ruined temple, a large overhead fan, like a propeller, whirs freely.

Setting aside *Red Desert* for the moment, this brief survey of Antonioni's films should suggest the atmosphere of *Blow-Up.* Yet faced with a murder witnessed by a photographer, Bosley Crowther inevitably recalled the Hitchcock of *Rear Win-*

dow, and this utterly misleading comparison has been perpetuated by many critics. In fact, the antiplot of *Blow-Up* is *vero Antonioni.*[1]

Like *L'Avventura, Blow-Up* concerns the search for something that is never found. As in *La Notte,* the peripatetic hero fails to accomplish anything. Like the other protagonists, the photographer is the embodiment of a role, although here he is so fully defined by his function that he is not even named. As in Antonioni's other films, the climax is reached when the protagonist comes to face his own impotence. There is even a concluding disappearance that recalls the absence of Vittoria and Piero from the last minutes of *Eclipse:* as the camera slowly draws away from the photographer, he slowly diminishes in size, an effect made more significant when Antonioni literally causes him to vanish before "the end."

The events in *Blow-Up* dramatize the same theme one finds in Antonioni's other films. The photographer, a creature of work and pleasure but of no inner force or loyalty, is unable to involve himself in life. He watches it, manipulates it; but, like all of Antonioni's male characters, he has no sense of life's purpose. Thus, when faced with a challenge, he cannot decisively act. Unable to transcend himself, except through ultimate confrontation with his soul, he represents modern paralysis.

Most reviewers have denied that this or any other theme is apparent in *Blow-Up,* while those few who believed that Antonioni was up to something were either uncertain or wrong, I think, about what it was. Since Antonioni demands closer attention than even professional film watchers are likely to be familiar with, and since reviewers usually have the sketchiest knowledge of a serious director's canon, the errors are not surprising. But what are we to make of the critical misconceptions perpetrated by John Simon?   *[124–125]*

Simon is, in my opinion, the best American film critic now writing. Expectedly, he was the one critic who saw the need to summarize *Blow-Up*'s events; yet in his exhaustive resumé, he missed the crucial moments. As a result, he determined that Antonioni's theme was Pirandellian, despite the total absence of any

---

[1] The Julio Cortázar short story on which *Blow-Up* is loosely based considers a question only hinted at in the film: does art have metaphysical and moral power over reality? Cortázar's hero is an amateur photographer but a professional translator, and the first part of his story is a characteristic dissertation on the difficulty of representing life in words.

The main event is the hero's encounter with a young boy and an older, blond woman in the square of an island in the Seine. Thinking he witnesses an act of sexual initiation, he takes a photograph. But when the woman asks that it be returned, an older man, who had been watching the scene from a car, interrupts their altercation. During the argument, the boy escapes, convincing the translator that, despite his meddling, "taking the photo had been a good act." When he returns home and blows up the photograph, however, he concludes that the older woman was apparently seducing the boy for the man. Revolted by what he has witnessed, the photographer now imaginatively relives the experience, trying to release the boy from the imagined horror just as he had released him from the actual scene.

Antonioni's transformations are nearly total: the ages of the couple are reversed, she becomes dark-haired, the scene takes place in a garden rather than a square, seduction becomes murder. More important, the art theme is made peripheral (by introducing a literal artist as a foil to the commercial, mechanical photographer), while Antonioni focuses on the social context that he invents for the episode. I can think of no better way to illustrate the profoundly social orientation of Antonioni.

Notice, too, that whereas Cortázar's hero never discovers whether his "good act" was really effectual, Antonioni's photographer learns that he accomplished nothing. Cortázar's territory is the imagination, where fabulous victories match equally fabulous defeats; Antonioni's world is sadly, unconquerably real.

metaphysical concern in the director's other work. Together with the common emphasis on Hitchcock, this Pirandellian analogy has done a great deal to obfuscate Antonioni's meaning.

Because the body vanishes, and because the photographer ultimately hears a tennis ball that doesn't exist, some people have thought that Antonioni means us to question the existence of the corpse. Incidental details such as the photographer's initial appearance as a bum who surprisingly enters a Rolls Royce have been cited in support of this interpretation. Yet the point of the first scene is that the photographer *isn't* a bum, that he took part in the doss-house life merely to exploit it for his picture book. The body exists; what is significant is that the photographer didn't realize he'd seen it.

When the narrator enters the park, we see him performing his first spontaneous gesture. Emerging from the antique shop, he notices it and, for no apparent reason, enters. Perhaps he is attracted by the lush greenness, the melodically rustling leaves. Chancing on the love ballet, however, the photographer responds automatically, according to a settled routine. Love, as his agent, Ron, later tells him, would make a "truer" conclusion to his picture book. But when the girl tries to get his film and a young man (apparently the murderer) peers through the restaurant window at his lunch with Ron, the photographer begins to suspect that he has witnessed something less than innocent. After the girl leaves his studio, he blows up the photographs; and it is here, I think, that Simon and every other critic I have read misinterpret the action.

What happens is this: While the photographer is studying the shots, he spies something suspicious in the still of some shrubbery behind a fence. What he does not see but what the audience does, as Antonioni's lens pans across the row of blowups, is the still showing a body. The audience, but not the photographer, knows that a body exists. (When Vanessa Redgrave ran away from the photographer during the park scene, she stopped to look down at the tree, from behind which a head was unmistakably visible.) But the photographer chooses to blow up only the still showing the murderer and his gun. Exulting in what he thinks is a meaningful action, he rushes to the phone to call his agent. "Somebody was trying to kill somebody else," he says, "I saved his life."

That the photographer jumps to this erroneous conclusion despite contrary evidence is logical in view of subtle but clear hints we got earlier of a latent dissatisfaction with his normal mode of behavior. His studio is dominated by photographs of a sky diver and a skin diver, his living room by a shot of camels (recalling a similar photograph in *Eclipse*), and he clearly would like to get away. Vittoria made her frail gesture in a plane; the photographer buys a propeller. Lydia had gone on a solitary walk; the photographer, so far as he knows, takes a stroll in the park. As he tells his agent, "I've gone off London this week. Doesn't do anything for me. I'm fed up with those bloody bitches. Wish I had tons of money, then I'd be free."

Freedom and mastery are cheaply purchased when the photographer allows himself to believe he has saved a man's life. Had he done so, his action would have symbolized a separation from the aimless mod world. What he witnessed, as he believes, was the attempt by a young swinger to murder a gray-haired, older man in a garden. Catching the snake hidden in the bushes, the photographer had preserved the intended victim. The fact of the matter is different.

While on the phone with Ron, he hears a noise at the door. Apparently suspecting the murderer, he opens it surreptitiously; in tumble two teeny-boppers. Although he had previously expressed contempt for these "bloody bitches," he now becomes involved with them. Meanwhile Ron rings [125–126] off. When the girls, who have come for some exploitation of their own, begin to undress before a clothes-rack, the photographer seizes the opportunity. An orgy ensues, and here Antonioni works his most audacious trick.[2]

While the photographer is romping with the girls (avidly attended by any normal spectator), for perhaps five seconds, in the upper right hand corner of the frame, above the purple paper, we see a man dressed like the murderer, watching them. Antonioni then cuts to the girls as they are pulling on the photographer's clothes, and the photographer, who is sitting up, now notices the shot he had previously overlooked. Much to their chagrin, he ejects the teeny-boppers, blows up the fatal still, and learns that he had saved nothing.

However, instead of calling the police, asking for help, or in any way dealing with what he now realizes, he returns to the park to prove that the murder took place (although in calling his agent, he had acted far more precipitately with no more evidence). Back at the park, he sees the body; but behind him he hears a click, as of a gun or camera, and he runs away. Again, he does not go for the police. Instead, he returns to his studio and looks longingly at the propeller, an old part without a plane, lying on a white floor—useless. He then goes to his friend's apartment, where he is shocked to find the wife fixing her attention upon him while having intercourse with her husband.

Reentering his studio, he discovers that the blowups have been stolen, presumably by the man who entered during the orgy sequence. After a brief, apparently fruitless conversation with his friend's wife, he takes off in his car. While driving, he thinks he sees the murderer's accomplice; but his attempt to chase her degenerates into his meaningless involvement with an absurd experience at a rock'n roll club. Once again, he has recourse to his agent; but he finds Ron in a marijuana trance, which he soon joins. In the last scene, returning to the park, he discovers that the murderer has made off with the body. He has accomplished nothing.

For he is part of his world. Hiding behind a tree, like the murderer, he shot with a camera what the latter shot with a gun; and he did not save the older man. He is blond, and so is the murderer. For all his aloof contempt, he is as frivolous as the mod clowns who frame his experience. In the last scene, when he hears their "tennis ball," he effectively actualizes the charade existence that they share in common. His final gesture of resignation—like Sandro's tears, Giovanni's loveless copulation, or Piero's and Vittoria's failure to meet—shows clearly that the photographer cannot change.

[2] This detail is perhaps a shade too audacious, but there is precedent for it in *L'Avventura*. When Anna disappears, she leaves two books behind her: the Bible and *Tender is the Night*. We get a brief glimpse of the latter, which I presume was meant to hint at Anna's relationship with her father and thus help establish a motive for her disappearance. Thus we have the father's response when Claudia gives him both volumes: "This looks like a good sign. Don't you think so? As far as I'm concerned, anyone who reads the Bible could not have committed an act of impropriety." (This, like all passages from the first three films, is quoted from *Screenplays of Michelangelo Antonioni*. New York, 1963.)

The actions I have sketched are nearly pantomimed; their larger implications are also established through visual means. As with the carabinieri's office in L'Avventura, the first shot in La Notte (showing a graceful old building standing in front of Pirelli's glass box), the forbidding sleekness of E.U.R. in Eclipse, Antonioni fills the background in Blow-Up with examples of tradition being razed to make way for a gray, anonymous wasteland. As the photographer drives through London, the camera pans along the colorful walls of the old city only to be abruptly lost in blank space surrounding a new housing project—all grays and browns. When he visits the antique shop, scouting real estate for his agent, he advises purchase since the neighborhood seems to have attracted homosexuals—those great contemporary buyers of the past. The old caretaker, however, refuses to sell him anything, but the young mod owner is only too anxious to turn the shop into cash for a trip to Nepal, where she hopes to escape [126–127] from the antiques. "Nepal is all antiques," the photographer dryly observes.

The modern world, however, seems bent on destroying its traditions. On the wall of the photographer's apartment, an old Roman tablet is overwhelmed by the hallucinatory violence of the modern painting at its side. More important, traditional human pursuits are being drained of their force. Politics is now playacting; a pacifist parade marches by with signs bearing inscriptions like "No," or "On. On. On." or "Go away." Pleasure is narcotizing, whether at the "pot" party or in the rock 'n roll club. Love is unabsorbing, as the photographer learns from his friend's marriage. Art has lost its validity. Murder is ignored.

These last implications are forcefully portrayed in the film's main scenes of human interaction. The first of these scenes shows the photographer visiting his friend Bill, who is a painter. When the hero enters his flat, the painter is standing affectedly before a large canvas. Attempting to engage the photographer's interest, he explains his condition:

> They don't mean anything when I do them, just a mess. Afterward, I find something to hang onto [pointing]—like that leg. Then it all sorts itself out; it's like finding a clue in a detective story.

Although we are likely to find Bill rather pretentious, particularly in view of the obviously derivative nature of his painting, the photographer seems unusually impressed. When the painter's wife enters, he tells her that he has wanted to buy one of the canvases. When we see her massaging his neck with obvious interest on her part but mere friendly comfort on his, we know what this oasis of art and domesticity might mean to a man so cynical and frenetic. Later, in his puzzlement concerning the murder, when he turns to them for help, he discovers that the oasis is dry.

In the second important scene, the murderer's accomplice meets the photographer at his studio because he blew his car horn when he reached his street so as to inform the pursuers of his whereabouts. When he tries to calm her, she replies:

> "My private life is already in a mess. It would be a disaster—"
> P: "So what? Nothing like a little disaster for sorting things out."

Through turning sparse, functional dialogue into a system of verbal echoes, Antonioni achieves the economy of tight verse. Yet he does not sacrifice naturalness. The painter, in an observation appropriate to the scene, had suggested that visual experience is comprehensible only through recollection, during which process it performs the function of a clue that helps to "sort things out." The photographer, in a casual remark to the girl, asserts that the sorting out process is facilitated by disaster. This verbal cross-reference points to the meaning behind the action.

The most subtle use of dialogue occurs in a sequence which has been either ignored or misinterpreted as a sign that Antonioni's theme is failure of communication. When the painter's wife enters his studio, she comes upon a distraught man; he has lost his evidence and his faith in his friends. Although laconically, they do communicate:

P: "Do you ever think of leaving [your husband]?"
W: "No, I don't think so."
P: [Turning away with annoyance] "I saw a man killed this morning."
W: "Where? Was he shot?"
P: "Sort of a park."
W: "Are you sure?"
P: "He's still there."
W: "Who was he?"
P: "Someone."
W: "How did it happen?"
P: "I don't know. I didn't see."
W: [Bewildered] "You didn't see?"
P: [Wry grimace] "No."
W: "Shouldn't you call the police?"
P: [Pointing to the one still the murderer didn't take] "That's the body."
W: "Looks like one of Bill's paintings. [Turning to him, helplessly] Will you help me? I don't know what to do. [He doesn't react. She looks at the shot.] What is it? Hmmmm. I wonder why they shot him."
P: "I didn't ask."
W: [Looks up at him, smiles sadly, and, after some hesitation, leaves.]

[127–128]

I record this dialogue to show how clearly and economically Antonioni establishes his meaning.[3] When the painter's wife comes to his apartment, she hears

---

[3] The dialogue at the "pot" party is equally clear. After great difficulty, the photographer succeeds in getting Ron to listen to his problem:

P: "Someone's been killed."
R: "O.K."
P: "Listen, those pictures I took in the park—[No response] I want you to see the corpse. We've got to get a shot of it."
R: [Bewildered] "I'm not a photographer."
P: [Bitterly] "I am."
R: [Nonplussed] "What did you see in that park?"
P: [Resignedly] "Nothing." [Ron, who can't focus his eyes well, motions the photographer to follow him. The photographer does. Next scene shows him walking up from the debauch.]

the photographer's confession of failure and declares her own. Bill's art is no alternative to the destruction symbolized by the murder; his art is another version of it. They can no more deal with their marriage than the photographer can deal with the crime. She can only slink away in compassion for their mutual impotence, leaving him to futile pursuit, marijuana, and his depressing moment of truth.

In *Blow-Up*, as in *Eclipse* and *L'Avventura's* island sequence, Antonioni achieves his meanings through the use of sound effects as well as speech. When the photographer shoots his model in a parody of intercourse, and when he poses the mannequins, music, as he says, is "noise" to inspire their artificial vitality. When Vanessa Redgrave comes to his apartment, fresh from the murder, he tries to teach her the lesson that music maintains one's "cool." While giving her some "pot," to which she sensuously yields herself, he shows her that really to enjoy it and the taped jazz he is playing, she must hold herself back—draw slowly and keep time against the beat. Before he begins to inspect the blowups, he turns the jazz on. But the music quickly fades when he becomes involved; as he looks deeply into the frames, we hear on the sound track a rustling of leaves.

The incredible greenness of a park that was the ironic setting for murder suggests another of Antonioni's means. When the photographer discovers the body's loss, he looks up at the tree, whose leaves now rattle angrily, and sees the leaves as black against a white sky. Like the sound analogies and the verbal cross-references, the color in *Blow-Up* aids comprehension.

The film is composed mainly in four hues: black, white, green and purple. The hero's studio is black and white, as are most of his clothes and those of Vanessa Redgrave. So too are photographs. In fact, the meaning of the event in the park was "as clear as black and white" before he photographed it, which is what makes for significance in his initial failure of perception as well as in his underlying failure to understand the implication of his way of life. The green park was penetrated by evil. Suitably, the door of the photographer's dark room, in which he brings to light the dark deed, is also green. Not, however, until he copulates with the teeny-boppers in a sea of purple does he realize that he did not prevent the crime. Appropriately, the door to the room in which he blows up the fatal still is also purple. One of the teeny-boppers wears purple tights; the other, green.

Colorful though it is, *Blow-Up* seems to be moving toward colorlessness, black and white—almost as if Antonioni were trying to make us face the skull beneath the painted flesh. But that is not what most reviewers have done. That they should, if my reading is correct, have missed the film's meaning so completely is a phenomenon almost as significant as the film itself. What, after all, does their error tell us?

The familiar things are aspects of a fixed condition. As I have said, few reviewers know the director's work; fewer still have sophisticated ideas about film art. Their collective sophistication, if not their intelligence, is modest; when they simulate brilliance, it is only through the perfervid prose we associate with *Time* magazine. I doubt that many serious readers would choose books on the advice of the same sources to which, *faute de mieux*, they are forced to turn for evaluation of films. This much, I think, is sadly inarguable, but not limited to consideration of *avant-garde* film-making in general or Antonioni in particular.   [*128–129*]

The confusion about Antonioni comes from the unusual demands he makes. Most films are to be looked at; Antonioni's are to be inspected. Decades of film as a commercial form of escapism have atrophied our perception; like all great artists, Antonioni insists that we see anew. Unfortunately, most reviewers can't see. Although many disguised their ineptitude by reporting little of what goes on in *Blow-Up*, distressing errors of fact tend to characterize the more venturesome accounts. Thus one reviewer (Richard Corliss, *National Review*) has the photographer buying an oar, while another (Joseph Morgenstern, *Newsweek*) has the orgy spread out on sky-blue paper. John Simon suggests that the photographer makes eyes at Sarah Miles, whereas the reverse is true. As a result of this error, he can give no accurate reading of the subplot. John Coleman (*New Statesman*) loftily deems *Blow-Up* a "very superficial film . . . about people reckoned as léading superficial lives"; but since he asserts that the photographer saw the body and the gun *after* the orgy sequence, Coleman is in no position to call anyone superficial.

Such errors of fact are less important in themselves than as manifestations of a cavalier attitude toward Antonioni's difficult style. More than their mistakes, the arrogance of reviewers is what rankles. Confronted with a famously complex director whose films are widely acknowledged to be important, the journeyman critic, both here and in England, treats *Blow-Up* as if it were indeed a mechanical piece of Hitchcock. Despite museum cults, the emergence of cinema's right to be considered a form of art is notoriously recent. A parallel growth in movie reviewing is long overdue.

Among critics, the source of confusion is more profound. Misunderstanding *Blow-Up* is not only failure to scrutinize with sufficient care a highly wrought method of expression; it is the consequence of some false, but currently powerful, ideas about the nature of art. Although these ideas are more blatantly damaging with an art form so ill-defined as cinema, they have their origin in wider cultural presuppositions.

The first of them, to use Norman Podhoretz's phrase, is the demand that art "bring the news." Widespread dissatisfaction with contemporary fiction, lack of interest in poetry, and the inflation of nonfictional forms like the book review all indicate the dominance of this aesthetic program. Thus Norman Mailer's lucubrations attain significance because he styles himself a social prophet, confessional poetry becomes the accepted fashion in verse, and nonfiction, a form defined by what it isn't, now begins to absorb whatever it lacks.

From the neonaturalist perspective, *Blow-Up* is offensive because it manipulates the materials of contemporary London to express not the city but Antonioni's version of modern life. If one can bear the hip language—not unrelated to the ideas—he can see this attitude clearly expressed in Richard Goldstein's article in the *Village Voice*, entitled "The Screw-Up." Condemning a lack of "understanding that can only be called Parental," Goldstein insists that Antonioni misrepresents the swinging Samarkand and derides the film for the expressiveness that—*autres temps, autres moeurs*—would have guaranteed its status as a work of art. Whatever can be said for such documentary emphasis, it easily degenerates into mindless fixation on the up-to-date. That people old enough to know better don't avoid the trap can be seen in Pauline Kael's review, where, amidst a veritable fusillade, she criticizes Antonioni for not catching "the humor and fervor and astonishing speed in youth's rejection of older values." Godard, *sí!* Antonioni, *no!*

The other new aesthetic barbarism has quickly filtered down to its rightful level, having been recently promoted . . . by the arts editor of *Look.* Given a more respectable formulation by Susan Sontag, Richard Gilman and other less conspicuous gurus, the conception of art as "sensuous form" might seem a useful antidote to excess verisimilitude, but it comes to much the same thing. Like those who wish art to be a form of sociology, the advocates of a "new sensibility" reveal a fatal [*129–130*] affinity for what's "in." Thus Miss Sontag finds that formal heights are scaled by happenings, pornography and science fiction, while critics like Gilman opt for novels (promoted by magazines like the *New Yorker*) in which insouciance becomes art by imitating the era's bafflement. (Collusion between the documentary and noninterpretive definitions of art was nicely indicated by the appearance of Robert Garis's review—which argues that the film is good because it is "exciting to watch"—in *Commentary.*)

One error encourages the sentimental social pieties of some reviewers; the other authorizes their imperception. Thus reviews of *Blow-Up* express outraged social optimism or a kind of aesthetic trance induced by globules of "surface beauty." The skillful creation of symbols for insight—art, in short—becomes an achievement of negligible appeal.

A third aesthetic error (born, in part, out of reaction against the other two), despite a devotion to artistic seriousness, runs the risk of blocking new modes. John Simon is rightly opposed to art without discursive implications or rational validity. In *Hudson Review* pieces concerning Albee, Pinter, and thinkers like McLuhan and N. O. Brown, Simon shows himself a powerful demolition machine for a culture beseiged on all sides. But in his splendid assaults, he sometimes finds himself forced backward into old-fashioned demands for situational realism, psychologically valid motivation, and humanistically oriented themes. These requirements should be suspended with considerably less alacrity than most critics now show, but they must be abandoned for those rare cases, like Borges, Beckett or Antonioni, in which authentic art is being produced in a new way. Significantly, Simon is receptive to such art when reviewing books—a further indication that people automatically relax their aesthetics when discussing films.

A similarly based lack of sympathy is detectable in the otherwise laudatory pieces on Antonioni's earlier films that Dwight Macdonald wrote for *Esquire.* Although Macdonald, along with Stanley Kauffmann, was one of Antonioni's few discerning American champions, he became displeased by the Italian's progressive refusal to motivate his characters. Even Kauffmann was made nervous by the abstractionism of *Eclipse,* although he rejoiced, wrongly as I think, in the colored abstractionism of *Red Desert.*

Still, despite a few hints of retrograde commitment, Simon, Kauffmann and Macdonald are the most sensitive of Antonioni's American critics and the most useful, intelligent film critics of recent times. The fumbling responses of their colleagues remind us that the always thinly staffed legion of competence is now threatened with depopulation. Macdonald has been replaced at *Esquire* by Wilfrid Sheed, while Pauline Kael has taken over from Kauffmann on the *New Republic*. (Fortunately, Kauffmann will review films for the *New American Review*, but only three times a year; and I suspect he will be pressed for space.)

As a novelist and book or theater critic, Wilfrid Sheed has behind him an estimable body of work. As a film critic, he has nothing—either in experience or rumination—a fact that he candidly admitted in his first *Esquire* piece. Despite his avowed respect for Antonioni's other films, his review of *Blow-Up* expresses nearly ruthless contempt. Much of the piece is not about the film at all, concentrating its attention instead (complete with feeble jokes about old musicals that Sheed *does* know) on Rex Reed's interview with Antonioni in the *Times*. The rest of his review repeats Judith Crist's complaint that Antonioni let a good story get away, Richard Goldstein's complaint that Antonioni didn't really capture London, and the blank raving about "surface beauty" that characterizes most other reviews. Finding the symbolism "nonorganic" and the ideas banal, Sheed disdains to argue either point.

Such offenses against criticism are compounded in Miss Kael's review by offenses against taste, logic and the reader's patience. In a piece so staggeringly verbose that one cannot, as in Sheed's case, attribute the lack of argument to lack of space, Miss [130–131] Kael serves up that combination of personal exhibitionism, obsession with fashion, and irrelevant inside dope that has become her special ragout. She reviews not the film but the audience.[4]

> Will *Blow-Up* be taken seriously in 1968 only by the same sort of cultural die-hards who are still sending out five-page single-spaced letters on their interpretation of Marienbad? (No two are alike, no one interesting.) It has some of the Mari-

[4] Space limits prevent me from detailing Miss Kael's other vagaries, but I should like to draw attention to her one valid point. Miss Kael accuses Antonioni of secretly loving the mod life he exposes. This brings me to *Red Desert*.

Antonioni's first color film is in most respects identical to its predecessors, although it is less successful. More even than *La Notte*, it employs rather embarrassing dialogue. Also, whereas we can accept the representational function of normal people without needing to know much about them, a sick soul inevitably raises questions of causality which Antonioni is characteristically unable to answer.

More seriously, *Red Desert* is spoiled by a confusion in perspective, and it is here that Pauline Kael's point about *Blow-Up* is relevant. Much of the film seems to indicate that the camera is essentially inseparable from Giuliana's twisted viewpoint. That presumably explains why we see things change color or lose definition as she looks at them. But in addition to several scenes in which she does not appear, there are examples of contradictory focus: in one scene, objects are in soft focus before and behind her, while she is sharp. This technical confusion reveals a deeper thematic uncertainty. Much of the film suggests that Giuliana is sickened by an actually terrifying culture, full of slag heaps, loneliness and exploitation. But since Antonioni is at pains to show that industrial Ravenna is also beautiful (he even paints steam pipes in gay colors), we begin to suspect that Giuliana's inability to adjust is culpable. This would support the apparent optimism of the ending.

Blow-Up suggests, for some people, a similar ambivalence. Isn't Antonioni fascinated by the mod scene, which, although empty, is certainly colorful? So far as I can see, people who answer "yes" are confusing their own response to the undeniably exciting materials with the film's theme. (Could Antonioni have convinced us that a film was set in mod London if he had photographed London the way he photographed the Lipari Islands or Milan?) Nevertheless, I think this is an arguable and important question. Were it possible here, I should like to consider the nostalgia for answers that Antonioni shares with most great modern chroniclers of the wasteland.

enbad appeal: a friend phones for your opinion and when you tell him you didn't much care for it, he says, "You'd better see it again, I was at a swinging party the other night and it's all anybody ever talked about!" (Was there ever a good movie that everybody was talking about?) It probably won't blow over because it also has the *Morgan!-Georgy Girl* appeal; people identify with it so strongly, they get *upset* if you don't like it—as if you were rejecting not just the movie but *them*. And in a way they're right, because if you don't accept the peculiarly slugged consciousness of *Blow-Up,* you *are* rejecting something in them. Antonioni's new mixture of suspense with vagueness and confusion seems to have the kind of numbing fascination for them that they associate with art and intellectuality, and they are responding to it as *their* film—and hence as a masterpiece.

Two bad reviews by two irresponsible critics prove little; but when we search for alternatives, the point gets made. There are frequently fewer interesting plays or books in a given season than interesting films. Yet I think the *Blow-Up* controversy suggests how ill-equipped American criticism is to discuss them. With the exception of John Simon, there is, at the moment, no aesthetically sophisticated and informed guide available for the growing audience that seeks enlightenment about films—and Simon writes for only thirty-five thousand readers a dozen times a year in the *New Leader.* Of the journalistic film reviewers, there is scarcely one to be taken seriously. The mass magazines used to employ men like Agee or Macdonald, but such critics have been ill-replaced. Smaller film quarterlies (when they last long enough to be useful) are made up either by film buffs capable, like the *Cahiers du Cinéma* crowd, of ontological analyses of Jerry Lewis, or they bear the same relationship to live film criticism that a philological journal bears to the vital discussion of books.

Artists like Antonioni will continue to progress, unperturbed by widespread ignorance. (Moreover, they will prosper; *Variety* says *Blow-Up* is "k.o.") But scores of interested viewers will be left behind.   [*131*]

1.   Mr. Samuels attributes what he regards as errors concerning *Blow-Up* to the reviewers' sketchy "knowledge of a . . . director's canon." Do you think it important to have such knowledge before judging a single film? What arguments can be made for and against this view?

2.   Mr. Samuels discusses the symbolic meaning of the hero's belief that he saved a man's life. But, of course, the hero must have had inner motives as well. What might they have been? Or would you disagree with Samuels' interpretation?

3.   None of the four critics spends much time discussing the film's rock n' roll sequence. What is its function in *Blow-Up*? Does this presentation of a rock n' roll club seem authentic to you? How accurately would you say Antonioni has caught the "youth scene" in his movie?

SELECTIVE GLOSSARY

Angle   The position of the camera relative to the subject.

Angle shot   A shot in which the camera is not parallel to the subject but is placed above, below, or to the side. The result is an unusual view of the subject that produces a special effect.

Auteur   French for "author." When used to designate a filmmaker, the word indicates his total control over the film, from writing the script to editing the shots. The filmmaker with such control is regarded as analogous to the author of a book and thus as a more authentic artist than one who shoots another man's ideas or submits to another man's shaping of his artistic expression.

Back projection   Action transpiring against a screen on which a second action is projected, as when a person seen driving a car is himself photographed against a photograph of moving traffic.

Cameraman   Either the man who actually does the photographing or one who plans the lighting for each shot. Sometimes one person does both jobs.

Close-up   A shot of some detail taken at close range. Most frequently, close-ups fill the frame with the actor's face, but close-ups may also be taken of other parts of the anatomy, of inanimate objects, etc.

Continuity   Smooth unobtrusive transitions among the shots in a sequence or entire film.

Crosscut   Rapid transition between two separate shots; frequently maintained for some time so as to make two actions simultaneous.

Cut   Any transition from one shot to another. Cuts are characterized by their speed and by their frequency within a given length of film. Thus "fast-cutting" indicates frequent, abrupt transitions, whereas "long-cutting" indicates a more theatrical succession of dramatic scenes. The former is used for effects of agitation, suspense, etc.; the latter avoids effects and helps us to concentrate on the content of the scene.

Director   Usually the chief artist in the actual filmmaking, the director tells the actors what to do and oversees the work of cameramen, editors, etc.

Dissolve   Marking the transition from one scene to another by having one emerge at the same time as the other fades out.

Dolly   A moving vehicle on which a camera can be mounted.

Dolly-shot   A shot taken with a moving camera.

Dubbing   Re-recording of the sound track; usually employed to impose a language comprehensible to the national audience on the language in which the film was originally shot.

Editor   The man responsible for joining shots, eliminating footage, and achieving continuity. Occasionally a director may make all the editorial choices, though the actual mechanics are performed by someone else.

Fade in   Gradual appearance from darkness.

Fade out   Gradual disappearance of a shot into darkness; marks the end of a scene.

Filter   Toned transparency placed over the lens to obtain special lighting effect.

Flashback   Shot or sequence out of chronological order. If a prediction of future action, called *flashforward*.

Focus   To present a sharp, clear vision of the subject. Softening of focus is used for special effects.

Frame   The single photograph. The illusion of motion is produced by the rapid succession of frames.

Freeze   A successive projecting of the same frame designed to hold the action before the viewer.

Grain   A particle of the film image. Large particles produce a "grainy" surface, cultivated for certain effects.

Hand-held camera   A camera not mounted on dolly or tripod; usually results in jerky image desired for certain effects of "naturalness."

Intercut   A short cut into a sequence to which it does not logically belong and thus productive of powerful effects of surprise, interpretation, etc.

Iris in/out   Gradual appearance and/or disappearance of the scene through an expanding circle.

Jump Cut   A deliberately abrupt cut used for emotive effect.

Mise-en-scène   French for "staging." Every film director is engaged both in "mise-en-scène" (i.e. telling actors how to deliver their lines and organizing physical movement) and in planning camera set-ups. Critics variously emphasize these two aspects of the director's art.

Montage   Literally, the assembling or editing of the entire film. But the history of film form makes it desirable to reserve this term for non-continuity editing, i.e. editing designed to call attention to itself by producing special effects. Thus prolonged crosscutting or parallel montage creates simultaneity of action. Constant intercutting, as in dream sequences, creates a new reality. Montage is the most frequently discussed and controversial aspect of film form. Consult the bibliography for sources.

Pan   To move the camera horizontally across the subject.

Scene   A numbered section of the script. Less technically, it is called *sequence*.

Score   Musical accompaniment or songs in a film.

Sequence   A series of shots thought to form an integral action. Corresponds to a dramatic scene.

Set-up   Positioning of subject and relationship to it of the camera.

Shooting script   The scenario complete with indications of how the set-ups are to be managed. Finished films are more or less enactments of the shooting script, though in the actual filming most directors improvise to some extent.

Shot   A single view of the subject. Three basic kinds of shots are usually designated: distance (long), medium, and close-up. The actual length of the projected shot is usually determined by editing.

Slow motion   An effect of retarded movement produced by projecting the film at a slower rate than the subject was photographed. The reverse technique, less often used, produces speed-up motion.

Sound track   The electronic band of sound (speech, natural sound, music) joined to the filmstrip in a sound film.

Stock shot   A shot not made for the film but taken from a library or stock of film kept for such borrowings.

Superimpose   To print one shot on another. Used for special effects of simultaneity.

Synchronization   The joining of film and sound tracks. Occasionally, special purposes dictate a deliberate mismating of the two, as, for example, when a director wishes a speech in one scene to be heard in the following.

Take   One photographing of a shot, scene, or sequence. Most moments on film represent the director's or editor's choice from among several takes.

Tilt   To swing the camera vertically.

Track   To move the camera toward or away from the subject.

Tripod   Three-legged mounting for camera used to prevent unwanted camera motion that might blur the shot.

Wipe   The effacing of a screen image by some other image. There are many varieties of wipe, but few are used in contemporary films since they increase artificiality. See bibliography of books on technique for full discussion of the wipe.

Zoom   Sudden close-up, usually accomplished with special lens.

PAPERS
AND PROJECTS

Short papers: The following suggestions for short papers (from 500 to 1500 words) do not require additional reading or viewing of films. In this section, and those that follow, the suggestions are listed in an order roughly corresponding to the order of selections in this volume.

1. Write a description of some event you experienced. Then rewrite it in cinematic form, stressing the space-time characteristics discussed by Profs. Panofsky and Hauser.

2. Describe a confrontation with some member of your family or a friend. Rewrite it as a scene, complete with camera angles and other designations for the shooting script.

3. Compare the essays in the section called "Defining the Form." Which one seems to you to provide the fullest definition of film art? Why?

4. Synthesize the arguments of all writers in this section except Nicola Chiaromonte so as to produce a single line of argument against his contention that films present "a world disinfected of consciousness."

5. Write a descriptive or evaluative account of some film performance that particularly impressed you. What standards are you using?

6. Neither Irving Pichel nor Basil Wright discusses the zoom shot. Write a paper in which you show when this technique might be effectively used in a film.

7. Write your own critic's credo.

8. Write a paper attacking or defending the institution of film criticism. You may wish to take up the issues defined by relevant articles in this book (by Simon, Houston, Samuels, etc.).

242

9. In "The Critical Question," Penelope Houston maintains that a good critic can admire the skill of a film whose meaning he dislikes or the meaning of a film which is not skillful. Use this standard to judge any of the critical reviews in this volume. Does the critic measure up, or is he confusing aesthetic and moral judgments?

10. Penelope Houston says: "To the generation which has grown up during the last few years, art is something for kicks. . . ." Using your own experience and that of your friends, support or refute this judgment.

11. Select an actor who qualifies as your film hero.

    a)   What does he represent?
    b)   In the light of Robert Brustein's essay, evaluate the implications of your choice.

12. Compare Robert Warshow's account of the function of sadism in the gangster film with its function in *Bonnie and Clyde*. How relevant is Mr. Warshow's analysis to this film?

13. In his review of *The Graduate*, Stanley Kauffmann says: "Moral attitudes, far from relaxing, are getting stricter and stricter, and many of the shoddy moralistic acceptances that dictated mindless actions for decades are now being fiercely questioned." Using your own experience and that of your friends, judge the accuracy of Mr. Kauffmann's assertion.

14. *The Graduate*, through its depiction of Benjamin, is widely held to portray the attitudes of young people toward adult society. Do you agree? Why?

15. Edgar Friedenberg refers to Benjamin as "fashionably unheroic." Do you agree that heroism is out of fashion today? Write an essay on this subject.

16. In his review of *The Graduate*, Mr. Friedenberg also says, "an honest movie about human disaster—even a comedy—must place that disaster in its cultural setting as well as make witty comments about it." Write a paper in which you support or refute this assertion.

17. Jacob Brackman attacks *The Graduate* as a misrepresentation of contemporary youth. Write a paper supporting his views. (To do so, you may first want to read the uncut *New Yorker* version of Mr. Brackman's essay.)

18. *Bonnie and Clyde* inspired many essays on violence in American life. Using the film as a starting point, write your own essay on this subject.

19. Many people seem to have accepted the Barrows' own conception of themselves. Write a paper in which you argue for the gang.

20. In defending *Bonnie and Clyde,* Joseph Morgenstern lists a number of acceptably violent films. Select one you know, discuss the way in which its violence is acceptable, and judge whether this serves as a precedent for *Bonnie and Clyde.*

21. Both *The Graduate* and *Bonnie and Clyde* contain many unusual photographic effects. Select one film and write an essay on its photographic style.

22. Write your own review of one of the three films discussed in this volume.

23. Jerry Richard deplores unanalytical enjoyment of movies. Write a defense or attack of his position.

24. *Blow-Up* is very difficult to understand in a single viewing. Write a paper on the problems and possible solutions in viewing such a film.

25. In discussing Antonioni, Charles Thomas Samuels points to visual parallels or motifs. Are there any such in *The Graduate* and *Bonnie and Clyde?* Pick one film and discuss such devices. What are they and what do they do?

Long Papers: The following topics, designed for papers of from 1500–5000 words, require additional reading or viewing of films.

1. Arnold Hauser compares film form to the philosophy of Henri Bergson. Read Bergson's *Time and Free Will* and write a paper in which you explore the connection.

2. Michael Roemer cites *The Best Years of Our Lives* as a film that uses stock responses while it seems to be showing actual life. Select a more recent film with the same defect and analyze its manipulation of the audience.

3. Select a scene from a play or novel and recast it in scenario form, using the guidelines set down by Dudley Nichols.

4. Camera technique has greatly influenced contemporary fiction. Select one of the following novels and show how its form may be called "cinematic":

        a. John Dos Passos: *Manhattan Transfer*
        b. Ernest Hemingway: *For Whom the Bell Tolls*
        c. Katherine Anne Porter: *Ship of Fools*
        d. William Faulkner: *Requiem for a Nun*
        e. Nathanael West: *The Day of the Locust*
        f. Norman Mailer: *The Naked and the Dead*
        g. Joseph Heller: *Catch 22*
        h. John Updike: *Rabbit, Run*
        i. Philip Roth: *When She Was Good*

5. Select any scene from a film that you particularly enjoyed and remember well. Then, by using Andrew Sarris' example of directorial interpretation ("Little Red Riding Hood"), show how that scene was interpreted by the way it was shot as well as by the things said or done in it.

6. Do the reviews in this volume justify Andrew Sarris' categories of "literary" and "visualist" film criticism?

7. Irving Pichel suggests that camera movements were, in effect, indicated in 19th century fiction. Test his hypothesis by picking some major 19th century novel. How is its form cinematic?

8. In moving from the spectator-oriented to the narrator-oriented camera, Irving Pichel naturally falls to the use of quotes around the word "see." For, in the first case, seeing is entirely physical, while in the second, it is intellectual, emotional, and interpretive. This implies that the way in which the camera sees an action tells us how the author or director "sees" (i.e. understands and feels about) it. Show how this works by discussing specific shots or sequences.

9. Since Irving Pichel wrote his article, many directors have preferred a hand-held camera to a tripod-mounted or dolly-mounted machine. Select one of the following films and show what the hand-held camera accomplishes:

    a.   A Godard film (e.g. *Breathless*)
    b.   Truffaut's *The 400 Blows* or *Jules and Jim*
    c.   Cassavetes' *Faces*

10. Select any book containing stills from a film. Using the article by Basil Wright for information, describe the likely means for shooting each frame.

11. John Simon asserts that a good critic must have a moral position. Read one of the volumes of film criticism listed in the bibliography and define what you think to be the position of its author. Does it qualify as a moral position?

12. Of the directors cited by Robert Brustein, several are still active. Select one of the following films and show whether or not the director is still involved in the same style and world that Mr. Brustein summarizes:

    a.   Elia Kazan's *The Arrangement*
    b.   Sydney Lumet's *Blood Kin*
    c.   Joshua Logan's *Paint Your Wagon*

13. Using Robert Warshow's essay as a starting point, plan a television documentary on the gangster film as an American genre.

14. Charles Thomas Samuels cites three sources for the ideas and plot of *Bonnie and Clyde*. Select one and show whether it might have influenced the film.

a.   Faulkner's *Sanctuary*
b.   the psychology of Erik Erikson
c.   the films of Jean-Luc Godard

15.   Using Kracauer's *From Caligari to Hitler* as a guide, write a psycho-historical study of some film or group of films.

16.   Read Ian Cameron's monograph on Antonioni (*Film Quarterly,* vol. 16). Compare and contrast his ideas with those of the critics in this volume.

17.   Stanley Kauffmann has reviewed all of Antonioni's films released in this country (in *A World on Film*). Write a synthesis of his articles in order to articulate the "Kauffmann thesis" concerning Antonioni.

18.   Several of the essays in this volume compare and contrast film and theatre. Using them and other sources from the bibliography, write an essay stating your own conclusions on this subject.

19.   Read Homer's *Odyssey*. Does it support Mr. Samuels' contention that *L'Avventura* contains an implied parallel?

20.   Compare Charles Webb's novel *The Graduate* with Nichols' film.

21.   Either through this comparison or any other of a novel and its filmed version, evaluate the position taken on this subject by George Bluestone in *Novels into Film*.

22.   After reading through the reviews of *Blow-Up* in this volume, and any others you can find, make a list of facts about which the reviewers disagree. Which are the most disputed facts? What does this say about the film?

LIBRARY RESEARCH PROJECTS

1.   Annotate this volume by making a separate note card for every proper name, title, or allusion with which you are unfamiliar. On the card, indicate how you researched the information and give full citations for the source from which you derived accurate information.

2.   Recently, some writers have contended that the movies have lost their influence to television. How would you go about investigating the accuracy of this contention? Make a list of definitions for the term "influence," locate sources of relevant information, and write a report on your conclusions.

3. Erwin Panofsky sketches the history of the motion picture. Amplify his sketch by reading about the subject in histories of film (start with the bibliography), encyclopedias, memoirs, etc. Assemble your own bibliography.

4. In distinguishing between stage and screen, Erwin Panofsky cites Olivier's production of *Henry V*. Any of Olivier's Shakespearean films provides a good testing ground for theories about the relationship between stage and screen. Select one of the films (*Henry V, Hamlet, Richard III, Othello*), compile a bibliography of reviews and essays about it, and write a paper in which you define the various critical assertions on the stage/screen distinction that can be inferred from the essays.

5. At Montreal's 1967 Expo, new film techniques were introduced. Read the accounts of these techniques in contemporary newspapers and magazines, and write a report in which you describe and analyze the innovations.

6. Go through the back numbers of either *Film Quarterly* or *Sight and Sound* to familiarize yourself with the subjects covered, writers, etc. Then write a report characterizing the magazine.

7. By reading a sampling of news features on the stars of the fifties and those of the sixties, test Robert Brustein's assertion that Hollywood has abandoned glamor. Assemble a bibliography of your sources.

8. Using newspapers and biographical dictionaries (e.g. *Who's Who*) write a report on the backgrounds and training of contemporary movie-artists. Is there as large a concentration of theatre people in films today as there was, according to Robert Brustein, in the sixties? What seem to be the main training grounds for film people now?

9. Using *Screen World's* annual volumes, the reviewing columns of major magazines, and any other reference aids you can find, compile a list of gangster films made in 1959–1969 and those made in 1929–1939. Is the gangster film still as popular a genre as it was during the Depression?

10. In Stanley Kauffmann's review of *The Graduate* he praises the casting of Dustin Hoffman. From newspapers and magazines, collect the important facts about Hoffman's background and any information you can find about the reasons for his casting. Is Kauffmann right in saying that this casting is off-beat, or does Hoffman fit the movie star model sketched by Mr. Brustein?

11. Make a bibliography of books and articles on violence. From what perspectives is it possible to analyze the effects of violence in films?

12. Helpful to Joseph Morgenstern's position about *Bonnie and Clyde* is the fact that violence in earlier films was not deplored. Select one of the films Mr. Morgenstern cites (*Public Enemy*, a Charlie Chaplin comedy, *My Little Chickadee*), read contemporary reviews of the film, and conclude whether Mr. Morgenstern's position is accurate. Include a bibliography of reviews in your paper.

13. Compile a bibliography for a paper on film censorship.

14. In 1968, a new rating code was established to deal with the problem of minors seeing objectionable films. Do a research paper on this device, and, by reading various responses to it, formulate your own conclusions about its feasibility.

15. Compile a full bibliography of criticism on one of the films treated in this volume.

16. One of the most interesting research possibilities in the field of art is the study of a work's reputation. Write a reputation study of some film at least ten years old by reading all the criticism of it that you can find. Include a bibliography in your paper.

17. In his essay on *Bonnie and Clyde,* Mr. Samuels refers to the irate letters inspired by Bosley Crowther's review. Read these (in the *New York Times* Sunday editions after the review appeared) and write a paper in which you summarize the various defenses made of the film by the viewers.

18. In his essay on *Bonnie and Clyde* Mr. Samuels distinguishes between "middlebrow critics like Bosley Crowther" and "reviewers whose very names stand for the setting and guiding of taste."

   a.) Read through a sampling of Bosley Crowther's reviews. What seem to be his guiding principles? In what sense is Mr. Samuels correct in calling these principles middle-brow?
   b.) Select one of the other critics whom Mr. Samuels cites (Pauline Kael of *The New Yorker,* Andrew Sarris of *The Village Voice*). How do their standards and methods differ from Crowther's?

SELECTIVE
BIBLIOGRAPHY

Backgrounds

Brownlow, Kevin. *The Parade's Gone By*. New York: Knopf, 1968.
Houston, Penelope. *The Contemporary Cinema*. Baltimore: Penguin, 1964.
Jacobs, Lewis. *The Rise of the American Film*. New York: Harcourt, Brace, 1939.
Kracauer, Siegfried. *From Caligari to Hitler: A Psychological History of the German Film*. Princeton: Princeton U. Press, 1947.
Powdermaker, Hortense. *Hollywood the Dream Factory: An Anthropologist Looks at the Movie-Makers*. Boston: Little, Brown, 1950.

Aesthetics

Arnheim, Rudolph. *Film as Art*. Berkeley: U. of California Press, 1957.
Balázs, Béla. *Theory of the Film*. New York: Roy Publishers, 1953.
Bazin, André. *What is Cinema?* Trans. and ed. by Hugh Gray. Berkeley: U. of California Press, 1967.
Eisenstein, Sergei. *Film Form and the Film Sense*. Trans. and ed. by Jay Leyda. Cleveland and New York: Meridian, 1957.
Kracauer, Siegfried. *Theory of Film: The Redemption of Physical Reality*. New York: Oxford U. Press, 1960.
Lindgren, Ernest. *The Art of the Film*. New York: Macmillan, 1962. Rev. ed.
Pudovkin, V. I. *Film Technique and Film Acting*. London: Vision Press, 1959. Rev. Memorial ed.

Technique

Feldman, Joseph and Harry. *Dynamics of the Film*. New York: Hermitage House, 1952.
Livingston, Don. *Film and the Director*. New York: Macmillan, 1953.
Reisz, Karel. *The Technique of Film Editing*. New York: Hastings House, 1968. Rev. ed.
Spottiswoode, Raymond. *A Grammar of the Film*. Berkeley: U. of California Press, 1950.

Criticism

Kael, Pauline. *I Lost It at the Movies*. Boston: Atlantic-Little, Brown, 1965.
_____. *Kiss Kiss Bang Bang*. Boston: Atlantic-Little, Brown, 1968.
Kauffmann, Stanley. *A World on Film*. New York: Harper & Row, 1966.

Macdonald, Dwight. *Dwight Macdonald on Movies*. Englewood Cliffs, N. J.: Prentice-Hall, 1969.
Simon, John. *Private Screenings*. New York: Macmillan, 1967.
Taylor, John Russell. *Cinema Eye, Cinema Ear*. New York: Hill & Wang, 1964.
Warshow, Robert. *The Immediate Experience*. Garden City: Doubleday, 1962.

Dictionaries

Graham, Peter. *Dictionary of the Cinema*. New York: Barnes, 1968.
Halliwell, Leslie. *The Filmgoer's Companion*. New York: Hill & Wang, 1967, Rev. ed.
Skilbeck, Oswald. *ABC of Film and TV Working Terms*. London & New York: Focal Press, 1960.

Periodicals

Periodicals Devoted to Film:
Film Quarterly. U. of California Press. Berkeley, Calif.
Sight & Sound. American office: 155 W. 15th St., N.Y.C.

General Periodicals:
Commentary   *New Leader*
Encounter   *New Republic*
Evergreen Review   *New Yorker*
Hudson Review   *Village Voice*

16 mm Distributors

Audio Film Center	34 MacQuesten Parkway S.	Mt. Vernon, N.Y.
*Avco-Embassy Pictures	1301 Sixth Ave.	N.Y.C.
Brandon Films Inc.	221 W. 57th St.	N.Y.C.
Columbia Cinematheque	711 Fifth Ave.	N.Y.C.
Contemporary Films	330 W. 42nd St.	N.Y.C.
Continental 16	241 East 34th St.	N.Y.C.
†Films Incorporated	38 W. 32nd St.	N.Y.C.
Janus Films	24 W. 58th St.	N.Y.C.
Museum of Modern Art Film Library	11 W. 53rd St.	N.Y.C.
Twyman Films	329 Salem Ave.	Dayton, Ohio
UA: 16	729 Seventh Ave.	N.Y.C.
United World Films	221 Park Ave. S.	N.Y.C.
††Warner Bros., Inc. (Non-Theatrical Distribution)	666 Fifth Ave.	N.Y.C.

---

*The Graduate
†Blow-Up
††Bonnie and Clyde